How Nietzsche Came
in From the Cold

How Nietzsche Came in From the Cold

Tale of a Redemption

PHILIPP FELSCH

Translated by Daniel Bowles

polity

Originally published as *Wie Nietzsche aus der Kälte kam. Geschichte einer Rettung* © Verlag C.H.Beck oHG, München 2022

This English edition © Polity Press, 2024

The translation of this work was supported by a grant from the Goethe-Institut

Polity Press
65 Bridge Street
Cambridge CB2 1UR, UK

Polity Press
111 River Street
Hoboken, NJ 07030, USA

ISBN-13: 978-1-5095-5761-5 – hardback

A catalogue record for this book is available from the British Library.

Library of Congress Control Number: 2023941291

Typeset in 11 on 14pt Warnock Pro
by Fakenham Prepress Solutions, Fakenham, Norfolk NR21 8NL
Printed and bound in Great Britain by CPI Group (UK) Ltd, Croydon

The publisher has used its best endeavours to ensure that the URLs for external websites referred to in this book are correct and active at the time of going to press. However, the publisher has no responsibility for the websites and can make no guarantee that a site will remain live or that the content is or will remain appropriate.

Every effort has been made to trace all copyright holders, but if any have been overlooked the publisher will be pleased to include any necessary credits in any subsequent reprint or edition.

For further information on Polity, visit our website:
politybooks.com

for Martin Bauer

I scribble something here
and there on a page while on my journeys,
I write nothing at my desk,
friends decipher my scribblings.

Friedrich Nietzsche

Nietzsche needs no interpreter.

Giorgio Colli

Nietzsche is a disease.

Mazzino Montinari

Contents

CONTENTS

List of Illustrations

to what happened in the military field, although there is
a definite and essential connection, certainly. The war of
position calls on enormous masses of people to make huge
sacrifices; that is why an unprecedented concentration of
hegemony is required and hence a more 'interventionist'
kind of government that will engage more openly in the
offensive against the opponents and ensure, once and for
all, the 'impossibility' of internal disintegration by putting
in place controls of all kinds – political, administrative,
etc., reinforcement of the hegemonic positions of the
dominant group, etc. All of this indicates that the
culminating phase of the politico-historical situation has
begun, for, in politics, once the 'war of position' is won,
it is definitively decisive. In politics, in other words, the
war of maneuver drags on as long as the positions being
won are not decisive and the resources of hegemony and
the state are not fully mobilized. But when, for some
reason or another, these positions have lost their value
and only the decisive positions matter, then one shifts to
siege warfare – compact, difficult, requiring exceptional
abilities of patience and inventiveness. In politics, the
siege is reciprocal, whatever the appearances; the mere
fact that the ruling power has to parade all its resources
reveals its estimate of the adversary." (Antonio Gramsci,
Prison Notebooks, ed. and trans. Joseph A. Buttigieg, vol.
III: Notebooks 6–8 [New York: Columbia University Press,

Acknowledgments

I am grateful to the employees at the Goethe and Schiller Archive in Weimar and at the Fondazione Mondadori in Milan – and especially to Maddalena Taglioli at the Centro Archivistico della Scuola Normale Superiore in Pisa. My gratitude goes to Alessandra Origgi for her transcriptions and to Wolfert von Rahden and Bettina Wahrig-Schmidt for their references. Wolfram Groddeck helped in deciphering Nietzsche's notebooks. Chiara Colli Staude gave her friendly support. To all of them I offer my heartfelt thanks. For their critical reading and important suggestions, I thank Andreas Bernard, Jan von Brevern, David Höhn, Yael Reuveny, and Martin Bauer, who provided the impetus for this book.

THE SPOILSPORTS
Introduction

In July 1964 at Royaumont, a former Cistercian abbey located north of Paris, a German–French summit meeting took place. The year prior, de Gaulle and Adenauer had signed the Élysée Treaty. As though feeling an obligation to the spirit of that friendship accord, the two nations' leading expositors of Nietzsche were now meeting to discuss the correct interpretive reading of his works. In hindsight, Royaumont is considered one of the events that inaugurated the postmodern era in French philosophy. The participants could not have foreseen, however, that their convention would one day be thought of as the germinal moment of a new *Zeitgeist*. During his lifetime, Nietzsche himself had wanted to be regarded as an "unfashionable" thinker, but only in the second postwar era following his death did this wish seem finally to come true. To be sure, he had been acquitted of the charge of National Socialism by Georges Bataille, and he had appeared in Camus and Sartre as a kind of remote precursor to existentialism. But the next big thing in France was structuralism. In the two German states, prospects looked even worse for the author of *Zarathustra*. In the German Democratic Republic (GDR), he officially rated as a "pioneer of fascism," and in the Federal Republic of Germany (FRG), too, his reputation had plunged to a historic nadir. If those diagnosing the times are to be believed, he had lost his core audience, the so-called "youth of today." The skeptical generation no longer had any use for his pathos. As late as 1968, Jürgen Habermas wrote, with palpable relief, that "nothing contagious" now emanated from Nietzsche.[1]

It is fitting that the majority of the speakers at Royaumont were Nietzsche veterans from the first half of the century: Boris de Schlözer, for instance, the eighty-three-year-old scion of the Russian branch of a German noble family, who spoke about the transfiguration of evil in Nietzsche and Dostoevsky. Or Jean Wahl, the Jewish Sorbonne professor who had been incarcerated during the German occupation and who at Royaumont, as honorary chairman of the Société française d'études nietzschéennes, played the role of a convivial figurehead. Or Karl Löwith, who, unlike anyone else, managed to personify the Nietzsche enthusiasm from the first half of the century, for he had, after all, experienced it first-hand; from the youth movement, to the euphoria around the world war and his studies with Heidegger, to the day the National Socialist racist laws put an end to his academic career in Germany, Nietzsche had been the lodestar of his own radical school of thought. Without this "last German philosopher," Löwith later wrote in his autobiography, drafted in Japanese exile, "the development of Germany" could not be understood – and in a turn of phrase redolent of the mood of many a scholar of the humanities today, he added with remorse that he heedlessly "contributed to the destruction."[2]

At Royaumont, the erstwhile avant-gardist had transformed into a white-haired stoic who was no longer intrigued by Nietzsche's theory of the will to power, but rather by his thought of the eternal return. Löwith argued for exiting the disastrous upheaval of modernism and returning to a classical equanimity that viewed humankind as part of the forever-immutable cosmos.[3]

Nothing could be more anathema to the French Young Nietzscheans comprising the other half of the conference attendees than this loftily standoffish conservatism. While Löwith showed the balance of an epochal disenchantment, they were already rehearsing the themes of a future philosophy of transgression. For Gilles Deleuze, *attaché de recherches* at the Centre national de la recherche scientifique and organizer of the colloquium, what the eternal return called to mind was in no way the contemplation of the ever-constant cosmos, but a Dionysian principle of upheaval that guaranteed the world never remained identical with itself.[4]

One of these young Frenchmen was Michel Foucault, who at the time, just like Deleuze, did not yet enjoy considerable renown. The fact that his lecture on "Nietzsche, Freud, Marx" is the only one still read today might be because he assumes the perspective of a second-order observer. Indeed, instead of adding another interpretation to those by the Nietzsche expositors, he made his object of inquiry interpretation as such. Well into the nineteenth century, Foucault argued, the practices of textual exegesis were limited by the regulative notion of an authentic source text. It was Nietzsche – and Freud and Marx – who cut this comforting ground from under hermeneutics with their writings. By replacing the idea of the original text with an abyss of interpretations nested inside one another, Nietzsche, in particular, transformed for his successors the business of interpretation into an infinite task no longer backed by an originary truth.[5]

The Birth of Tragedy, Nietzsche's first book, which appeared in print in 1872 and simultaneously heralded the beginning of the end of his academic career, has an unusual dramatic structure. Readers must first follow the dialectic of the Apollonian and Dionysian for twelve chapters before – halfway through the text – Socrates, the actual protagonist, finally enters onto the narrative stage. Or more precisely: he does not enter the stage where the god of dreams and the god of ecstasy celebrate their tension-filled unification in the form of ancient tragedy, but instead sits inconspicuously among the audience, where, together with his sympathetic comrade, the poet Euripides, he eyes what transpires, full of misgivings. The worldview that underlies tragedy remains incomprehensible to him. Unlike the others present, Socrates embodies "theoretical optimism," the ethos of Enlightenment science, the belief that it was possible "to separate true knowledge from semblance and fallacy" and to escape the tragic hero's fate with existential slyness. The real drama Nietzsche unfolds in the second half of his book is not between Dionysian and Apollonian principles, but between Dionysian and Socratic ones.[6]

It was with the same skepticism and the same unobtrusiveness as Socrates and Euripides that Giorgio Colli and Mazzino Montinari must have sat among the philosophers assembled at Royaumont. They have left virtually no trace among the records of the conference's discussions. Aside from the short lecture Montinari delivered on the morning of the second day, not one query, not one hypothesis, not so much as a single marginal comment of theirs has survived. And yet they must have lodged their objection after Foucault's lecture on unregulated interpretation at the very latest. As their correspondence in the run-up to the conference reveals, however, they felt out of place among the Nietzsche experts. Colli, who in his mid-forties taught ancient philosophy as an adjunct professor at the University of Pisa, normally gave academic functions a wide berth, and Montinari, who in his time as an operative of the Italian Communist Party had grown accustomed to dividing the world into friends and foes, was afraid the "bigwigs of Western Nietzscheology" wanted to make an example of him. Even on the bus from Paris to Royaumont, they chanced to overhear a French professor inquiring of an Italian colleague about the identity of the two unknown Italians whose names appeared in the program. They belonged to none of the camps represented at the colloquium, they felt no affinity for either the German Apollonians or the French Dionysians, and in the coffee breaks, which are inescapable at such events, they surely stood around largely by themselves. "The many, and among them the best individuals, had only a wary smile for him," Nietzsche writes about Euripides the skeptic, and the pair of Italians may have fared similarly.[7] In the eyes of the Nietzscheologists, to be sure, they played an ignominious role; they had come to Royaumont as spoilsports.

What one must also bear in mind is that this German–French exchange of ideas was burdened with a troubling legacy. In the late 1950s, as a result of publications by Darmstadt philosophy professor Karl Schlechta and French Germanist Richard Roos, it had come to light in both Germany and France in quick succession that the respective Nietzsche editions issued by the Nietzsche Archive in Weimar under the aegis of Elisabeth Förster-Nietzsche contained posthumous interventions and manipulations, even falsifications. There had not been a solid textual foundation since that time.[8]

The body of research on what is perhaps the most famous scandal in more recent philosophical history now fills a small library unto itself. Erich Podach, one of the many Nietzsche scholars to weigh in on the debate then, wrote that Nietzsche was the "most severely distorted figure in modern literary and intellectual history with respect to his life and works." And while one may, with good reason, cast doubt on this assertion, it is true that there may hardly be another instance of literary and philosophical inheritance in which this suspicion plays so crucial a role.[9]

For reasons subject to continual speculation, Nietzsche had suffered a mental breakdown in Turin toward the beginning of 1889 and spent the following decade until his death in 1900 largely under the care of his mother and sister, who, along with guardianship over him, had gained power of disposition over his published and unpublished oeuvre. To be sure, the image of the money-grubbing sister ruled by the anti-Semitic obsessions of her deceased husband and personally profiting from the celebrity of her mentally ill brother has since yielded to a more nuanced appraisal. Credit is nevertheless due to Elisabeth, who from the outset endured exceptional mistrust for her role as female executor of the estate, for having chased after Nietzsche's scattered *Nachlass*, or literary remains, down to the last scrap of paper that bore his handwriting and, as George disciple Rudolf Pannwitz wrote in *Merkur* in 1957, for having "hurled [his message] into the world at the seminal moment." That she did not shrink from telling strategic lies all the while, that she possessed the criminal energy to suppress, alter, and falsify documents, and that she offered up her brother to the *völkisch* Right and the National Socialists, however, remains equally true. Under his sister's direction, no fewer than four different complete editions were launched. She herself became influentially active in publication, parlayed Weimar's Nietzsche Archive into a national pilgrimage site, and contributed decisively to the transformation of her brother into the icon with a mustache that he remains – among everything else – to this day.[10]

Elisabeth's campaign essentially turned on the fact that she had secured for herself the copyright to Nietzsche's *Nachlass* in 1896. By placing snippets and teasers in newspapers, she kept interest alive in the fast-growing Nietzsche community. With the publication of *The Will to Power* in 1901, the year after Nietzsche's death, she unveiled the purported magnum opus his adherents had long been waiting for. Her efforts ended up fomenting belief in an esoteric tradition that surpassed in significance those writings published during his lifetime – a belief which according to Schlechta's and Roos's revelations was to be regarded as a fiction.[11]

While *Der Spiegel* devoted a ten-page lead story to the affair in the culture section, the majority of philosophers brushed it off like a pesky nuisance. Heidegger, who himself had been involved in the preparations for a historical, critical edition of the complete works as a consultant to the Nietzsche Archive in the 1930s, declared that *The Will to Power* remained for him as ever the definitive reference. Even Schlechta, who had edited the incriminated book's aphorisms into a corrected, chronological order, voiced opposition to the need for a completely new edition. Toying with such thoughts, moreover, seemed purely hypothetical to most of those concerned anyway since, as Rudolf Pannwitz, cited above, had written, Nietzsche's *Nachlass* "in the Eastern Zone" – in the GDR, that is – was beyond the reach of all well-intentioned friends of Nietzsche until further notice.[12]

Montinari was the sole conference participant in attendance from the "Eastern Zone." When the invitation from Deleuze arrived, he was about to relocate his place of residence to Weimar. In those days, anyone who moved from Tuscany to the GDR had to have good reasons. In Montinari's case, these reasons dated back to a day in April 1961. While the rumor was still circulating among quite a few West German Nietzscheans that Nietzsche's *Nachlass* had been loaded onto a Soviet truck after the war and ended up in Moscow's catacombs, it was on this day – four months before the Berlin Wall was built – that Montinari, who still maintained good contacts in the GDR from his time as a party functionary, entered the Goethe and Schiller Archive in Weimar to consult Nietzsche's manuscripts. Is it an exaggeration to suggest that he never got over this experience? "This journey to Weimar is perhaps the most important event of my life," he wrote a few days later to Colli. "I was moved in a very peculiar, ineffable way when I held a manuscript of Nietzsche's in my hands for the first time."[13]

Nietzsche himself had fled from Thuringia to Italy via waypoints in Switzerland and France. Under the spell of Nietzsche's manuscripts, Montinari chose the opposite path. As a matter of fact, in Weimar he had only wanted to check the textual basis for an Italian translation, planned together with Colli, yet after his return they decided to edit a new German-language edition of Nietzsche's complete published and unpublished writings. While Colli used his media contacts to drum up financial backers and publishers, Montinari began deciphering Nietzsche's *Nachlass* on site in Weimar – a task that would occupy him until the end of his life. As Nietzsche had written in the preface to *Dawn*, he wanted to be read "slowly, deeply, with deference and caution, with ulterior motives, with doors left open, with delicate fingers and eyes." In Montinari, he found his perfect reader. "He is perhaps the only person among the living who has read every surviving line, every preserved missive in the original," Frank Schirrmacher, the literary section editor of the *Frankfurter Allgemeine Zeitung*, wrote shortly before Montinari's death in 1986.[14]

There is a sense of astonishment at the outset of this book not unlike that of the French professor on the bus to Royaumont. Who were the two Italian dilettantes, and how did they end up editing Nietzsche's writings? What was the source of their commitment to the work of a philosopher who in the 1960s – especially for leftists – was still an ambassador of evil? Colli and Montinari were an improbable pair in multiple respects: a bourgeois independent scholar with philhellene obsessions and, twelve years his junior, an apostate foot soldier of the Communist Party with a proletarian family background. Their mutual acquaintance extended back to the 1940s, to the Tuscan town of Lucca, where Colli had been Montinari's high school philosophy teacher. "The one taciturn, aristocratic, captivated by the radiance of a distant past; the other vivacious, electrifying, empathetic, preoccupied by the present and its transformation," wrote Antonio Gnoli, who devoted a series of insightful portraits to the two in the daily *La Repubblica*.[15]

Not even in their enthusiasm for Nietzsche did they jibe with one another. While Colli saw in Nietzsche a modern-day mystic who enabled him to flee to an imaginary Greece, Montinari viewed him as a radical figure of enlightenment, a proponent of inconspicuous insights won through methodological stringency. In Montinari's letters, one can trace the gradual metamorphosis of a communist intellectual into a philologist. Did his fidelity to the text provide him with ultimate stability after the loss of his political conviction? "All luxury leaves him unmoved, he only wants to work," reported the informal collaborator surveilling Montinari at the Goethe and Schiller Archive for the Ministry for State Security. Amid the cultural and political acceleration of the 1960s, it was the very doldrums behind the Wall that made possible the staying power of this epic deciphering project in the first instance. To Montinari, Weimar seemed to have fallen "out of time." There, of all places, in an educated middle-class enclave of

actually existing socialism, the maverick found his personal *posthistoire*. Transcribing a single page from Nietzsche's notebooks could
take days. After the reading room closed, Montinari would immerse
himself in autodidactic study of the theoretical and technical details
of editorial philology. In time he arrived at the conclusion – characteristic when dealing with sacred scriptures – that in Nietzsche's texts
"not one image, not one word, not even one punctuation mark in lieu
of another" was random. He intended to ignore the arguments over his
worldview and get back to the "genuine Nietzsche." What drove him,
he wrote to Colli, was a "raging passion for the truth."[16]

It was with this sensibility – and full of reservations about these
philosophers fond of interpretation – that Colli and Montinari
traveled to Royaumont in 1964. No wonder the encounter was colored
by mutual distrust; while the "bigwigs of Western Nietzscheology"
grappled with the correct interpretation, the two Italians staked their
claim to represent the authentic Nietzsche. Colli, who liked reading
his texts as one might listen to an "unknown music," held the opinion
that anyone who attempted to interpret Nietzsche did him the first
injustice. Lacking an academic title or pertinent publications but
equipped with the authority of his first-hand knowledge, Montinari
in his lecture detailed the deficiencies of existing editions. He went
so far as to suggest a moratorium on interpretation until philological
questions under dispute were resolved. Instead, however, Michel
Foucault called for wild exegesis. If indeed no authoritative foundation
in the form of an *Urtext* existed, then there was no alternative but to
indulge in ever more novel readings. "The only valid tribute to thought
such as Nietzsche's is precisely to use it, to deform it, to make it groan
and protest," he explained a few years later. "And if commentators
then say that I am being faithful or unfaithful to Nietzsche, that is of
absolutely no interest."[17]

This sounds like French theory, to whose global success story
Nietzsche the author owes his lasting renaissance up through the
present day: as a theorist of transgression, as a pioneer of "absolute
encoding" and all manners of Deconstruction. This French Nietzsche
could not have been more alien to Colli and Montinari's intentions.
In their deference to literality, their philological ethos, and their belief
in truth, they were evocative of figures from a distant past when

compared with Foucault and Deleuze. In their claim to represent the definitive Nietzsche, their edition intruded like an atavism into the landscape of late twentieth-century theory. Even Heidegger, who is said to have disparagingly termed their *Kritische Gesamtausgabe* [Critical Complete Edition] Nietzsche's "Communist edition," saw the spirit of the nineteenth century at work in philology. He felt "a revulsion at this thoroughness and rummaging," he had written in the 1930s before withdrawing from the advisory body of the historical-critical edition – not without adding that Nietzsche himself would have felt "a much greater one."[18]

To be sure, no one may have contributed more to the affect against philology in the German-speaking world than Nietzsche, who within the span of a few years had gone from a promising talent to a renegade of his field: ancient philology. Not even as a young professor in Basel had he been able to resist sneering at the insipidness of his colleagues: "Improving texts is entertaining work for scholars [. . .]; but it should not be regarded as too important a matter," one reads in the notes for the never-published fifth *Unfashionable Observation*, the title of which was to be "We Philologists." Later, too, after the end of his academic career, the love–hate relationship with his discipline never left him: philology was "science for cranks," "repetitive drudgery," and "intellectually middle class." In his autobiography *Ecce homo*, he wrote that the "junk of dusty scholarship" had ensured intellectual stagnation for ten years of his life.[19] Today, when the discipline at best occupies a marginal position within the humanities and has gone from a flagship subject to a rare and exotic one, the energy Nietzsche invested in his feud comes off as oddly over-ardent. In the course of its momentous loss of importance, little more seems to have remained of philology, in spite of all provisional attempts to salvage it, than its bad reputation.[20]

Why, then, tell the story of Colli and Montinari, which leads, to quote Nietzsche once more, straight through the "dust of bibliographic minutiæ"? Whoever opens one of the volumes of commentary from the *Kritische Gesamtausgabe* enters a desert of philological exactitude in which variants and preliminary stages are listed, citations and sources are identified, and punctilious descriptions of Nietzsche's manuscripts are given. "Nietzsche's aggressive intelligence apprehended by means of the most tedious pedantry," Schirrmacher once wrote about the two Italians' endeavor.[21] All the admirable meticulousness notwithstanding, does it not constitute a betrayal of Nietzsche's thought?

Much has been written about the irony inherent in the fact that Nietzsche of all people, that spurner of philology, has become the object of a philology so excessive. The circumstances of his transmission history and the character of his writings – aphoristic and marked by contradictions and constant revisions – have, on the one hand, made him into a Protean figure among modern philosophers. It would be difficult to find another body of work in the history of European thought that proved so adaptable to all imaginable interpretations: right-wingers and leftists, enthusiasts and skeptics, dictators and democrats have all invoked Nietzsche, and none of them had trouble producing the textual passages appropriate to his reading. Perhaps because he himself acted out the antagonistic tendencies of his age, Nietzsche played the role of a canvas onto which the entire spectrum of twentieth-century ideas could be projected.[22]

On the other hand, the promiscuity of his writings has given cause, time and again, for what might be termed a "philological caveat": every audacious reading, every claim to explicate the actual meaning of his thought, is met by the converse promise to reconstruct the "genuine," authentic Nietzsche freed from all post-hoc "legends," by bringing to light his buried, misconstrued, or repudiated *Urtext*. The thicket of interpretations thus stands in opposition to an almost equally confusing abundance of editions on the basis of which the history of Nietzsche's influence may be divided into periods. One almost has the impression he had to be edited anew each time in order for him to be interpreted anew – and vice versa.[23]

In this way, *The Will to Power*, the magnum opus compiled by his sister and the showpiece of the editions issued under her direction, dominated the Nietzscheology of the first half of the century, which sought the central idea, the systematic nexus, the philosophical essence of his aphoristic style. In Alfred Baeumler, Nietzsche became an apologist of power, in Karl Löwith, a denier of the linear temporal order of the modern age, while Heidegger conferred on him the final starring role in the drama of Western forgetfulness of being. It was Jürgen Habermas who in 1968 pointed out the paradox that only unsystematic thought possessed the requisite flexibility to be compatible with such different systematic schemata.[24]

Habermas's verdict coincided with the rise of the second wave of Nietzsche enthusiasm; centered in Paris, its perspective on Nietzsche's writings was one of diametrical opposition to preceding approaches. Within the attempts to conceptualize his oeuvre, the need to reappraise the ideological writer as a philosopher to be taken seriously had always been articulated as well. In contrast, Nietzsche's French interpreters, from Deleuze to Derrida, perceived the true explosive power of his thought to be located precisely in its aphoristic fragmentation, in its lack of a central viewpoint, in its transgression of the order of philosophical discourse. With this theoretical revision comes a philological one; the textual basis for the French Nietzsche was provided by Colli and Montinari's edition, which was published concurrently. Throughout the 1970s, the poststructuralist Nietzsche debate reads at times like a commentary on their editorial project. Despite contrary intentions and mutual animosity, Italian philology and French theory converged at a common intellectual sensibility. "Philology is in league with myth: it blocks the exit," Theodor W. Adorno wrote regarding the futility inherent in insisting on naked literality in the face of unpopular readings. Colli and Montinari were not spared this insight either. "Today one can say," Montinari wrote after encountering the first Zarathustra graffiti on the walls of the University of Florence during the "autonomous" turmoil of 1977, "that a new myth is forming around Nietzsche, lumping together elements of conservative ideology with some of leftist theory. Our edition has contributed significantly to this resurgence."[25]

Anyone who wishes to tell the story of this resurgence and this edition holds one inestimable advantage: they can draw upon the correspondence between Colli and Montinari, which, interrupted by briefer and longer pauses, spans four decades, from the 1940s to the 1970s – the documentation of an erotically charged teacher–student relationship, the *Bildungsroman* of two Italian intellectuals, and an intimate journal of an editorial project. As reflected in this correspondence, the "repetitive drudgery" of editorial philology loses any sort of technical routine and becomes a matter of existential and political relevance. On the basis of his biography, a large portion of

Italy's postwar history can be reconstructed, Adriano Sofri, founder of Lotta Continua, remarked after Montinari's death.[26] Yet not just that of Italy: with the *Kritische Gesamtausgabe*, a chapter of Cold War intellectual history comes into focus as well. Undergirded by the intimate insights that Colli and Montinari's letters afford, this book pursues a perhaps all too ambitious enterprise: cracking the cover of their edition a second time, but this time with the aim of releasing four decades of affective, intellectual, and political energies that lie stored within its sober critical apparatus.

1

BEYOND THE GOTHIC LINE
Lucca, 1943–4

For Mussolini's sixtieth birthday on July 29, 1943, Hitler gifted him a complete edition of Nietzsche, bound in blue pigskin. "Adolf Hitler to his dear Benito Mussolini," read the Führer's handwritten dedication in the first volume. The book shipment made its way across the Alps in time for the big day, but Field Marshal General Kesselring, Commander in Chief South stationed with the Italian high command in Frascati, near Rome, found himself incapable of delivering it personally because all attempts to locate the Duce had failed. A group of conspirators from the Fascist Grand Council had deposed him four days before his birthday and had taken him to an undisclosed location under the pretense of providing for his safety.[1]

Not until August did German intelligence operatives learn that Mussolini was being held captive on the island of Ponza, in the Tyrrhenian Sea. Accompanied by a note from Kesselring wishing him "a bit of joy," the Führer's gift was sent on to him by the new Italian government. According to Mussolini's notoriously unreliable memoirs, Nietzsche did in fact make the days of his imprisonment more bearable. Did he feel transported back to the beginnings of his political career when he had learned German specifically in order to read Nietzsche in the original? Was he comforted by Nietzsche's maxim "live dangerously!," which had been the slogan of his young movement in the 1920s? In order to prevent his liberation by the Germans, the Duce was taken from one hideout to the next. Only when the rebels relocated him to the Abruzzi did the Nietzsche edition remain behind on the isle of La Maddalena, north of Sardinia. In September, when Hitler put Italy under occupation, a Wehrmacht detachment is said to have been tasked with recapturing the volumes, but the story goes that the officer responsible obtained a revocation of the order by pointing out the expected casualties. A luxury set of Nietzsche volumes from Mussolini's personal library with a dedication from Hitler: there could scarcely be more striking proof of Nietzsche's political discreditation. But the edition's trail goes cold on La Maddalena. Its current where-abouts are unknown.[2]

The Chosen Few

Giorgio Colli also recommended his pupils read Nietzsche in German – at least those he met outside of class. After his arrival in Lucca as a teacher of philosophy and Greek at the Ginnasio N. Machiavelli in the autumn of 1942, it did not take long for him to gather a circle of devotees around him. At the beginning of the school year, he had surprised the students by asserting that philosophy was neither about juggling abstract notions, nor about memorizing classical systems of thought – and as though to prove this conviction, he displayed a provocative nonchalance toward the official syllabus.[3]

We must also bear in mind that philosophy instruction in fascist Italy was no minor matter. A former journalist, the Duce himself had a soft spot for intellectual speculations. The field owed its defining gain in prestige, however, to philosophy professor Giovanni Gentile, who had defected from the bourgeois-liberal camp to the fascist one in the early 1920s and been rewarded by Mussolini with the post of Minister of Education for doing so. Gentile had seized the opportunity to bolster the historical, literary disciplines over the scientific ones and to introduce as a principal subject a new manner of philosophy instruction tailored exactly to the profile of his own thought. He championed an idealism inspired by Hegel and Fichte according to which reality consisted of nothing but the "pure act" of cognition. He understood the world as the process of a consciousness gradually coming into its own, all while bringing about the beautiful, the true, and the good, and tasked philosophy classes with making pupils aware of this progress of Reason in its astonishing rigor, from its beginnings with the Greeks to its political realization in the "ethical state" of fascism.[4]

Giorgio Colli, by contrast, proclaimed Hegel anathema – a battle cry with which he fell between two stools, for Hegelianism, or *storicismo* as they called it in Italy, was not limited to Gentile's loyalist variant. Benedetto Croce, Gentile's adversary and the voice of antifascist Italy, also preached the grand narrative of the world-historical progress of Reason – even though in his version this process led not to Mussolini, but to a liberal state. Between Gentile and Croce there was no escape. With their Hegel-based systems, these two hostile *dioscuri* delimited the space of what was conceivable. The Prussian privy counselor Carl Schmitt, who had traveled to Rome in 1936 to lecture on the "total state" at the Italian–German Cultural Institute, was amazed at the soundness of his hosts' knowledge of Hegel. Even the Duce apparently assured him during an audience he was a staunch Hegelian. Mussolini's enthusiasm for Nietzsche had long since cooled; one might get the idea that Hitler chose the wrong gift seven years later.[5]

Without a doubt, Colli would have agreed with this supposition. While *storicismo* represented the false whole, for him Nietzsche's thought constituted the way out. According to Benedetto Croce, history was the "last religious faith" left to the modern subject. "Whosoever does not close his heart to historic sentiment," he had written, was "no longer alone," but united with the "spirits at work on earth before him," indeed, "with the life of the universe." It was notions like these that Nietzsche fought against half a century earlier. Colli delighted in citing Nietzsche's polemic against historicism from the second *Unfashionable Observation*, "On the Utility and Liability of History for Life," in which he had denounced the cult of historical education as a symptom of a dying culture. Although written as a reckoning with the history-obsessed climate in the Second German Empire, the text struck the Italian *Zeitgeist* of the 1940s on the nose. Was it justified to speak of cultural backwardness? To Karl Eugen Gass, a disciple of the Bonn scholar of Romance literatures Ernst Robert Curtius, who had studied at the Scuola Normale Superiore in Pisa in the late 1930s and had left behind a journal full of interesting observations about this

FRIEDRICH NIETZSCHE
GESAMMELTE WERKE

MUSARIONAUSGABE

ACHTZEHNTER BAND
DER WILLE ZUR MACHT
ERSTES UND ZWEITES BUCH
1884–1888

1926. 566

MUSARION VERLAG MÜNCHEN

The Musarion luxury edition – presumably also the same edition as Hitler's birthday present

FRIEDRICH NIETZSCHE GESAMMELTE WERKE

ACHTZEHNTER BAND

DER WILLE ZUR MACHT

VERSUCH EINER UMWERTHUNG ALLER WERTHE

ERSTES UND ZWEITES BUCH

PLÄNE UND ENTWÜRFE

1926. 566

MUSARION VERLAG MÜNCHEN

period, the professors and students of the elite institution seemed, at any rate, to be "stragglers" from the nineteenth century. While Heidegger's illusion-less existential philosophy prevailed at German universities, he wrote, the Italians' belief in the victory of progressive Reason remained undaunted.[6]

It was not, however, because he considered it backwards that Colli combatted idealism. On the contrary: the real problem for him was expressed in the claim to be fashionable. In its beginnings among the Greeks, philosophy, he explained to his students, had been a reflection on the correct life. In their hubris about being able to discern the laws of history, modern philosophers had abandoned this legacy. It was about time to restore thought to its old, practical purpose. "How are we to live?," he asked, allowing silence to work its magic in the classroom and looking at his pupils through his thick lenses. Luigi Imbasciati, one of the middling students, recalled: "He did not seem to me like one of the other teachers, but like a great intellectual."[7]

This impression might have been enhanced by the fact that Colli did not bother meeting the class at its current state of knowledge. From the outset, his interest was directed primarily at individuals, at those especially receptive to his ideas with whom he could meet after school. Walks atop Lucca's walls; conversations about philosophy, music, and their first amorous adventures; joint sessions lasting long into the evening: for his "Chosen Few," as they were dubbed, the encounters with the man hardly ten years their senior opened up a new world. Colli promised a superior, "Dionysian" knowledge accessible only to initiates. Fellow schoolmates must indeed have puzzled over what that meant, for – as was usual among inspirited collectives – limiting oneself to allusions and cultivating a telling discretion constituted half the allure. "Keeping the truth hidden from the many," Colli wrote later, after the war. "Winning over the few by means of this ploy. Giving cause neither for suspicion, nor for condemnation. Let's content ourselves with arousing curiosity with the secret." Among his favorite references was Plato's so-called Seventh Letter, in which the philosopher had warned about writing down the truth in order to protect it from vulgar misunderstandings. Colli himself also viewed books as a kind of hindrance to knowledge. The first step of his initiation consisted in gaining insight into the deficiency of "dead signs," the inevitable "corruption" and "ossification" to which every genuine idea was subjected in the course of being transcribed.[8]

One would hardly suppose that for this notion – aside from Plato – he would invoke Nietzsche of all people, the maniacal writer who constantly inveighed in his letters about the quality of his ink and his quills. A tragic self-contradiction, however, revealed itself to Colli in the existence Nietzsche had led as a man of letters after the end of his academic career. As an enlightened, even deeply religious thinker, Nietzsche had known about the futility of his authorial ambitions. "What is best and essential can only be conveyed from person to person, it can and should never be 'public,'" reads one letter to his friend Franz Overbeck. Such sentences struck a chord with Colli. The truth, he explained, arises only from the spirited discussion of a group of people: "If wisdom is your aim, you can toss out all your books."[9] No wonder he did not seem like an ordinary teacher to his pupils.

Standard Positions of Nietzsche Reception

It was almost as though Colli resented Nietzsche for ultimately having been a mere *homme de lettres*. "After *Zarathustra*," he wrote, "he should have concentrated on gathering a group around himself and proceeded with a concrete cultural campaign." What Nietzsche had failed to do, Colli intended to put into action with his Chosen Few. He imagined himself less a reader than a successor, called to "undertake something in [Nietzsche's] direction." In these aspirations, he was not alone. The Nietzscheanism of the first half of the century was full of charismatic leaders and inspirited circles laboring away at incarnating the prophet's words.[10]

Nietzsche himself had demonstratively renounced his era's state educational institutions. While he was discharging his duties as a university instructor with growing reluctance, a closer relationship with his students had long been on his mind. In his third *Unfashionable Observation*, "Schopenhauer as Educator" – the first of his works that Colli and Montinari later translated into Italian – he sketched out the prototype of a charismatic teacher who inspires his disciples less through his knowledge than through his example of breaking with the *juste milieu* of their age. In his unpublished notes from this period, he dreamed alternatively of a "society of the unfashionable" or a "monastery for freer spirits." As becomes clear from a letter to his university friend Erwin Rohde, he even set aside a portion of his professorial salary to found their "new Greek academy": "Then we shall be teachers to each other," he wrote, "our books will be merely fishhooks for catching people into our monastic and artistic community. We shall [live], work, enjoy for each another – perhaps this is the only way in which we can work for the *whole*."[11]

It was part of Nietzsche's tragic nature that he never succeeded in making this dream of a pedagogical cloister a reality. For his self-declared successors, however, an instruction manual sprang from this incapacity. The poet Stefan George, too, stylized himself as the heir obliged to complete the failed mission. Nietzsche may have understood "the fundamental big things," he wrote to Ernst Gundolf, but he lacked the "plastic god": the ability to practice his doctrine within the protective space of an intimately connected community. George himself famously developed a particular talent in this arena. His circle was the most prominent case of a confederation inspired by Nietzsche, with the very highest pedagogical and political aspirations. For Colli, who took note of this circle's publications with interest, George constituted an important font of inspiration. The identification with Nietzsche, the urge to action, the initiation rituals – they could have been adopted directly from the master. It would be nice to know whether the same was true of Colli's "Dionysian" secret. Clad in ancient costumes, the "Cosmic Circle" of Schwabing, which George had joined around the turn of the century together with Ludwig Klages, attempted to bring about Dionysian ecstasy with monotonic, "droning, nasal chants."[12]

What lay in closer historical proximity was the Parisian secret society Acéphale, which Georges Bataille and Pierre Klossowski had founded in the late 1930s as a combat league against fascism. Instead of spurring the forces of enlightened reason to action, the conspirators looked to defeat the reactionary camp with its own weapons by creating an antifascist counter-myth. As the guarantor of their new mythology, they had, naturally, chosen Nietzsche. Bataille, too, was loath to interpret Nietzsche as a canonical philosopher; he also advocated for taking action in his name. "I am the only one," he wrote, "who presents himself not as an expositor of Nietzsche, but as his equal." Among the ritual practices were an initiation ceremony sealed with blood, a vow of silence toward outsiders, and the order to alternately practice asceticism and ecstasy. At the new moon, the group would convene in the Bois de Boulogne at the foot of an oak tree split by lightning to perform Dionysian rites. On one of these nights, Bataille was even supposed to have asked his co-conspirators to make a human sacrifice of him.[13]

Seduction of Youth

It is impossible to claim that Colli's charisma is immediately evident to the onlooker. With his heavy glasses, sweater vest, and tie, he gives the impression in later photographs of a typical Italian academic. With respect to the younger Colli, there is the addition of something at once both penetrative and withdrawn. One can picture him gazing out over the rows of his pupils to watch for suitable candidates. In his notes from the 1930s, he presumed to be able to look into "the interior of people" and ferret out the "noblest" among them in order to estrange them from prevailing opinions and initiate them into a profound knowledge that would change their lives for ever.[14]

Colli must be imagined as a magnetic figure. Later, too, after he had left the Ginnasio N. Machiavelli and was teaching as an adjunct lecturer at the University of Pisa, he was always gathering a circle of students around him whose adulation he graciously accepted. "Modesty is no virtue," he recorded as his personal credo. Born into a bourgeois Turinese family in 1917, Colli hailed from a milieu that was to set the tone in Italy's cultural life after the Second World War. His father had been managing director of the liberal daily *La Stampa* until the fascists forced him into an early retirement in 1931 on account of his antifascist disposition. His mother's parents owned a large hotel in Turin's city center. Colli attended the same preparatory school as Leone Ginzburg and Cesare Pavese, who in the early 1930s, together with Giulio Einaudi, founded an antifascist publishing house inextricably linked with twentieth-century Italian intellectual history. In 1935

Giorgio Colli, 1942

– Colli was just completing high school – Pavese was arrested and sent into exile in southern Italy. In theory, Colli could have appeared as an introverted nerd in the margins of Natalia Ginzburg's autobiographical novel *Family Lexicon*, in which the author described Turin's intellectual environment under Mussolini.[15]

Only in theory – because aside from being not quite ten years younger, Colli was segregated from Ginzburg's friends by a formative experience of paramount importance to his intellectual biography. It is Anna Maria Musso-Colli whom we have to thank for the story of Colli's illness that relegated the eighteen-year-old to a long stint of bedrest. As he walked through spring-time Turin on unsteady legs following his recovery, he was made aware of his call to become a philosopher by a sudden epiphany. We can only speculate whether on this day he also passed by the site on the Via Po where Nietzsche's philosophical career had ended in January 1889. What is certain is that Colli perfected his

Ancient Greek while still in school, learned German on the side, and read all of Plato's dialogues in the original – and that, concurrently with his Graecophilia, his lifelong enthusiasm for Nietzsche began.[16]

Cesare Pavese described in his memoirs how, during the years of fascism, American literature became for him an "ideal fatherland."[17] Giorgio Colli had a similar experience, but instead of the modern United States, ancient Greece became his inner refuge. Where Pavese discovered Walt Whitman and *Moby-Dick*, he stumbled upon Plato and Empedocles. And while Pavese identified with literary modernism, Colli retreated into a Greek parallel universe.

Strictly speaking, it ought to be called a Greek–German parallel universe, for the Greeks about whom Colli so enthused had spawned from a German fantasy. Since that sojourner in Italy from Saxony-Anhalt, Johann Joachim Winckelmann, had discovered the Hellenes' "noble simplicity" and "quiet grandeur" in the eighteenth century, German poets and thinkers especially had dreamed their way back into an imaginary Greece. In *The Birth of Tragedy*, Nietzsche had conjured an outlandish "Dionysian" culture whose radiant counter-image he juxtaposed with an impoverished modern civilization. "I wouldn't know what purpose classical philology might have in our age if not to operate within it in an unfashionable manner – which is to say, against the age and thereby upon the age and hopefully for the benefit of a coming age," he wrote two years later in the foreword to his third *Unfashionable Observation*. Nietzsche's Greeks were, essentially, the cipher for a cultural program of reeducation. The great renewal he dreamed about coincided with the return to a "tragic" worldview. "We are becoming *more Greek* from day to day," he noted, still in the mid-1880s. "Herein lies (and has ever lain) my hope for the German character!" – a hope that Nietzsche connected with sweeping pedagogical fantasies. Although he initially looked primarily to the counter-revolutionary effect of Richard Wagner's music dramas, he began, on his own initiative, finding receptive disciples among his students in Basel. According to his first biographer, Lou Andreas-Salomé, he possessed an extraordinary talent for "attaching young people to himself." "At some point no thought will exist at all but *education*," read his unpublished notes from the period – all the more unfortunate that his pedagogical utopia never really came about. It is understandable why his life was overshadowed by "student panic," at least from the end of his academic career.[18]

After completing his studies in law and philosophy, Colli wanted to remain at the university, but unlike Nietzsche, who had become a professor in his mid-twenties, he found himself compelled to move to the provinces as a schoolteacher. He probably felt he was not living up to his potential, yet at the same time, the new assignment must also have jibed with his ambitions. Perhaps a high school in a Tuscan town was just the right place to found a "monastery of freer spirits." Inspired by his readings of Nietzsche and full of Graecophile fantasies, Colli reinvented himself in 1942 as a charismatic pedagogue.

He was not concerned with conveying the prescribed school curriculum; he was concerned with "beginning life from scratch in the Greek manner." What fifteen-year-old with intellectual proclivities would this prospect not have enticed? All the more so since the shift in attitudes Colli promised depended not just on the right thinking, but also on erotic and musical experiences. What was just as important as reading Nietzsche and Schopenhauer were the evenings when the teacher gathered his pupils around his gramophone to play Beethoven symphonies for them. Beethoven alone, as Colli later put it, could convey an intuitive sense "that this life – precisely in its harrowing vehemence, in its monstrosity – deserves to be lived." The Greeks as the blossom of human culture, and music as an experience capable of touching the ineffable: were these students aware how deeply their teacher carried them off into the mythology of that country which occupied Lucca with its troops in the autumn of 1943?[19]

Colli was guided by a German, philhellenic model in an erotic sense as well: his notions of schooling were inspired by the Platonism of German progressive education. Linda Bimbi, one of the Chosen Few who later went to Brazil as a political activist, recalled a dramatic reading of Plato's *Symposium*.[20] The dialogue is about a banquet at the home of the prize-winning Athenian playwright Agathon at which the guests vie to give the best speech praising Eros, god of love. Pausanias, Agathon's young lover, extemporizes about the merits of pederasty; the comic poet Aristophanes tells the famous myth of the humans divided in half; only Socrates refrains from delivering a festive speech and instead recounts the teaching of the priestess Diotima, according to which love gives voice to the unquenchable desire of mortals to participate in the immortality of the gods through union and procreation.

When the drunken Alcibiades shows up, the evening devolves into an orgy of drinking. Asked to contribute a hymn of praise to Eros as well, Alcibiades instead vents his disappointment in Socrates, who seeks company with beautiful youths – it is absolutely no coincidence he is seated beside the host Agathon on this evening – but who in the past has always resisted Alcibiades' own attempts at seduction. Afterward, the dialogue experiences a sort of blackout, and we suddenly find ourselves at the end of the party. Only Socrates, handsome Agathon, and Aristophanes can still keep themselves upright and are discussing which of the genres they represent professionally, so to speak – tragedy, comedy, or philosophy – is superior to the others. At dawn, after Socrates has also drunk his last two interlocutors under the table, he leaves, takes a bath, and as always goes about his daily labors.

It is possible to work out who took which part in the dramatic reading of the *Symposium*. The roles of the rival protégés, Agathon and Alcibiades, were reserved for Colli's favorite students, while the teacher, whom Linda Bimbi half ironically called "our Socrates," surely insisted on playing Plato's idol, desired by all, and executed in 399 BCE for "corrupting the youth."[21]

The *Symposium* deals with how best to slip into a banquet as an uninvited guest, what remedies there are for hiccups, and whether it makes sense to drink more to get rid of a hangover. What makes this dialogue – with which Plato had introduced Socratic philosophy in his day – a must-read in Colli's eyes, however, is the fact that it calls to mind what this mode of thought once was; the triumph of philosophy over rhetoric and poetry was expressed not only in Socrates' dialectical refinement, but also in his tolerance of alcohol. For his initiation into the mysteries of love, though, Socrates had the seer Diotima to thank. As philosophy was celebrating its dominance over tragedy and comedy, then, it simultaneously admitted its dependence on the sources of an esoteric knowledge.[22]

In Plato's biography, Colli explained, this dialogue marked a decisive turning point. Just as the elder Greek sages, he, too, first had had to pass through a mystical initiation whose deeper truth could not be expressed in language. But with the *Symposium*, he had returned to the communicative collective of the *polis* in order to dedicate himself to educating the youth – also the moment the new figure of the philosopher was born. At this juncture, Colli came back to Socrates' speech on Eros. It numbered among the worst aberrations of the modern age to have conflated love with the sex drive, since it was in reality a matter of the universal desire of mortals to elude their mortality by means of procreation and propagation. And the ultimate form of this "production amid the beautiful" was the desire to beget the values of "sophrosyne" and "righteousness," or in Plato's words: to propagate oneself in the "beautiful, generous, and naturally gifted soul[s]" and "beautiful bodies" of students.[23]

The Blue Light

"*Carissimo pedagogo*," dearest pedagogue, begin the letters Mazzino Montinari wrote to Colli between the autumn of 1943 and early 1944 while the teacher was off staying with his family in Piedmont. They are the letters of a fifteen-year-old boy who made no secret of his intense feelings. "How I wish you were here!" – "Come, come back to Lucca!" – "I think of you every day at least four or five times!" – so much for the general tenor of this correspondence, only one side of which survives, unfortunately. From playful flirtation to openly acknowledged longing, Montinari pulled out all the stops. One moment he feared his teacher could have fallen victim to the bombings of Turin. Another moment he was haunted by the notion that Colli had taken a different favorite pupil in his hometown. "Watch yourself! I would be terribly jealous . . . and resentful! But I am sure it isn't true and banish this ugly thought."[24]

Montinari's letters are signed with "*pais*," the Ancient Greek term for pupil. In the winter of 1943–4, he had long been playing his role in Colli's Platonic fantasy of education. The pair never again emerged from their Graecophilic role play; even twenty years later, when Colli reported on his progress in Weimar's Nietzsche Archive, Montinari adopted the tone of a student seeking his teacher's approval or fearing his censure. "If you were to drop me, I would suddenly no longer feel loved," he wrote in early 1968. "An Alcibiades without Socrates."[25]

Mazzino Montinari, 1946

As the letters from young Montinari show, he listened to Brahms and Beethoven, read Kant and Nietzsche, and, to improve his Greek, translated Plato's *Gorgias*. "If it weren't for the bombing raids, I would've already completed a lot more." He wanted to live out philosophy "in its complete etymological sense." "By that I mean constantly striving for wisdom in every aspect of my external and, much more importantly, my internal life. – Does that seem right to you?" Colli's answer may no longer be extant, unfortunately, but it is beyond all question that his pupil's avowal suited him. "Mazzino is now my new *pais*," he wrote to his wife, "and an especially good one at that. He is the first philosophical person who responds to me – philosophical in my way."[26]

In reminiscences about Montinari, there is often talk of his "radicality." For a scholar who spent half his life deciphering a *Nachlass* and who died peacefully among his books, it is not immediately clear what that is supposed to mean. It is necessary to read his letters if you want to discover the enthusiasm underlying his philology. His former schoolmates remember his religiosity, his moral rigidity, and his need for meaning, which within a handful of years will prompt him to try out a smorgasbord of worldviews, "from atheism to religious crises to communism." Before meeting Colli, he had toyed with the idea of joining the Dominican order, but his new teacher steered his existential search on to a new path.[27]

In a letter from December 1943, Montinari broached the subject of a night not long before on which they had sat side by side beneath a "blue light" "obsessed with Dionysus" while the "faint glow" of his faith was snuffed out. Regardless of how we are to imagine the scene, Colli apparently succeeded in winning over a proselyte for his Greek gods. In a letter to his wife, he mentioned the incident from his own point of view: "Mazzino does not disappoint me. I have already managed to talk him out of the notion that he's called to be a monk. I've taught him the Dionysian. Now he's in the enthusiastic phase." Which is no exaggeration: according to his friends' recollections, Montinari celebrated his new faith by pan-frying a crucifix on both sides.[28]

You can picture what sorts of rumors circulated in Lucca about the new philosophy teacher who ignored the curriculum, consorted with his pupils in private, and seduced them away from the Church. Linda Bimbi remembered her parents shaking their heads when she came home late one night after one of their symposia. The German occupation and the war ensured that school discipline went to seed and young people were left to their own devices – a favorable starting position for Colli's pedagogical ambitions. That he shepherded his pupils from the twilight of Catholicism into the light of an imaginary Hellenism was, without a doubt, an act of liberation. That he also encouraged them to talk openly about their love affairs was, in a town like Lucca in the 1940s, a gesture the progressiveness of which can scarcely be imagined. But what about the Graecophile role play, the cult of Platonic eroticism, the apologia vis-à-vis homosexuality? What about the murmured rituals of initiation, Montinari's obvious infatuation, and Colli's obvious cravings for authority? Subordinating oneself to a "leader who instills in us respect and admiration," Colli later wrote in his introduction to the Italian edition of Nietzsche's "Schopenhauer as Educator," was the first step toward developing one's own personality. Just as in other enlightened circles, competition for the leader's favor was part of this game in Lucca as well. Montinari's rival was Angelo Pasquinelli, two years his senior, who still occupied the position of the first *pais* ahead of him. Pasquinelli, too, agonized his way through Plato in the original, attempting to adopt a Dionysian sensibility and be a good philosopher. And while the writing in his letters does come off as somewhat more mature, he idolized his teacher just the same.[29]

As things are, one might not really suspect girls to be among Colli's pupils – the mixture of enthusiasm for Greece, secret-mongering, and the emphasis on the master-relationship having generally involved their exclusion, at least in German conclaves from the first half of the twentieth century. In the case of the Chosen Few, however, things are different. As it emerges from the extant correspondence, Colli seemed to have even encouraged his *paides* to bring their fellow female schoolmates along. At any rate, Pasquinelli did not allow his Dionysian feelings to prevent him from keeping Colli updated on the progress of his relationship with Gigliola Gianfrancesco, coveted by all, and submitting her to a crucial test, perhaps at Colli's suggestion. "I gave her *Zarathustra* to read; this is trial by fire. Do you think she'll pass?"[30] Gianfrancesco evidently showed herself to be up to the task, for not much later she belonged to Colli's circle as a permanent member.

"[I]n Italy it's the family which accounts for everything, justifies everything, is everything," wrote Leonardo Sciascia in his investigation of the abduction of Aldo Moro. One might tentatively apply his diagnosis to the Chosen Few; perhaps it is less a matter of gender politics than the proverbial Italian sense of family that put a stop to the excesses of male homosocial relationships in Colli's circle. In time, at least, the initial confraternity of *paides* transformed into an agglomeration of couples, which is to say, future families. When Colli's wife followed him to Lucca after the war with their young daughter, she was also incorporated into the group, by which their gatherings took on an addition familial note, since Anna Maria assumed the function of the housewife hostess. In Italy, even the Dionysian had a culinary character. Yet in spite of the classical division of duties, the emancipatory effect of Colli's coeducation should not be underestimated. As Clara Valenziano, who was later part of the founding editorial staff of the communist daily newspaper *il manifesto*, recalled, irrespective of

NIETZSCHES WERKE

BAND VII

Also sprach Zarathustra

Ein Buch für Alle und Keinen

Aus dem Nachlass 1882-1885

ÜBERSETZUNGSRECHT VORBEHALTEN

LEIPZIG, 1925

The first Italian edition of Nietzsche's collected works appeared in the late 1920s with Casa editrice Monanni. The publisher actually specialized in anarchist literature.

FEDERICO NIETZSCHE

COSÌ PARLÒ ZARATHUSTRA

UN LIBRO PER TUTTI E PER NESSUNO

INTRODUZIONE E APPENDICE
DI ELISABETTA FOERSTER-NIETZSCHE
PRIMA EDIZIONE ITALIANA AUTORIZZATA
TRADUZIONE DI DOMENICO CIAMPOLI

CASA EDITRICE MONANNI - MILANO (38)

the homoerotic atmosphere among the Chosen Few, a climate of intel-lectual equality predominated.[31]

The defining period lasted only a few months – but it left a deep impression on all those involved. Just how deep is clear from a letter that Montinari wrote in 1981, two years after Colli's death, to the latter's widow. As a professor in Florence, an internationally renowned Nietzsche expert, and a Fellow at the Wissenschaftskolleg in West Berlin, Montinari was then at the pinnacle of his academic success. But, as ever, he was plagued by old demons. "My past and present life is backward," he wrote, "everything is disintegrating and leaving behind a feeling of failure." If it were not for that recurrent dream in which beautiful Gigliola Gianfrancesco played the lead role.

> Gigliola and you, you both were the living symbol of something strong, archaic, youthful, of those divine moments we experienced in those days, in the brief time when we were all together: Giorgio, Angelo, you, Gigliola, and me. Never again have I experienced moments of inner fulfillment comparable to those when I was together with Giorgio listening to him talk. And in those days it was you who already belonged to Giorgio, with your enthusiasm and your intensity. The highpoint and the end of this archaic time were the months between December 1943 and April 1944, when I turned sixteen and Giorgio had to leave Lucca. – After that, "normal" life began, with many fine moments and some bad ones, but during that time everything began for me. That was when Giorgio imprinted his seal on my life forever.[32]

Magic of Letters

Wherever he was, there was Greece, Stefan George supposedly indicated to his disciples. The possibility cannot be ruled out that Colli made a similar pronouncement. His maxim, too, was "to begin life from scratch in the Greek manner," and he, too, was fully aware of his charismatic impact on his adherents. Yet while he absolutely possessed a poetic streak, Colli must be pictured less as the inspired poet than as the introverted scholar. To make present what was of the

The circle and the family: Gigliola Gianfrancesco, Clara Valenziano, Anna Maria, and Giorgio Colli (from left). In front, Chiara and Enrico Colli. Lucca, 1947

past, he looked not to lyric incantations, but to the means of strict erudition.[33]

Among the texts he had written in the late 1930s during the period of his emergent enthusiasm for Greece may be found a sort of intellectual self-affirmation bearing the title "Il filologo" – "The Philologist." The choice makes sense – after all, philology was the discipline that had taken on the task of officially maintaining philhellenism since the nineteenth century. In the generation after Winckelmann, the Graecophile *Zeitgeist* was established in advanced school instruction and in classical studies. The price for its institutional success? Academization. In the second half of the nineteenth century, the zeal for Greece that had sent the likes of Hölderlin into peak lyric form was threatening to solidify into philological scholasticism. It was for this very reason, to breathe new life into the genre, that Nietzsche, the classical philologist, had devised a new tenor for *his* Graecophilia. With his Dionysian Greeks, who had not yet lost touch with the wild heart of the world, he had set in opposition to Winckelmann's classicist Hellenes the harshest antithesis imaginable, their confident equilibrium in reality an embodiment of the virtues of the German educated middle classes. The break with his discipline had been unavoidable. His colleague Ulrich von Wilamowitz-Moellendorff had even bluntly called on him to vacate his professorship: "But let him step down from the lectern from which he is supposed to teach knowledge. He may gather tigers and panthers around his knees but not Germany's philologically interested youth, who are supposed to learn – in the asceticism of self-denying work – to look everywhere for nothing but the truth."[34]

For Colli's idol Nietzsche, philologists embodied the epitome of mental mediocrity. And yet, Montinari later recalled, Colli nevertheless led him and his schoolmates "through the stubble field of philology" and – entirely out of keeping at the school – familiarized them with difficult questions about the transmission of Plato's dialogues, the fragments of the pre-Socratics, and Nietzsche's *Nachlass*. As becomes apparent from his manuscript about the philologist, Colli reveled in bookishness, though not for its own sake, but rather merely as a means to a higher end. He was just as incapable of warming to philology as an academic study, of glorifying footnotes and appendices, as Nietzsche had been.[35] But just as for Nietzsche, the philologist for him was not an antiquarian whose responsibility was to restore ancient tradition, but a mediator – or, better yet, a prophet – who roused a foreign culture to new life.

What fascinated Colli about the Greeks were all the things that appealed to his own mystagogical streak: the rituals of initiation and divination as well as the tradition of an esoteric wisdom, which he viewed as the buried wellspring of philosophy. His "*filologo*" epitomized the attitude, lost in the modern era, of "interpreting the world as a secret"; he read the cosmos as a forest of signs or, as he put it, as an "expression" that implied "a common thread running through the essence of things." The "path of philosophy" that Colli wanted to walk together with his pupils was, in other words, a magic of letters, a philological mysticism that penetrated through the veil of words into the ineffable "Dionysian" heart of the world.[36]

It is now time to return to the arcanum in which the Chosen Few cloaked their gatherings. Compared to the sexual escapades of the George circle or Bataille's rites in the Bois de Boulogne, it appears almost alarmingly harmless. Ritual incantations do not survive from Lucca, nor is it known if Colli tried to persuade his *paides* to perform a human sacrifice on him. Neither is there even any credible recollection of how much drinking took place at their symposia. We must assume that the mystery the teacher celebrated with his pupils consisted in nothing more than reading together. In his afterword to the Italian edition of *The Birth of Tragedy*, Colli later spoke of an "ecstasy," one "which seems to spring up wholly from the typographic signs, consuming itself within them." He wanted to penetrate into Nietzsche's writings deeply enough that they would reveal, congealed into letters, the epiphany of the tragic worldview responsible for them – a practice of textual immersion that aimed at conjuring up a past experience. For this sort of inspirited reading, too, precursors could be identified, especially in German cultural history, from the circles of early Romanticism to the "speaking halls" of the German Youth Movement. Reanimating texts was the real trade secret of the Chosen Few.[37]

For that reason, it makes sense that Colli felt himself especially drawn to writings, so to speak, on the edge of writtenness. Among his favorite Greek authors, aside from Plato, were the pre-Socratics, whose entire written record consists of no more than a handful of abstruse fragments. And as a reader of Nietzsche, he harbored a special predilection for the material left unpublished during the former's lifetime, being of the opinion that Nietzsche the mystical thinker committed his most profound discernments, at the "limit of the inexpressible," only to his notebooks.[38]

In an exposé for the newsmagazine *Panorama*, Adriano Sofri characterized Colli as a thinker full of self-contradictions. There is indeed a deep irony in Colli's philological mysticism. On the one hand, he exhorted his pupils to go beyond bookish knowledge. The philosophy he modeled for them in his own life was to be nothing short of an initiation into an oral way of thinking and living. Yet precisely by attempting to repeat the ecstatic experiences seeding the writings of the philosopher he found relevant, he drove his pupils to practice a philological rigor that far exceeded the standard measure – a paradox that also characterized his own intellectual existence. "What is the point of alluding to Dionysian affirmation, to madness, to the play against all manner of abstraction and ossification, all the while consuming one's life with writing?," Colli asked with respect to his alter ego Nietzsche. Yet as much as he himself longed to accomplish something "that transcends paper and inkpot," he for his part scarcely managed to escape the "meagerness of literary activity."[39]

Hiding behind Colli's bookishness is a cultural paradigm: moving from the ideal world of culture into political praxis had forever proven difficult for Graecophiles. In its search for political grandeur, Europe of the modern era had always preferred looking to Rome. Identifying with the Greeks – who had been subjugated by the Romans – made sense, however, only if one intended to persuade oneself that it was the highest ridges of culture, not the lowlands of politics, that were of actual significance for humankind. While the bourgeoisie in France was securing its political rights to be heard, German intellectuals were forced to come to terms with their own sustained powerlessness. In order to transform their hardship into a virtue, they resorted to imagining themselves the belated successors to the allegedly apolitical and yet therefore culturally all the more superior Greeks. This self-image may have unleashed an impressive productivity in literature and philosophy. Politics, however, to the extent it played any role for the *Dichter und Denker*, thereby took on an unworldly, idealistic tone.[40]

In terms of politics, even Nietzsche, who declared himself the "last *anti-political* German," displayed the reflexes of a philhellenic German pastor's son. Shortly before his mental breakdown, he began to foretell "*grand politics*" and send letters in which he called his scattered adherents to prepare themselves for an imminent event to exceed all expectations. But Nietzsche did not want "*grand politics*" to be interpreted as politics in the customary sense, but as a cultural revolution that would unsettle the foundations of European civilization. Because he predicted in the near future a "spiritual war" of a scope never considered possible, many of his readers saw in him the dark prophet, if not the instigator, of the First World War.[41]

Colli would not have dreamed of viewing Nietzsche as a warmonger, seeing as how it was the latter's genteel distance from politics that he valued. "Nietzsche is the anti-political man par excellence," he declared to his pupils. "His doctrine aims for mankind's total distance from social and political interests." As with much that Colli said about

Nietzsche, there is of course a nagging suspicion here, too, that he was essentially referring to himself. At any rate, Montinari was of the opinion that his teacher was "even more classical, even more Greek," than Nietzsche himself. While Nietzsche at least discovered politics toward the end of his life, Colli had always completely ignored the sphere of human coexistence.[42]

The schoolteacher made no secret of his loathing for fascism, though. Whenever he contrasted the nobleness of the ancient Greeks with the vulgarity of the Romans, Mussolini's raucous cult of *romanità* is of course also meant. Whenever he claimed Nietzsche has been "dragged through the mud," it was superfluous to ask to whom the allusion is referring. Like his father, the former managing director of *La Stampa*, Colli was inclined toward liberal convictions, but to call him a liberal is a half-truth at best, for unlike with the bourgeois antifascists, no sort of political agenda emerged from his liberalism. The freedom of the individual that he believed in is the freedom *from* politics. In February 1943, when news reached Lucca of the defeat of the German 6th Army in Stalingrad, Colli implored his *paides* to remain with Plato and Beethoven. Since life in its lack of redemption could only be justified on aesthetic grounds, such external events were inconsequential. "It's not about changing the world of history," he later wrote. "In light of what a handful of people are capable of thinking and saying to one another, the changes in societies and states amount to little. What a dirty business politics is."[43]

The School of Higher Ignorance

It is by this point, at the latest, however, that we stumble upon Colli's second self-contradiction, which, within the context of the times, may run even deeper. For just as he turned his Chosen Few into precocious philologists – in spite of his aversion to books – so, too, did his apolitical teachings contribute to their politicization. In any case, among the pupils at the Ginnasio N. Machiavelli who were drawn into the maelstrom of politics, a disproportionate number of *paides* stand out. This is also of course due to the fact that Colli had chosen an inauspicious moment to inaugurate his school of higher ignorance:

in the summer of 1943, Italy became a war zone. The events coming thick and fast from July onward could no longer be shrugged off as irrelevant. On the tenth of the month, the Americans landed in Sicily; two weeks later, the Duce was deposed. After the new government under General Badoglio officially capitulated on September 8, having thereby de facto abandoned the alliance with Hitler, Italy came under occupation by the Wehrmacht in its "Operation Axis." The war the majority of Italians knew primarily from their newspapers up until then, aside from the Allied bombings, suddenly plagued them on their own territory. This was especially true for Tuscany, where a few miles north of Lucca, along the southern edge of the Apennines, the so-called Gothic Line ran, that neuralgic German defensive position that might best stop the advance of the Allied armies from the south.[44]

While the enemy armies were taking up their positions throughout the late summer, the collapse of the fascist regime, including among the Italian populace, released political energies long bottled up. In September, the first antifascist partisan leagues formed. Yet after Mussolini, liberated by the Germans and installed in Salò on Lake Garda, proclaimed the Repubblica Sociale Italiana on the twenty-third of that month, fascism in northern Italy experienced a convulsive renaissance as well. New military formations, new police units, and a new Guarda Nazionale were mustered. In addition, paramilitary Black Brigades were formed to battle the partisans. The conflict waged by the international powers on Italian soil unraveled into a bloody civil war. The waves of conscription that coursed through the country in subsequent months left Italians fit for military service no choice but to join either one of the new fascist combat leagues or the *Resistenza* – or to seek their salvation by hiding and fleeing.

The surviving correspondence gives an inkling of how the war burst into the lives of Colli's *paides*. Angelo Pasquinelli was the first one no longer capable of concentrating on his Greek under the prevailing conditions. His enthusiasm for Nietzsche and Gigliola Gianfrancesco notwithstanding, he suffered a personal crisis at the beginning of the summer holidays that made school, friendship, and even Colli's initiation project appear pointless. "It is sad! I'm not in the mood for anything anymore, least of all reading. Whenever I think of my future and try to imagine my life, I'm groping around in total darkness."

Shortly thereafter, the coup d'état took place. In the letters he wrote to Colli after this incident, Pasquinelli comes across as a different person. Instead of Plato and Nietzsche, he read Marx and the Italian Marxist Labriola. Instead of cluelessness, he articulated resoluteness: "I have decided to look reality in the eye, whatever it may be; I don't want to deceive myself or pacify myself with emotional outbursts. As soon as you return, I will explain everything to you." That he reverted to using the formal "*Lei*" with Colli instead of the intimate informal "*tu*" is indicative of a sudden need for distance. It is quite possible, in proletarian Viereggio, where he had family, that Pasquinelli had come into contact with the *Resistenza*. Rather than return to school in the autumn, he joined the partisans.[45]

It was only at this point that Montinari rose in rank to Colli's favorite student. The night of "Dionysian obsession" on which his teacher disabused him of his faith must have occurred a short time after Pasquinelli went to ground. In Montinari's letters, too, there are allusions to "important decisions," but he mostly seemed resolved to "withdraw from the world" and be a good, which is to say Stoic, philosopher. What kept him busy was progress on his translation of *Gorgias*. At the same time, his letters reveal that he did not remain impassive in the face of historical events. "My brain is in constant turmoil," he informed Colli in November. He hoped not to do "anything stupid."[46]

It is to Luigi Imbasciati, the aforementioned schoolmate who admired Colli as a "great intellectual," that we owe the depiction of the events that made Montinari violate this resolution. In mid-December, at a propaganda evening put on by the fascist youth organization Gioventù Italiana del Littorio, a scandal erupted when the grammar school students in attendance refused to sing along to the concluding "Vincere." It did not help matters that the event organizers initially threatened not to let anyone leave the hall and then sent the schoolboys into the street between ranks of soldiers with fixed bayonets. In the exhilaration of their triumph, some of them showed up the next morning at the Ginnasio N. Machiavelli school singing *Risorgimento* songs to win over their classmates for an impromptu antifascist procession. As Imbasciati recalls, the authorities soon identified Montinari as the ringleader. He was arrested, interrogated, and beaten by militiamen from the Guarda Nazionale before he was allowed to go home. A few weeks later, the Capo della Provincia leading the investigations ordered him, along with the rest of the rabble-rousers, among whom were more *paides*, to be expelled from school.[47]

In one of the letters composed between his arrest and his expulsion, Montinari described his disposition. He no longer recognized himself, he wrote; the turmoil in his mind had subsided. "I feel the need to be alone and to reflect in silence" – as if the act of rebellion had put him into a state of inner clarity. Yet unlike with Pasquinelli, his political awakening did not involve distancing himself from his teacher. On the contrary, he wanted to dedicate himself to Greek even more earnestly than before, to work even harder than ever to be a good *pais*. He was intent on leading a Dionysian existence; philosophy, music, and love were to be the benchmarks of his life from now on.[48]

One of the lessons learned in the twentieth century is that cultivation and the intellect possess no intrinsic political or moral value. According to critics of German cultural history, the malevolent spirit of National Socialism emerged from the lofty tone of Graecophilia. Making the exaltation of an idealistic cultural sphere into the origin of all evil, however, is simply to pervert the old pathos of the poets and thinkers into its opposite. As the history of the George circle demonstrates, if nothing else, belief in an ideal body politic *did* inspire quite a few of its adherents to political resistance. Apparently, Colli's instruction had a similar impact. Linda Bimbi regarded him as a "wordless taskmaster of antifascism." As his students' reactions show, contempt for the political, particularly in a society that had been continuously politicized for two decades, could itself prove to be a political act – an interrelationship of which Colli also seemed, at least in retrospect, to have been conscious. "The secret is the invention of a terrible weapon against the state," he noted in 1957 in regard to the intentions behind his arcane group formation. In *Critique and Crisis*, his dissertation on indirect politicization in European Masonic lodges written during that same period, German historian Reinhart Koselleck came to a similar conclusion. Montinari also later insisted on having acquired from Colli not only his enthusiasm for Nietzsche and the Greeks, but also his "opposition to fascism." Far from forming spheres separate from or even antithetical to one another, culture and politics fused together into a singular nexus of experience in the months between December 1943 and April 1944.[49]

Looking back, the particulars of what happened at the time can no longer be reconstructed. Doubtless, the meetings of the Chosen Few took on further heightened importance in light of their exclusion from school, the state of exception providing immediate evidence of Colli's ideas about the autonomy of the individual. From the beginning of 1944, their gatherings were no longer conducive just to reading *Zarathustra* together, but also to preparing for what Italian historiography has termed "civil resistance." No further details about the *paides'* activities, however, are known. We know only that Montinari was temporarily forced to hide out in the attic of the Teatro del Giglio, that nevertheless he fell back into the hands of the fascists – and that he felt the "irresponsible euphoria" of heroism in prison. Decades later, in conversation with Frank Schirrmacher, he described the experience of that "unsurpassable" intellectual freedom which Colli had preached as the aim of his Dionysian exercises. To provoke his jailers, he asked them to send to his cell a copy of Plato's *Republic*. "The work about ethics of the state and the freedom of the spirit," Schirrmacher remarked, "ought to have been recognized as a danger if the militia hadn't been so stupid." Instead: "the victory of the book over the machine gun."[50]

While Montinari was experiencing the power of philosophy, the Allies advanced northward. In April 1944, Giovanni Gentile was murdered by partisans in Florence – an incident that unleashed a frenzy of high spirits among the Chosen Few, for even if he had not played an important role for a long while, in their eyes, Gentile, Mussolini's Hegelian, embodied false utopian thought and its corruption by the promises of power. Lasting into the wee hours of the morning on account of the night-time curfew, the party for Montinari's sixteenth birthday became a final culmination of their "archaic" time together. Ten days later, on April 14, "awful news" arrived – as Colli recorded laconically in the journal he had kept since that spring. It may have had to do with his conscription, which up until now he had successfully dodged. The following day, he cleared out his apartment in Lucca and traveled to his parents' home in Turin, probably to see whether any alternatives would present themselves, for going to war on Mussolini's behalf was – especially in the spring of 1944 – not a conceivable option. Evidently, these inquiries proved fruitless, because on April 19 Colli's journal read "decision" and on April 20 "Milano Mazzino." From Milan, Colli and Montinari traveled on toward the Alps, into the Valtellina. There, two days later, the student, familiar with the area because his mother was from here, led his teacher, along with an unspecified group of Italian Jews, over a lonely mountain summit in the Bernina massif into neutral Swiss foreign territory.[51]

Colli largely spent the following year in a refugee camp near Lugano, tracking the Allied advance by radio, forging plans for the future, and looking back at the twenty-seven years of his life hitherto. According to a sullen self-portrait in his journal, he discerned in himself "egoisms large and small," cravings for domination, and a "grave lack of self-criticism." To judge by his letters to his wife, however, his exile was generally characterized by a feeling of lightheartedness. "You don't need to worry about me. The best of health, easy work, good mood." Unafflicted by genuine existential doubts, Colli alternatively pondered publishing his "youthful writings" or formulating a "definitive philosophical system." Any trace of Montinari, back in Tuscany following his rescue operation, is missing from this period, however. Clara Valenziano described how Lucca transformed into a city of women over the summer of 1944. While the men were stationed at one front or the other, on the run, or living an underground existence, it was up to women to see to their survival. With their bicycles, they sallied forth into the surrounding land on extended foraging rides. In the deserted fields, these new matriarchs were privy to the experience of an unknown freedom. "We lived like prehistoric gatherers, rummaging through the bushes, eating berries and roots, and browsing the rows of the vineyards."[52]

Because of the proximity to German defensive positions along the Gothic Line, the *Resistenza* was especially active in the area around Lucca. It was here that the German occupation troops carried out some of their bloodiest acts of reprisal to weaken support for the partisans among the population. At daybreak on August 12, 1944, units of the Waffen-SS killed over 400 residents of the mountain village Sant'Anna di Stazzema, just thirty miles northwest of Lucca. "Everything is awful. What will become of our friends?," Colli wondered to Anna Maria. A short time later, he reported "that our Lucca is under fire by artillery at this very moment." When American troops moved into the city on September 5, the war was over. Soon afterward, the new school year began, and Montinari and the other agitators were allowed to attend classes again. In the spring of 1945, Colli returned from his exile. Full of enthusiasm, the *paides* resumed their meetings, but for those who had experienced resistance and liberation, the evenings with Plato and Beethoven no longer generated the same intensity. In November, Montinari passed the entrance exam for the Scuola Normale in Pisa and, for the time being, left Colli and Nietzsche and the Greeks behind him.[53]

2

PAINSTAKING CARE AND CLASS WARFARE
Pisa, 1948

In his posthumously published diary from academic year 1937–8, Karl Eugen Gass – the German exchange student mentioned in the previous chapter – left behind interesting, detailed impressions of studying at Italy's elite university, which Napoleon founded at the beginning of the nineteenth century. His descriptions recounted the beauty of existence in the palazzo, restored by Vasari, where the Republic of Pisa's council of elders had once convened; the interactions between professors and students, which, to an observer accustomed to the hierarchical set-up of German universities, seemed extremely nonchalant; but also, on the other hand, the "lack of any sort of social life," which consisted of little more than occasional visits to the cinema and evening walks down the Borgo Stretto, a promenade lined with arcades.[1]

Gass, for whom his dissertation advisor Ernst Robert Curtius had held very high hopes, was killed while deployed at the front toward the end of 1944. One year later, Montinari was part of the first generation to resume studies after the wartime closure of the Scuola Normale. He himself did not keep a journal, alas. What we know about his university studies stems, therefore, to a large extent from second-hand sources. We may assume that the new first-years also groaned under the burden of the workload, promenaded down the Borgo Stretto, and met up in one another's rooms for harmless carousing – although there were dire supply shortages after the war. With the exception of

Students in front of the Scuola Normale, Pisa, early 1940s

Giovanni Gentile, the last rector, the academic staff was even largely the same. What had changed, however, was the intellectual atmosphere in the war-torn city. For although Gass had stumbled upon a skeptical faculty already widely disillusioned by fascism in 1937, in 1946 a spirit of optimism was in the air. Perhaps we might imagine the atmosphere a bit like that in a neorealist Rossellini film. The self-image of a large number of professors and students had been shaped by the experience of antifascism and resistance. What resulted from this was the expectation of involvement in building a new society.[2]

On the Joy of Being Communist

At the end of the first semester in March 1946, Palmiro Togliatti, head of the Communist Party and Minister of Justice in the antifascist government of national unity, came to visit. The impression Togliatti had made on Jean-Paul Sartre, who had gotten to know him in the 1950s, was "as though through magic some giant had infiltrated the body of a grammar school teacher." His speech beneath the dark ceiling joists of the medieval auditorium was dedicated to the "Italian utopians and social reformers" who had been dreaming of a better society since the eighteenth century. The hour had come to realize this dream: "We all feel we have arrived at the point where either something fundamental will change in the structure and organization of modern society or we will inevitably be headed toward a new, unspeakable catastrophe." *Socialisme ou Barbarie*, as a group comprised of Marxist intellectuals founded a short time later in France would dub itself: this was essentially the choice Togliatti presented as well – that barbarism might win out, however, was something almost none of his listeners considered possible in the spring of 1946. The triumph of Labour against Churchill's Tories the previous year seemed to portend a reversal of the trend: the Left was on the move, not just in England, but throughout Europe.[3]

Montinari also seemed to have been impressed by Togliatti. In his search for a spiritual home, he, like many of his age-mates, would become a communist. There may seldom have been a better time or a better place to do so. Half a century later, Toni Negri would recall the "lightness and joy of being communist" in his theory bestseller *Empire*. It is quite possible that the collective experience of Italian intellectuals in the postwar period is contained in that phrasing. At any rate, the lightness and joy of communism must have been palpable at the Scuola Normale in those days.[4]

Having returned from his exile in Moscow in 1944, in just a few years Togliatti had procured for the Partito Comunista Italiano (PCI, Italian Communist Party) an electoral base spanning all classes. In this endeavor, he profited as much from the aura surrounding the *Resistenza* as he did from the new luster of the Soviet Union. We must not forget that Stalin emerged at the end of the war not as a mass murderer, but as Europe's illustrious liberator. Togliatti's political style can be gleaned from the tenor of his speech in Pisa: by calling on his auditorium to close ideological rifts, he evoked the antifascist united front; by emphasizing the compatibility of revolution and reform, he legitimized his parliamentary policy; by retracing the history of a native millenarian tradition, he made the just society the business of all Italians. As in Greece, where the war would devolve into a civil war in

1946, a climate of smoldering violence prevailed in Italy after liberation as well. That communist resistance fighters relinquished their weapons to assume power by legal means was due in no small part to Togliatti's influence. "No adventures, Comrades, no adventures!," he himself is said to have whispered in 1948, even as an assassin's bullet wounded him and Italy again stood at the precipice of an armed conflict. For some, this was how he became a hero of democratic socialism. From the others, he must put up with the accusation of having missed the *kairos* of the revolution.[5]

Under Togliatti, the PCI became not only the strongest in membership, but also, to use the wording of Sartre, the "most intelligent" among Western communist parties. When in his speech he appealed to the "men of research" to lend their support to the "men of action" in order to create a "renewed Italy," these were not then empty words, for it was precisely the sphere of the cultural superstructure to which the chairman accorded special significance. He replaced the old Leninist-Bolshevik guard with a younger generation of operatives with academic backgrounds. He was responsible for founding newspapers, like *La Rinascità* and *Il Poletecnico*, that became forums for avant-garde culture and Marxist theoretical debates. Above all, however, he invoked an author at every opportunity who conferred upon intellectuals a central role in the class struggle.[6]

Comrade Job

Thanks to his belated celebrity, Antonio Gramsci's fate is widely known today. Sentenced by the fascist judiciary in 1928 to a long prison term for inciting civil war, this cofounder and general secretary of the PCI died from the consequences of his incarceration just under ten years later at the age of forty-six. His biography alone would have predestined him to play the part of a symbolic political figure. His lasting fame, however, traces its origin back first and foremost to his written legacy. The *Lettere di Carcere*, Gramsci's letters from prison, harrowingly document the battle of an intellectual passionately interested in the world for his physical and mental survival. The *Quaderni di Carcere* (*Prison Notebooks*), his encyclopedic reflections on Italian history, the role of intellectuals, and the strategy of the modern class struggle, are today counted among the classics of Marxist literature. After Gramsci's death, they were smuggled into the Soviet Union by a female relative, where they fell into the hands of the expatriate Togliatti, who brought them back to Italy in 1944 and set about their expeditious publication.[7]

In early 1947, one year after Togliatti's visit to Pisa and in time for the tenth anniversary of Gramsci's death, the time had finally come. Luigo Rosso, director of the Scuola Normale, introduced the first volume of the collected works of Gramsci published by Einaudi. From his address, one might glean all aspects of the role intended for Gramsci. Russo called to mind Gramsci's life and death and his heroic bravery. By characterizing him as a thinker "deeply rooted in the Italian tradition," he took pains not to cede the martyr solely to the radical Left. And finally, he provided insights into the "2,848 clearly and evenly handwritten pages" of the long-awaited *Prison Notebooks*, which were devoted to the theme of Gramsci's life: the function of intellectuals in the battle for hegemony.[8]

Considering that Theodor W. Adorno would become the master thinker of the New Left in West Germany just a few years later, it becomes clear why the tenor of theoretical debates in both countries was so different. To be sure, it is customary to class both Gramsci and Adorno with the economically heedless wing of "Western Marxism," but their commonalities essentially end with their general interest in the phenomena of the cultural superstructure. For while there is little left for intellectuals to do in the *posthistoire* of Adorno's "administered world" but cultivate their lack of consent, with Gramsci they are permitted to feel like the vanguard of the class struggle as they had been in their best years. Adorno may have employed the notion of the "message in a bottle" for his own writings, but the image is a much better fit for Gramsci. Attracting scholarly notice with a delay of almost two decades, his "philosophy of praxis" – which ironically exists only because the fascists had hindered him in his praxis – preserved the conditions of the 1920s and 1930s for the postwar period.[9]

As was the case for many other leftist intellectuals, the catalyst for Gramsci's theoretical work lay in asking why the revolution, which had eliminated feudalism in Russia, had failed in the more advanced

Western European countries, counter to the predictions of Marx's theory. Proceeding from this question, the German sociologist Max Weber had developed the theory of bureaucratic domination, the "iron cage" of which resisted all revolutionary upheavals. By contrast, Gramsci's response – which interested both the postcolonial Left and the New Right in the early twenty-first century – consisted in elaborating the concept of "hegemony."

In essence – and disregarding all nuances and facets that differentiate it further in the labyrinth of the *Prison Notebooks* – the term directs our attention toward the fact that domination is based not just on "power," but also on "conviction," not just on "politics," but also on "culture," or simply – to employ another of the dialectical pairs of concepts Gramsci so enjoyed using – not just on "authority," but also on "hegemony." What results from this is the strategically significant implication that – at least in states where the power of the bourgeois classes can draw upon schools, universities, and the mass media – a subversion of power relations has no chance without a long-term strategy of grassroots work in cultural policy, without gradually shifting attitudes, convictions, and manners of speaking. "Without a new mode of thought, without a high culture, no single political movement can be victorious in the modern world." Thus reads the conclusion that Luigi Russo drew from Gramsci's reflections. It goes without saying that the agents of the cultural struggle Gramsci also dubbed the "war of position" are the intellectuals, who in the history of Marxist theorizations neither have ever before been, nor will ever again be, accorded such a significance.[10]

No wonder, then, that Montinari felt drawn to communism. As a budding toiler in the vineyard of culture, he stood before a clearly delineated task here. Still, in exchange he had to relinquish the idea of "culture" that Giorgio Colli had conveyed to him. Using Nietzsche, Colli had transfigured culture into a sphere of liberated humanity threatened by politics and the state, while Gramsci saw in it a "molecular" form of domination alongside the monopoly on the state's use of force. In this respect, the two thinkers could hardly be more different. On the other hand, however, the path from Nietzsche to Gramsci appears straightforwardly logical. Had Colli not commended to his pupils Nietzsche's prototypical philosopher, who operated less

"§[138]. Past and present. Transition from the war of maneuver (and frontal assault) to the war of position – in the political field as well" (left side, middle). Italian postwar Marxism was under the spell of Gramsci's Prison Notebooks (cf. List of Illustrations, pp. ix–x])

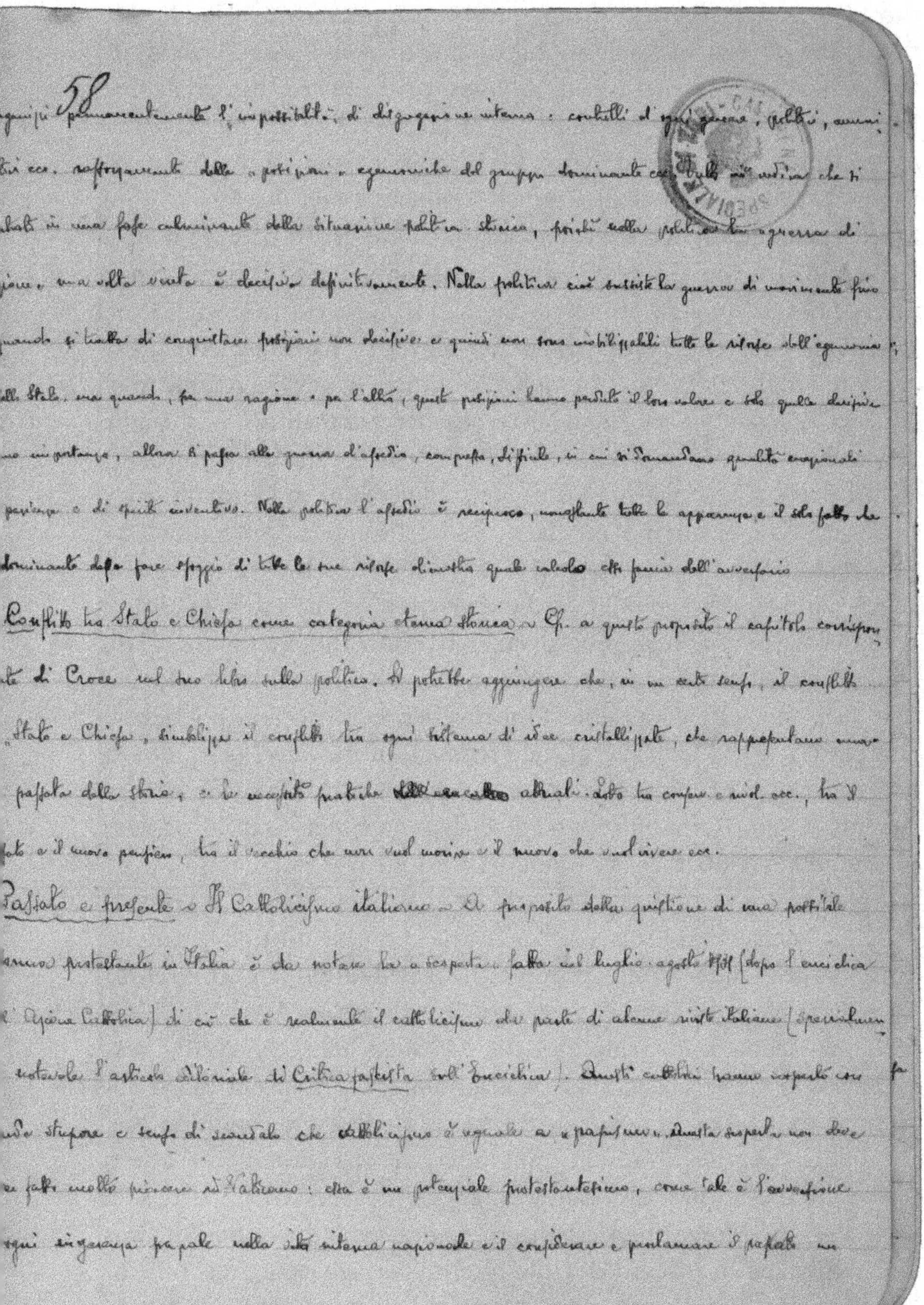

58 guisce permanentemente l'impossibilità di disgregazione interna: controlli d'ogni genere, politici, ammini-
strativi ecc. rafforzamento delle «posizioni» egemoniche del gruppo dominante ecc. Tutto ciò indica che si
rati in una fase culminante della situazione politico-storica, poiché nella politica la «guerra di
zione», una volta vinta, è decisiva definitivamente. Nella politica cioè sussiste la guerra di movimento fino
ando si tratta di conquistare posizioni non decisive e quindi non sono mobilizzabili tutte le risorse dell'egemonia
llo Stato, ma quando, per una ragione o per l'altra, queste posizioni hanno perduto il loro valore e solo quelle decisive
no importanza, allora si passa alla guerra d'assedio, compressa, difficile, in cui si domandano qualità eccezionali
pazienza e di spirito inventivo. Nella politica l'assedio è reciproco, nonostante tutte le apparenze e il solo fatto che
dominante debba fare sfoggio di tutte le sue risorse dimostra quale calcolo esso faccia dell'avversario.
Conflitto tra Stato e Chiesa come categoria eterna storica. Cfr. a questo proposito il capitolo corrispon-
te di Croce nel suo libro sulla politica. Si potrebbe aggiungere che, in un certo senso, il conflitto
«Stato e Chiesa» simbolizza il conflitto tra ogni sistema di idee cristallizzate, che rappresentano una
passata della storia, e le necessità pratiche attuali. Lotta tra conserv. e rivol. ecc., tra il
to e il nuovo pensiero, tra il vecchio che non vuol morire e il nuovo che vuol vivere ecc.
Passato e presente. Il cattolicismo italiano. A proposito della quistione di una possibile
ma protestante in Italia è da notare la «scoperta» fatta nel luglio-agosto 1931 (dopo l'enciclica
l'Azione Cattolica) di ciò che è realmente il cattolicismo da parte di alcune riviste italiane (specialmen-
notevole l'articolo editoriale di Critica fascista sull'Enciclica). Questi cattolici hanno «scoperto» con
de stupore e senso di scandalo che cattolicismo è uguale a «papismo». Questa scoperta non deve
fatto molto piacere al Vaticano: essa è un potenziale protestantesimo, come tale è l'avversione
ogni ingerenza papale nella vita interna nazionale e il considerare e proclamare il papato un

through his writings than through his personal example? Had he not traced the poverty of modern philosophy, time and again, back to its academization? "I benefit from a philosopher only to the extent that he is capable of setting an example," Nietzsche wrote in *Schopenhauer as Educator*. Who could have set a more persuasive example for the power of thought than Gramsci? He embodied the rare case of a modern philosopher who demonstrated the truth of his theories first-hand. During Gramsci's trial, Mussolini's state prosecutor had uttered the infamous words that one had to "prevent this brain from functioning for twenty years." By the power of his mind alone, the condemned thwarted this attempt. "Pessimism of reason, optimism of will," was his morale-boosting, Nietzsche-derived mantra, by which he elevated patience to the rank of a cardinal virtue for the revolutionary.[11]

The crop of students who attended universities in Germany after the war were given the moniker of the "skeptical generation" by sociologist Helmut Schelsky in 1957. He regarded their pragmatism, sober-mindedness, and political aloofness as a reaction to the political apocalypse of National Socialism. Just how differently the two countries exited the epoch of fascism can be inferred from the fact that the trend in Italy was almost the reverse: *not* to become politicized at a place like the Scuola Normale seemed, in the late 1940s, almost to be a matter of impossibility. In the elections for the Constituent Assembly, the Communists and Socialists together won 40 percent of the vote. Democrazia Cristiana (Christian Democracy), however, emerged as the strongest party, and its chairman, Alcide De Gasperi – Italy's Adenauer – also served as the head of the unity government. This was the initial configuration that provided the background for the polarization of Cold War camps in subsequent years. In 1947, with the Truman Doctrine and the Marshall Plan, the course was set. In economic respects, Italy was among those to profit most, but because the United States attached to its pledges the condition that the influence of the powerful Communist Party be curbed, De Gasperi provoked the antifascist coalition's split with the leftist parties in early 1947. The following year, the configuration of the Cold War was already locked in place. With the alternative between "freedom" or "Communism," Italy experienced a factional electoral campaign waged with great intensity by both sides.[12]

By this point, Montinari had long been championing the PCI. His more recent conversion seems to have taken place in the mode of existential crises as well. According to the recollections of a fellow student, he was still clearly pervaded by "religious spirit." Because of his friend's mood swings, Angelo Pasquinelli, who was likewise studying in Pisa, was concerned that "things might end up poorly" for him. We have one of Montinari's professors to thank for a character study that in its terse concision possesses an almost clinical quality: "extreme highs and lows, big problems, the tendency to torture himself and others and want to solve everything in an emotional manner."[13]

Montinari's politicization had an existential component for the very reason that it signified a break with the man to whom he owed his intellectual awakening. In the first *colloquio* the *Normalisti* have to pass every year to demonstrate their progress in learning, he still requested an examination on Parmenides. But to the extent that his fascination with the ancient Greeks waned, he also lost contact with Giorgio Colli; Colli's culture-as-religion, his arcane murmuring, and his elitism suddenly came off as reactionary. Conversely, communism was everything he had wanted to safeguard his pupils against: the belief that history is the manifestation of reason, that political involvement is the purpose of thought, and that a political utopia proceeds from the perfectibility of humankind. Did Colli, for his part, perceive it as a bitter irony that the party comrade who co-edited Gramsci's *Prison Notebooks* together with Togliatti bore the name Felice Platone, the "happy Plato"? Another twenty years later, Montinari would complain about his partner's having nothing but disdain for his political convictions.[14]

Le goût de l'archive

In one regard, Montinari nevertheless remained loyal to his *pedagogo*; it was not merely the *Zeitgeist* that alienated him from his former opinions, not merely the glamour of the party that converted him to a new worldview. The initiation into communism took on the form of personal fealty for him as well. This constellation is familiar from Thomas Mann's *The Magic Mountain*. While Colli embodies Mann's

Settembrini, the voice of bourgeois-liberal humanism, Montinari came under the influence of a radical in Pisa who in many respects resembles the Jesuit and Hegelian Leo Naphta.[15]

Delio Cantimori, who taught modern history at the Normale, was reserved, scornful, prim, but at the same time had a paternally approachable manner. That quite a few of Montinari's fellow students described him as "God" was due less to his personal charisma than to the fact that he epitomized the high art of historical learnedness, vesting it with unimagined relevance in the cultural battles of the Cold War. Cantimori had a reputation for spending every spare minute in the library. His seminars were exercises in a study of source material, the concreteness of which made the long speculative arcs of leftwing dialectics seem like relics of the bourgeois epoch. In this regard, his influence can be compared to that of a younger French scholar: like Michel Foucault a generation after him, Cantimori lent archival work a subversive aura of danger. Apart from their *goût de l'archive*, the two historians were further linked by an interest in marginal figures, in subversives and those excluded from modern society. Cantimori's scholarly renown was predicated on a study concerning Italian heretics of the late Renaissance first published in 1939, *Eretici italiani del Cinquecento*, and based on far-flung sources from German-language libraries – a study invoked by a school of Italian Church historians that still exists today.[16]

Yet what was impressive about Cantimori was not just the breadth of his historical knowledge. He was just as well versed in the theological subtleties of each heretical movement in the early modern period, however apocryphal, as he was in the state of class struggles. He read both the *Studi storici* and the international press. He was just as concerned with delivering lectures as he was with translating *Das Kapital* into Italian. The spectrum of his intellectual interests was held together by a political agenda: the professor in whose writings the French historian of antiquity Paul Veyne recognized the "cosmopolitan, enlightened, genuine-congenial atmosphere" of Italian postwar Marxism made no bones about being a communist.[17]

He was the unofficial representative of the PCI at the Normale, which students could tell from the mere fact that Palmiro Togliatti referred with his aforementioned address on "Utopisti e riformatori sociali" to Cantimori's book published three years earlier, entitled *Utopisti e riformatori italiani* (*Italian Utopians and Reformers*). The latter was devoted to the successors of the religious heretics, to the Italian freethinkers, Jacobins, and utopian socialists of the eighteenth and nineteenth centuries, whom the party chairman claimed in his speech as *his* predecessors. In the cultural battles on the Italian Left, Cantimori occupied a special position: he was the encyclopedist of dissidence whose research furnished proof of an autochthonous tradition of communism in Italy, untouched by Bolshevism and Stalinism.[18]

From Cantimori's lectures, Montinari became acquainted with a world of nonconformists, deviants, and rabble-rousers stretching from the Anabaptists of the sixteenth century to the professional revolutionaries of the twentieth. The plots of dialectical materialism played no role in them; Cantimori's political orientation was distinguished more by his skepticism of grand narratives. For him, being a Marxist meant having more rigorous empirical thinking, displaying greater exactitude, and practicing the asceticism of archival work. What lent this archival work its currency was its sectarian aura, the impression that, amid the latent civil war raging in Italy, Cantimori was surveying a hidden history of revolt and of messianic thought in which he himself was embroiled as a political intellectual.[19]

Without taking into account the influence of his Naphta, we cannot understand Montinari's latter stamina as a Nietzsche philologist. A letter – his first – that he addressed to the professor in February 1948, in the middle of that year's dramatic electoral campaign, contains thematic suggestions for the upcoming annual colloquium. There is no more mention of Parmenides, or any other Greeks besides. Instead, we see Montinari immersed in the document holdings of the various archives in his hometown, where, in line with Cantimori's motto to conduct "first-hand historical research," he compiled material on the sixteenth-century Counter-Reformation in Lucca. The following year, in his *tesi di laurea* (master's thesis), he turned to the other side, to the Protestant heretics who had stood their ground for almost twenty years before being put to flight by papal troops. In this unpublished study of his based on trial records from the Inquisition, he aimed to show that the new denomination was widespread among the lower classes of Lucca's population in particular, and that Protestantism had been not just a matter of faith, but also an act of social rebellion.[20]

Cantimori's history of religious deviance appealed to many leftists of the day. Echoes may be found in Italo Calvino's historical novels as well as in the microhistorical studies of his perhaps best-known pupil, Carlo Ginzburg, who in 1976 managed an international bestseller with his book on Menocchio, the heretical miller from Friuli. In his introduction to *The Cheese and the Worms*, Ginzburg revealed how deeply his preoccupation with the unknown Friulian miller had been motivated by political projections. In Menocchio's "aspirations for a radical reform of society," in the "eating away at religion from within," which his apocryphal ideas had contributed to, Ginzburg saw the beginning of a "line of development" reaching into the present. "In a sense he is one of our forerunners," he wrote. Calvino, too, had chosen the overarching title *Our Ancestors* for his trilogy of historical novels from the 1950s. In each case, the first-person plural refers to the Italian leftist intellectuals from the second half of the twentieth century.[21]

In his foreword to the German edition of *Eretici italiani del Cinquecento*, Cantimori himself suggested that his book was about a chapter in the history of "Italian intellectuals" which had remained Antonio Gramsci's unfinished life's work. Yet the foreword to the German edition dates from 1949. What his students did not know was that their professor had joined the National Fascist Party in 1926, the year of Gramsci's arrest. He had kept secret the fact that he had been fascinated by a very different breed of modern intellectuals when he had begun his studies on ecclesiastical history.[22]

Only after his death did a debate flare up in Cantimori's case about the submissiveness of Italian intellectuals. According to his defenders, Cantimori's fascist episode was an instance of youthful indiscretion, while his critics think they detect in it the expression of an antiliberal affect to which he remained true even later during his communist phase – for which reason his conversion proves nothing for them but his opportunism. If his own apologetic retrospective from the 1960s is to be believed, then in a fit of "mental confusion" he had made a mistake, amid the intellectual climate after the First World War, about the color of the revolution. Like many other intellectuals of his generation – at the time still more at home in philosophy than in history

– he had hoped fascism would finalize the incomplete project of the *Risorgimento*, the national unification of Italians into one strong state. The conceptual world of his politics, spelled out in books and articles since the late 1920s, had been shaped just as much by anticapitalist ideas as it had by anticlerical ones. Like his mentor Giovanni Gentile, he also sympathized with an organically divided "ethical-corporate" state, though with autonomous professional features, making him into a typical proponent of leftist fascism.[23]

Still, in his political thought experiments, Cantimori not only derived inspiration from the intra-Italian debate, but also tracked the developments in the antiliberal, antidemocratic milieu of the Weimar Republic with great interest. Aside from the attempts by National Bolsheviks and *Querfront* (cross-front) intellectuals to conceive of *völkisch* and socialist principles simultaneously, what primarily fascinated him was the ideological, fateful-existential – indeed, as he wrote in one of his essays, "religious" – intensity that seemed so characteristic to him of many authors from the national-revolutionary scene. Historians argue over whether Cantimori was guided by his studies of Church history in his analyses of the new German Right, or whether the events in Germany incited him to turn toward ecclesiastical history in the first place. At any rate, his conservative revolutionaries and his heretics exhibit conspicuous similarities. In the racist "sects," in the "new mystery cults" and "irrationalist movements" populating the political landscape of the Weimar Republic, he glimpsed "a need for renewal and for reform of social life" that had not existed in Germany to this degree since the time of the Reformation.[24]

After 1933, by dint of Hitler's seizure of power, an unexpected role as expert fell to Cantimori. Thanks to his familiarity with Germany, further deepened by multiple sojourns for study and research, he was able to make a name for himself as a cultural mediator – one might also say as an "Axis intellectual" – who helped the educated Italian public gain a deeper understanding of the new German regime through his essays, reviews, and translations. Carl Schmitt, whose treatise *The Concept of the Political* he had translated into Italian as *Principi politici del Nazionalsocialismo* in 1935, was full of praise for Cantimori's rendering. With regard to the extensive introduction the translator of the Italian edition had contributed, he was aware of "no other

depiction of Germany's intellectual position from outside Germany
that delves so far below the surface and displays so many insights into
details of intellectual-historical importance." Evidently, it had escaped
Schmitt, who even proudly bestowed the book on the Duce during his
audience in 1936, that Cantimori had at the same time also translated
into Italian the disquisition "Politischer Dezisionismus" ("Political
Decisionism"), which had been published under a pseudonym by his
friend Karl Löwith. In razor-sharp sentences, it stated that Schmitt,
theorist of the friend–foe distinction, himself ranked among the

Delio Cantimori with his wife Emma Mezzomonte (center) and an unknown
woman, around 1940

political romantics whom he had so severely taken to task elsewhere. It would be nice to know the cause of Cantimori's dual-track politics of translation. Did they have to do with his mercurial ideological flexibility, which, according to Löwith, who had been staying in Rome since 1934 to escape the German race laws, we have to hold responsible for the fact that Italian fascists, unlike German Nazis, were still "humane even in a black shirt," or was it owing to the fact that Schmitt's understanding of politics, in its fixation on the worst-case scenario of war, ran counter to Cantimori's own conceptions of a firmly structured authoritarian order in an "ethical state"?[25]

On one point, Cantimori unquestioningly accorded with Schmitt. For him, too, politics was not a necessary evil, but an expression of a higher reality of life, superordinate to the existence of individuals. As such – as a mode of human conduct related to the sphere of state and nation, or later to class – the political could be reduced neither to economic principles nor to moral ones. Insofar as the idealistic overtones elicited by Gentile faded and Cantimori renounced philosophy in order to turn toward historical empiricism, the latter cultivated a hard-nosed realism, condemning "moralists" and "beautiful souls" for their political naïveté.[26]

Cantimori maintained the cold style of disillusionment even after his conversion to Marxism – the timing of which is essential for its political and moral assessment. Had he already switched sides soon after his marriage in 1936 to the militant communist Emma Mezzomonte? Had the Hitler–Stalin Pact brought him closer to Bolshevism, or had he become a "staunch" leftist only after Mussolini's demise? Was it a sudden conversion experience or a gradual change of heart? Evidence may be found for each and every variation. No wonder Cantimori was said to have had "demons." Defying all efforts toward a historical reappraisal of his case, he remains to this day a dubious character.[27]

Everyone Else's Nietzsche

When Montinari was studying with him, Cantimori's primary interest did in fact involve those Enlightenment figures and utopians whom the contemporaneous Left claimed as their "ancestors." Nevertheless, they gadded about the fringes of his courses as ever: the renegades of the Second International, the *Querfront* intellectuals, Conservative Revolutionaries, and others who despised the bourgeois way of life – and with them Nietzsche, whom they had all invoked almost without exception. This Nietzsche, however, had hardly anything to do with the Nietzsche of Giorgio Colli. The author for whom Colli had stoked enthusiasm among his Chosen Few had shown contempt for modernity, while judging the present at a distance of 2,000 years. Cantimori's Nietzsche, on the other hand, was an unsettlingly contemporary thinker who had not merely surpassed the claim first formulated by Hegel that philosophy must keep pace with its own time, but had done it one better. "When I once wrote the word 'unfashionable' on my books," Nietzsche himself had been forced to realize when looking back on his early writings, "how much youth, inexperience, isolation expresses itself in this word! Today I comprehend that with this kind of lament enthusiasm and dissatisfaction I actually belonged to the most modern of moderns." In declaring war against bourgeois civilization and its values, he had in no way succeeded in escaping the momentum of modernism. On the contrary: he had actually shifted it into a higher gear.[28]

For Cantimori, this was simultaneously what constituted the political character of Nietzsche's thought – though not political in the sense that Nietzsche had allied himself with one of the existing parties or interest groups of his age. He had, to be sure, regarded democracy as the "disease" of the modern state, but he had not championed the cause of a restoration of the Old European order either. "We 'conserve' nothing, nor do we want to go back to any past; we are absolutely not 'liberal,' we do not work for 'progress,'" it reads in *The Joyful Science*. As Cantimori put it, Nietzsche's radicality consisted in his having negated the "field as such on which the political debate of modernity takes place." If Nietzsche had moved even beyond Marx in his critique of the status quo, according to Hugo Fischer – a German nationalist revolutionary, from the circle of Ernst Jünger, whom Cantimori considered one of the most important interpreters of Nietzsche during the interwar period – then that was because, as an apostate of the bourgeois world, Nietzsche had been a provocation for all those of its camps bonded by mutual resentment: for "nationalists and socialists, militarists and pacifists, monarchists and republicans, reactionaries and revolutionaries, capitalists and communists, chauvinists and pan-Europeans, Christians and atheists." In Nietzsche's own words: "I spoil everyone's taste for their party." That was why he had become a sloganeer for adherents of that "third path" which had rattled the political geography of European societies after the First World War: for the aristocratic radicals, the Conservative Revolutionaries, the Nationalist Bolsheviks, the German Socialists, the creative destroyers, the "believing doubters," and whoever else gave their political ambitions a paradoxical moniker.[29]

Academics in the War of Position

For the Italian Left, the memory of 1948 is linked to a trauma. Democrazia Cristiana emerged as the clear victor from the first elections of the young republic. Togliatti's strategy had therefore failed. Struck by the bullets of a rightwing assassin, the general secretary of the PCI was in a critical condition three months later. As in many Italian cities, spontaneous demonstrations erupted in Pisa as well. On the Piazza dei Cavaglieri, a fascist provocateur was beaten to death. In nearby Volterra, communists declared the Proletarian Republic. Even at the Scuola Normale, there were students making the case for an armed uprising, but as a classmate's memoirs recount, the moderates, among them Montinari, succeeded in persuading the radicals to participate instead in the general strike called by the leftist unified trade union.[30]

It is said that Gino Bartali's victory in that year's Tour de France saved the Italians from civil war. The far more crucial role, however, might have been played by Togliatti himself, who even from hospital managed to impose discipline on his party and even more emphatically committed it to toeing the constitutional line. After the turning point of 1948, the Catholics and the communists finally geared up for their culture war. While the PCI established a *commissione culturale* to coordinate its activities on that front more effectively, the Right, sitting at the long arm of power, made its first moves amid the new "war of position." To prevent the threat of the Scuola Normale transforming into a "cell sympathizing with the extreme leftwing parties," as the prefect of the Pisan administrative district suggested to Rome, Luigi Russo was ousted from his directorship in November 1948 and replaced with a Catholic scientist. The "Lex Andreotti," named after the eponymous young state secretary, prohibited funding for neorealist films. Having acted as an anticommunist crusader in the electoral campaign, Pope Pius XII expelled the PCI and its members from the Catholic community of faith in 1949.[31]

Rossana Rossanda, one of the few women who succeeded in rising to the Central Committee of the PCI, was among those assigned at the time to "pick up the pieces." From her memoirs, the shifts in atmosphere among the leftist camp are evident: "At a time when we needed nothing as urgently as friends, we let ourselves be seduced by the Cold War and by old Stalin's final fantasies of omnipotence into moronic modes of behavior, into assuming hubristic know-it-all attitudes toward anyone who did not share our views or follow the 'party line.'" Cantimori also had to discharge his duties more forcefully than before. The correspondence with the relevant bodies of the PCI preserved in his literary estate gives a good impression of a prominent academic's deployment in the war of position. Alluding to Machiavelli, Gramsci had dubbed the party the "modern prince." There is indeed an element of feudalism audible in the way the various subdivisions called on their foot soldier:

Dear Comrade, we have decided to adopt new and important measures with respect to the labor of intellectuals in the party, and would like to undertake a concrete allocation of tasks. It is therefore necessary for you to attend the meeting of the propaganda department of party headquarters scheduled for next Wednesday. Fraternally yours.

Or:

Dear Comrade, in consultation with the party secretary's office and as part of the membership recruitment campaign, our department has resolved to organize a series of lectures on the topic "Why I Am a Communist" to be delivered by intellectual comrades in Italy's fifteen largest cities. I am sure the significance of this initiative will not escape you despite the brevity of these explications. I would therefore be grateful to you if you could confirm with me your participation as soon as possible. Fraternally yours.

Or (Togliatti himself):

Dear Cantimori, upon reviewing the status of our editions, I have noticed that it has also not been possible for you in recent months to adhere to the agreed-upon rhythm of submitting seventy to eighty pages per month. You know what expectations are held for a reputable and scholarly translation of *Das Kapital* both in and outside the party, and so I beg you to devote your best efforts to this work for a certain period of time and to do everything possible so that submission is not further delayed.

With mild consternation, Cantimori realized in hindsight that he "in fact always did the bidding" of the party directives. It was difficult to avoid the impression that the love affair of Italian intellectuals with communism bore subservient features.[32]

For Montinari as well, the year 1948 represented a caesura. Affected by current events, he became a member of the party. After defending his *tesi di laurea* the following year, he would find his niche in the communist culture industry in the autumn of 1950 as an editor for Edizioni Rinascità in Rome. At least by the time of his move to the capital, he later recalled, he was living in a state of "total politicization." Snapshots from Montinari's life as a Roman leftist intellectual: PCI headquarters in the Via delle Botteghe Oscure; the party bookstore Libreria Rinascità; the trattoria on the Piazza dei Santi Apostoli; the *rosticceria* on the Corso Vittorio Emanuele; fish soup in Anzio, where his old classmate Clara Valenziano accepted a job as a schoolteacher in the mid-1950s . . . In Italy, which Ernst Bloch called the land of "porosity," communism and hedonism cannot be divided. It is all the more difficult to imagine Montinari eating a lonely supper at the Christliches Hospiz in Weimar ten years later. Yet, according to his colleague Cesare Cases, who witnessed him both in Rome and in the GDR, he had two souls within his breast, one "epicurean" and the other "ascetic." That may indeed be a cliché, but it helps us to understand why he found a second home in the State of Workers and Farmers.[33]

Montinari recalled his years in Rome as an era of ideological certainties. He corrected translations, set print manuscripts, and planned affordable editions of Marxist classics. A good communist, he headed to the local party office after working hours to undertake practical tasks. "The happy connection between politics and culture that had formed during the *Resistenza*," according to Valentino Gerratana, his boss at Edizioni Rinascità, had "not yet been affected by the political defeat of the leftists in '48." Still, the openness to avant-garde experiments had subsided. The *commissione culturale* focused its efforts on translating the poetry of Gramsci's theory into the prose of readings, film screenings, and those cultural centers one can still find today in certain small towns in Emilia Romagna and Tuscany. The notion of helping the proletarians achieve autonomy through education recalled the era of the Second International, during which the party functionaries then in charge had undergone their own political socialization. By comparison, conservative and reactionary forces must be given credit for understanding the present better, for while the communists sent their intellectuals throughout the country, sang their *Resistenza* songs, and organized reading competitions, Democrazia Cristiana and the Catholic Church were looking to photonovels, Hollywood films, and – a bit later – even the new medium of television to win over their compatriots to *their* version of a better world.[34]

Travels in Germany

Dear Professor, it has now been a month since I arrived in Germany. So far I am doing well, also owing to the somewhat favorable exchange rate. I was able to spend ten days in the German Democratic Republic and at the Leipzig book fair. I've experienced many interesting things, heard gorgeous music, and even bought a few books (among them the first volume of the Selected Works of Marx and Engels in two volumes, Moscow 1950). I've been to the Leipzig party headquarters of the SED [Sozialistische Einheitspartei Deutschlands, Socialist Unity Party of Germany], of course strictly privately; the comrades received me with enormous kindness, and since I had asked for information on their agricultural reform, they drove me to a tractor lending station. These are not just economic centers, but also political and cultural ones; in the station I visited, for instance, there was a cinema and a library with reading rooms and lounge spaces. In the administrative office, I saw, to my great delight, a portrait of Thomas Müntzer. The East is completely different than the West of Germany: here you can learn up close about the tough reality of building a socialist society. The supply of food, especially fat and meat, still presents a problem. That's because of the task imposed on the national economy by the Two-Year Plan, which aims to establish a strong heavy industry in order to be able to pay for necessary foodstuffs with industrial goods. The republic is pinning its greatest hopes on young people, for whom plenty is being done. Both men and women receive jobs with responsibilities – all doors are open to them. In West Germany, on the other hand, the newspapers are reporting on the problem of unemployed teenagers who live without any prospects and often stoop to delinquency, but absolutely nothing is being done about it.[35]

The letter in which Montinari told Cantimori of his first trip to Germany dates to the beginning of 1950. Even before he embarked on his professional life as an editor at a publishing house, an opportunity had presented itself to go to Frankfurt am Main on scholarship. "I cannot say I have achieved much in the way of my studies," Montinari wrote in a later letter. His point of contact in Frankfurt was historian and connoisseur of Italy Otto Vossler. (A certain Theodor W. Adorno, who had only just returned from Los Angeles for the first time shortly before, in October 1949, had not yet established his reputation.) From Montinari's letters, we learn that he spent a great deal of time reading the newspapers, that he established contact with the Communist Party in Frankfurt, and that, at twenty-two, he suffered a "nervous breakdown," which doctors diagnosed as a heart attack. "The political experiences are certainly the most interesting ones," he informed Cantimori. The proximity between the two German states provided plenty of illustrative material. Nevertheless, his comparative observations probably only confirmed for him his prior convictions: even if the meat supply was still wanting, the GDR represented the better

Germany, whereas in the FRG, where the principle of competition reigned supreme, the past was perpetuated.[36]

Reflected in Montinari's dualistic thinking is the division in postwar Italian society. While relations with West Germany normalized and an occasionally almost Germanophile atmosphere prevailed in large portions of the Italian populace – at least until rearmament in the mid-1950s – leftist and left-liberal travelers to Germany described a nation of apathy and repression resembling either a film noir or an Expressionist nightmare. "These days the Italian newspapers continue their very favorable coverage of Germany, almost without exception," the Rome correspondent of the *Frankfurter Allgemeine Zeitung* reported to his editors in 1950. Meanwhile, a "Letter from Germany" appeared in the left-leaning Florentine *Nuovo Corriere* in which the scholarship holder Montinari wrote about anti-Semitic violence, political indifference, and "spiritual neglect": in short, about the unremitting National Socialism of the West Germans.[37]

Montinari's school friend and fellow student Angelo Pasquinelli, living in Munich for research purposes over the winter of 1951–2, was also astonished at the Germans' self-righteousness: "It makes you want to smash their skulls in with a hammer to see what's inside," he wrote in a letter to Colli.

> But beneath the hard shell there's probably nothing at all: that's the only explanation. What the world owes poor Germany, which had only wanted to save European civilization in the war against Russia (before, they spoke of "Aryan," but now they confine themselves to small-scale badmouthing of the Jews): so goes the platitude, for us akin to the legend of military treason that the fascist newspapers disseminate.[38]

The "Lettere dalla Germania," which the aforementioned Germanist Cesare Cases published in the Communist Party magazine *Il Contemporaneo*, may be regarded as a particularly drastic case of West German noir. That West Germany was the "most soullessly Americanized country in Europe," where also, at the same time, "the worst German traditions live on," was something Cases thought he was able to gather from, among other places, *BILD-Zeitung*, the coverage of which he characterized as "Auschwitz in small doses" – "or, rather, they are those small doses, those black obsessive fantasies of the German Philistine, that sometimes under favorable circumstances combine with one another to produce the butchers of Auschwitz."[39]

Cases, who as a Jew had fled to Switzerland from the Italian race laws, would rather have gone to the GDR. Since the official cultural exchange was limited to the Federal Republic, however, that would have required private contacts or party channels. When two years later he made it to the East after finally securing an invitation to the University of Leipzig as an Italian instructor, his expectations were not disappointed. "What I want to tell you about," he wrote to his friend Delio Cantimori,

> is the almost complete disappearance of German megalomania, which is due on the one hand to socialism and on the other to the simple fact that defeat was felt much more severely here and that reconstruction took longer and didn't turn on individual initiative, whereby there is none of the arrogance of the Germans at believing themselves to be masters of the world solely because they invented the "Volkswagen." The "inwardness defended by might" which Thomas Mann spoke of no longer exists because there is no more might and also because their inwardness was severely shaken. Unlike in the Bonn Republic, here I actually no longer perceive the resentment toward the Germans that prohibits me from relating to them like normal people.[40]

The letter from Cases is quoted here in order to convey a sense of the mood in which Montinari arrived – when in spring 1953, three years after his stay in Frankfurt, he was sent to East Berlin for a year by the PCI as editor of the radio show that the East German sister party produced for Italian listeners. It is a notable shortcoming that there are no documents from this period, given that it constituted a key moment for everything else. In East Berlin, Montinari found himself once more surrounded by German–Italian cultural mediators, by GDR whisperers, Italy aficionados, and leftist Germanists, some of whom used the city as a hub into the other Eastern bloc states. He went to the cinema, had numerous love affairs, followed public debates, and made contacts in the cultural sector. Among his acquaintances were antifascists like Heinz Riedt, the translator of Primo Levi who had emigrated to the GDR, East German intellectuals such as the author Ingeborg Rauschenberg-Nimz, and schemers like Sergio d'Angelo, who in 1955 would smuggle the manuscript of *Doctor Zhivago* out of the USSR on behalf of Feltrinelli.[41]

Among the cultural events of the season was the publication of Georg Lukács's polemic against bourgeois irrationalism, *The Destruction of Reason*. In this book, which was to shape Western and Eastern European leftists' view of Nietzsche for years, Montinari read about how he himself had been seduced as a young intellectual by the "leading philosopher" of the bourgeoisie. According to Lukács, Nietzsche's entire oeuvre was to be understood as an assault on the progressive forces of socialism. His glorification of the agonistic Greeks: a "mythicizing of capitalist competition." His exaltation of culture: an expression of an ideological rearguard action able to assert itself only in the battle against the promising tendencies of his age. His aphoristic form: a symptom of the inevitable disintegration of the bourgeois worldview. Even so, Lukács conceded that Nietzsche fulfilled his historic mission – that is, to coopt those members of the intelligentsia enamored by the workers' movement – on the strength of his "not inconsiderable talent." By having substituted a "cosmic, biological" revolution for the idea of a social one, he had imparted to his adherents that "pleasant moral feeling" of being rebellious while nevertheless releasing them from their duty to engage earnestly in the battle against the bourgeoisie at the same time.[42]

For all his reading in Lukács, however, Montinari also ended up on ideologically precarious terrain in the GDR. He rediscovered his old predilection for German literature and intellectual history, kindled by Colli, read bourgeois authors like Thomas Mann, Heine, and Kafka, and witnessed the East German popular uprising. In March 1953, shortly after his arrival, Stalin died. Just as in the other Soviet satellite states, the event roused vague expectations in the GDR as well, but the hardliners under Walter Ulbricht made no moves at all toward a course correction. In Bulgaria and Czechoslovakia, workers demonstrated against rising prices. After an increase in labor standards, their East German comrades also took to the streets. "I was in Berlin on June 17, 1953," Montinari later recalled, "I saw the tanks move in to defend the party, I heard the people curse socialism." The tanks did help successfully get the situation back under control, but the political signals they sent were disastrous. Even Bertolt Brecht, who normally exercised severe restraint when it came to critiquing socialist Germany, sarcastically advised the government to dissolve the people and elect itself a new one.[43]

Drinking, Smoking, Reading

Nor did the events pass Montinari by unmarked. Back in Italy, and now twenty-six years old, he was drafted into military service. The fifteen months in a barracks in Bari, where Gramsci had once served time in prison, constitute a biographical nadir. "I suffer greatly," he wrote to one of his new German girlfriends, comparing himself with the bumbling soldier Švejk. The southern Italian heat bothered him; the events of East Berlin continued to resonate. "Many memories tie me to your homeland," he wrote, "cheerful and grim, beautiful and bitter." In the forced repose of his term of service, the conflicting experiences grew into an intellectual crisis. "I think I am incapable of practical work," he noted down in one of his attempts at self-understanding. His task was to strive for "knowledge and truth"; it was up to others to organize people "for the revolution." In awkward German, he sketched out a telling self-portrait:

> My favorite occupation: to read; my main vice: to smoke; my favorite authors: Heine and T. Mann; the German *"Tonsetzer"* [composer] I like most: Johannes Brahms; my favorite sport: does not exist. I drink enough wine, I don't like beer, nor do I like liqueurs at all, with the exception of egg liqueur. German cuisine I love passionately I like very much. My worldview: materialist rationalism; my party: CP [Communist Party] of Italy.[44]

This was the self-characterization of a political intellectual who flirted with the possibility of retreating into the realm of culture.

As one can glean from this letter, Thomas Mann played an especially important role in Montinari's intellectual explorations. With the publication of *Doctor Faustus*, the parable of the German composer Adrian

Leverkühn, Mann had confirmed his status after the war as the most significant living German author. Yet in still another regard, he occupied an almost singular position; he numbered among the few German emigrants not to be coopted by either of the two parties in the Cold War. He had returned neither to the Federal Republic (like Adorno) nor to the GDR (like Brecht), but had chosen neutral Switzerland, from which he might undertake the balancing act of dividing his moral authority between both German states. While that elicited outrage among Western anticommunists, Mann represented a trump card for the Left. A reactionary bourgeois par excellence, he had not only transformed over the 1920s into a "republican of Reason," but had later even realized as well that the future of humanity, as he informed one of his critics, had long since become "unimaginable without communist features." As his visits to the GDR proved – most recently in the Schiller anniversary year of 1955 – he did not consider that a poor outlook either. Although not a communist himself, Mann was living proof of the compatibility of communism with bourgeois humanism. At the same time, he was a trustee who permitted his leftist readers to venture deep into the domain of bourgeois decadence. It was from Heinz Riedt that Montinari had the new complete edition of Thomas Mann by Aufbau Verlag sent to him in Italy. In the party magazine *Il Contemporaneo*, he translated excerpts of Mann's correspondence with communist authors like Lukács, Peter Huchel, and Anna Seghers. After his military service ended, he returned to Rome and in early 1958 became founding director of the Centro Thomas Mann.[45]

By this point at the very latest, Montinari ceased being an observer and intervened in the cultural war both German states were waging on Italian soil. For, as *Der Spiegel* hastened to enlighten its West German readers, the Centro Thomas Mann, housed in the Palazzo Lancelotti in Rome, was financed by the GDR. In the calculus of SED leadership, cultural politics in these years served to compensate for the absence of diplomatic relationships. When East Berlin got wind that plans for a "pan-German" cultural institute were circulating among Italian leftist intellectuals – to whom, aside from Montinari, Cesare Cases and the philosopher Galvano della Volpe belonged – the Ministry of Culture signaled its support. It expected, as an internal memo reads, to be able to advance "the recognition of the GDR by the Italian government" through indirect means. According to *Der Spiegel*, it was the "enterprising frequent traveler to East Berlin Dr. Mazzino Marinari [*sic*]" who made his way to the GDR in January 1957 "in order to hammer out a program of action for the 'Centro Thomas Mann' in the capital, in week-long talks with the cultural functionaries of the Pankow-based Kulturbund zur demokratischen Erneuerung Deutschlands [Cultural Association for the Democratic Renewal of Germany]."[46]

Among Montinari's papers, no traces of this trip survive. It is not out of the question, however, that *Der Spiegel* relied on data from the Bundesnachrichtendienst (Federal Intelligence Service), which advised the Italian government to monitor the center. In the press, Montinari emphasized that they did not want to disseminate "one-sided propaganda, but to reunite Germany in Rome, at least culturally." Nonetheless, the Centro's mission, according to its own

Montinari in the culture war, 1957

promotional brochure, consisted not just in deepening "in Italy direct knowledge of Germany's current political and cultural reality," but also in "contributing to an increase in commercial exchange between Italy and the German Democratic Republic." Aside from such tangible interests, *Der Spiegel* surmised, GDR functionaries were gambling on "being able to spend [their vacations] in Capri instead of Crimea" in the future. In actual fact, the Centro appears to have served a series of SED members as a refuge, and even to have brokered contacts in Italian politics by recruiting prestigious leftist celebrities. Montinari's core business, however, consisted in organizing a mixed cultural program. On the popular Heinrich Heine exhibition he opened in Palazzo Marignoli in 1957, the Italian correspondent for *Die Zeit* wrote: "Enlivened by reproductions of contemporary engravings and etchings, this deftly contrived exhibition – which is now to be shown in several other Italian cities – presented Heine as a progenitor of communism, a crafty falsification that was dispensed in homeopathic doses and attuned to the inclinations of Italian enthusiasts of the Left from all walks of life." That the West German ambassador lodged a protest with the Italian government may also have stemmed from the fact that the so-called German Library, which the Federal Republic had opened in Rome two years earlier, had so far not been nearly as successful with its events among the Italian "enthusiasts of the Left."[47]

The GDR's edge in cultural politics, however, cannot hide the fact that postwar communism was facing its most serious crisis. In early 1956, at the 20th Congress of the Communist Party of the Soviet Union (CPSU), Khrushchev, the new general secretary, confessed to the crimes of Stalinism for the first time. Instead of instituting reforms, though, he sent tanks to Budapest nine months later. If the uprising in East Berlin could be dismissed as a counter-revolutionary reflex on the part of workers blinded by the West German Economic Miracle, then what the Soviets crushed in Hungary in 1956 was a genuine democratic-socialist revolution. The communist parties of Western Europe found themselves in the quandary of having to formulate a position. After the delegates to the 8th Party Congress of the PCI in December 1956 condoned the invasion, the intellectuals bolted from Togliatti. The aura that had surrounded Soviet communism beyond Stalin's death was lost. The New Left, the schism of which was given its initial impetus by the events of 1956, was to rediscover it over the course of the 1960s – no longer in Moscow, however, but in liberation movements in the Third World.[48]

Montinari's latent disenchantment materialized in 1956 as well. The "peaceful, all-encompassing worldview" of dialectical materialism, he wrote in hindsight, had finally become obsolete for him, owing to the events in Hungary. This does not mean he did not still identify as a communist – the grand utopian narrative of the Left simply no longer played a role for him from this point forward. As in the past, the decisive impulse for his conversion was of a personal nature. Shortly before the Soviet tanks rolled into Budapest, Montinari's past would catch up with him; due to an unforeseen incident in the summer of 1956, he would cross paths with Giorgio Colli.[49]

3

OPERATION NIETZSCHE
Florence, 1958

We lost sight of Giorgio Colli in 1945 when he had returned to teaching after a year's exile. Following the rupture of the war, the teacher had seen a bright future for himself. "We must start over, first in a material sense, then in a spiritual one," we read in his private records from this period. He imagined that a radical new beginning awaited him, too, and not just Italy. He reflected on his existence up to this point, steeped in the conviction that everything would be different in the future. "My first life draws to a close," he wrote to Anna Maria, "and my soul is about to migrate into another Giorgio."[1]

There was no dearth of fantasies about this new Giorgio. It is not merely that Colli imagined him to be more ambitious and more masculine. He was also not the kind of person to lead the life of a simple secondary school teacher. Colli viewed himself as a professor, as a journalist, as the foreign correspondent for a large daily newspaper. "Publish, primarily on politics. Develop original ideas," was his reminder to himself. He wanted to succeed in the milieu of the capital city, which, thanks to his family connections, did not seem unrealistic. "I could find something in Rome," he wrote his wife, implying that Luigi Einaudi, the newly appointed senator from Turin, was ready to take up his cause.[2]

Off the Beaten Track

Initially, he looked to gain a foothold in journalism. His father, then the managing director of Milan's *Corriere della Sera*, assisted him in placing articles with various national dailies. In 1946, Colli became a salaried critic for Turin's *Nuova Stampa*, but he seemed to struggle with the journalistic tone. Even with current events, his pieces were straying so far into the philosophical that his father ultimately confronted him with a bitter truth: "It may be that your thinking is generally superior to that of journalists," he wrote in 1948. "What is certain is that journalism does not accord with your disposition. You aren't cut out for writing articles like those you recently sent to me. I find myself incapable of offering them to any newspaper. There can be no expectation, at least for the time being, of journalistic achievement on your part."[3]

Instead, Colli published his research on the pre-Socratics, dating back to the 1930s, under the cryptic title *Physis Kryptesthai Philei* – essentially, *Nature Likes to Hide*. Produced in a run of 500 copies by the print shop of the *Corriere della Sera*, the book attracted no attention to speak of, but did earn him a *libera docenza* – the Italian equivalent of a lectureship – at the University of Pisa. In the academic year 1948–9 – Montinari was just graduating from the neighboring Scuola Normale – he offered his first courses. This did not, however, satisfy his drive for success in the media. After his failed journalistic endeavors, in the late 1940s he turned to the Einaudi publishing house to offer his services as a translator. With Cesare Pavese, the Einaudi editor he knew from his schooldays, he agreed on a series of German-language titles, among them Schopenhauer's *Parerga and Paralipomena* and Karl Löwith's *From Hegel to Nietzsche*. Pavese did not regard as opportune his suggestion to reissue works by Nietzsche himself as well.

As it soon turned out, their collaboration was ill-fated: because of the devaluation of the lira, Colli demanded a renegotiation of his fee, which at the publishing house earned him a reputation for being a "gadfly"; the completed Löwith translation went missing under suspicious circumstances; and Pavese's suicide in 1950 deprived Colli of his advocate with the publisher. Still, this concatenation of small and large catastrophes was not the sole reason for Colli's poor track record. Einaudi was the mouthpiece of progressive postwar culture. With his anticommunism, his predilection for mystics and figures from the Counter-Enlightenment, and his aversion to everything having to do with politics, Colli remained an outsider in this environment.[4]

As a former exile, he could not even point to a heroic past. While his *paides* had been participating in the political struggle, he himself had followed the events over the radio. In the moral establishment of Italian postwar society, this was no minor matter: a categorical difference persisted between those involved in the resistance and those who fled to safety.[5]

The turning point arrived when the publisher suggested to Colli he provide Italian translations of Aristotle's *Organon* and Kant's *Critique of Pure Reason*. With his idiosyncratic ideas, he had had little success, though with his translations of the classics, he managed to persuade even Giulio Einaudi. In 1952, he received the offer to edit a new series, the Classici della Filosofia. Finally, he was granted the power to set the conceptual agenda. "Many feel vaguely drawn to philosophy," Colli wrote in his programmatic introduction. "In a certain regard, everyone is a philosopher in his own way. If, however, one wishes to pursue this urge in earnest, help is required. One must turn to the past to see what has already been done."[6] Just as with his Nietzsche edition later, he did not have specialists in mind with these philosophical classics, appealing instead to everyone prepared to challenge their common sense. Angelo Pasquinelli, who never broke off contact with his old teacher and who was by then married to Gigliola Gianfrancesco, became Colli's coworker. In the winter of 1951–2, Pasquinelli traveled to a Munich devastated by war to scout out extant editions of *Die Fragmente der Vorsokratiker* (*The Fragments of the Pre-Socratics*) by Hermann Diels and Walter Kranz at the Bayerische Staatsbibliothek.

Colli did not, however, limit himself only to his editorial occupation. Inspired by Aristotle's dialectics, he returned to one of his favorite topics: the roots of Western rationality. In order to better grasp the structure of the dominant mode of reason, he conducted his own experiments in logic. His notebooks from this period are full of sequences of letters and columns of formulae that only trained logicians understand.[7]

In the thin air of logic: Angelo Pasquinelli, Giorgio and Anna Maria Colli, Gigliola with Andrea Pasquinelli and other relatives (from left). Lucca, 1953

In 1956, when leftist intellectuals grew exasperated with actually existing socialism, Colli felt he had achieved a breakthrough in his research. In a letter to an old schoolmate, he took stock of his own postwar period:

> I, too, have fought hard, in particular to solve the practical question, which is to say, to arrive at a point where I am able to earn my living. All without excessively large concessions regarding what is truly important to me. The path was arduous and lonesome. The results are not brilliant, but acceptable. As you know, I have been a visiting lecturer at the University of Pisa for nine years. I haven't yet landed a professorship, but instead I've carved out a career in publishing and edit the series Classici della Filosofia for Einaudi, in which my translations of the *Organon* and the *Critique of Pure Reason* have appeared as the first volumes. With these works I've also made a certain name for myself, even internationally. But the most significant and least anticipated result of these difficult years is that I have succeeded (through my engagement with Aristotle) in gaining some novel speculative insights.

These concern certain fundamental logical propositions which, if I ultimately manage to prove them, will make any subsequent search for a "system" superfluous. My theoretical interests are thus satisfied. And so I would like to address the only problem remaining for me. I'm talking about the problem of action. By that I mean – to return to old and new ideas – the realm of expression, of *paideia*, of communal life, of the battle of culture, in order to assert oneself in life against politics, etc. Even in the old days, we were talking, if I remember correctly, about a joint project, a magazine, for example. Now, at long last, I'd like to proceed with the matter concretely. And of course all the while I think of old friends and long to see them again.[8]

What Colli left unmentioned was the fact that it was not just a productive period of work coming to an end in 1956. That summer, out of the blue, Angelo Pasquinelli died of a heart attack at age thirty. The funeral service took place in Lucca on June 16. In the history of the Nietzsche edition, this date marks an important event: after a ten-year estrangement, Colli and Montinari crossed paths once more.[9]

Beauty and Horror

Subsequent events can be either interpreted through depth psychology or – like Colli's ancient Greeks – viewed as fateful entanglement. Montinari, at rock bottom of his crisis concerning his political convictions, was confronted again in 1956 by a long-forgotten past. Suddenly, they were all together again: the teacher, the *paides*, the newly widowed Gigliola . . . only the crown prince, the partisan, the favorite of their hearts was absent – leaving behind a void in which his former rival began a new existence. This is not to ascribe to Montinari any sort of intention or calculation, but over the course of the following year, he gradually, de facto, took up the role of Pasquinelli. That he himself sensed he was maneuvering on forbidden territory emerges from a letter to Colli in early 1957:

Dear Giorgio, the time has come to write you, also because what I'd like to tell you can't wait any longer. The last time I was in

Florence, something great and terrible happened that I never would have expected, even though it was long present deep down inside me: I found Gigliola. And she found me. And that's it, I'm incapable of telling you more. I have the sense of being on a road that leads neither in a direction nor to a destination I know. I only know that I don't want to stop now, but to experience this moment as clearly as possible without thinking about the future. I experience these moments with a kind of tragic desire, as if I were in the epilogue of something: everything comes together, I rediscover bygone youth in a moment of grace, in a present which is at once alive, vast, and terrible.[10]

With religious fervor, Montinari confessed to Colli his feelings of bliss and guilt. One can only speculate what portion of them may be attributed to the confusing emotions surrounding his ideological conversion. To be sure, the "epilogue" he found himself in concerned his rediscovered youth at least as much as it did his existence as a communist cultural official. While he was still advocating for friendship between the nations of Italy and the GDR as the director of the Centro Thomas Mann, the decision was made to become heir to his deceased friend, in a professional capacity as well. In January 1958, Montinari resigned from all party offices and moved to Florence to begin collaborating with Colli. "What the hell are you doing?," wondered Sergio d'Angelo, his friend from their East Berlin days. Delio Cantimori told Montinari that he was about to do something "enormously stupid."[11]

Ten years later, in an especially candid profession of friendship, even by his standards, Montinari recalled the decisive factor that had been impossible for those on the outside to comprehend. "There were critical moments, even genuine crises between us," he wrote to Colli.

But as far as I am concerned, that has never changed anything about a fundamental fact that I have a hard time describing. It has roughly to do with the following: that I've perceived you as a person, since I was fifteen, in a very particular way; that I have been intensely drawn to you in a way I am not with anyone else; that I said yes to you as this person, just as you are. That is the underlying reason I returned to you ten years ago.[12]

The Other Library

No such outpourings of emotion from Colli survive. "Mazzino is back again," reads the laconic notation in his diary. But for him, too, the reunion with the prodigal student signaled a turning point. It is quite possible that Montinari fueled the urge Colli had been feeling to have some practical impact after long years spent in the ivory tower with Aristotle and Kant. It is quite possible that he encouraged him to turn to an author he had lost sight of for a long while. "Desire to fight. Return to Nietzsche," Colli noted in his diary in March 1957, shortly after his fortieth birthday. In July, he traveled to Sils Maria, where he experienced an epiphany when confronted with the sublimity of nature. "The waterfall. Understood Nietzsche," reads the cryptic entry in his diary.[13] Could it be that he identified with Zarathustra in his newly perceived need to take action? At the age of forty, Zarathustra had descended from his mountains to share his teachings with the people on the plains.

Colli, for his part, harbored the thought of drafting a "book about our crisis," according to the heading of his posthumously published notes from 1957. The collection of pages was written with constant reference to Nietzsche. To all those, Colli wrote, "who feel uneasy, who are alarmed, repulsed, disgusted by our century," this author "provided something valuable": his unreserved disdain for the modern world. In many respects, Colli's thoughts about the relationship between culture and politics, between philosophy and education, draw upon older reflections. Alongside them, a panorama of conservative cultural criticism unfolds, omitting scarcely a single one of the motifs typical of the 1950s, from the quantification of the world and the estrangement of the individual to the annihilation of natural spatial and temporal relations by technology. In those days, cultural criticism from the Left and from the Right looked strikingly similar sometimes. That it was not a progressive speaking in these notes becomes obvious when Colli diagnosed what, in his eyes, was the greatest failure of the modern education system: namely, recognizing the natural inequality of humankind and meeting the needs of the "superior ones" among them. By contrast, any critique of consumer culture, of "affluent society" and Americanization, played only a subordinate role – and that although Italy, too, experienced its *miracolo economico* in those years. It was not the economy, but the "dirty business" of politics which constituted the true evil, even in democracy. While the Italian communists endeavored to put literature, film, and education to the service of politics, Colli dreamed the opposite dream of a new sacralization of culture: "Whatever is left of religious feeling has been absorbed by the state. The masses revere only certain political idols (fatherland – democracy – freedom – work – social justice, etc.). Dethrone these idols and shift religious sensibility to culture."[14]

This is why Colli now returned to his penchant for forming arcane communities, along the lines of the ancient schools of philosophy. Unlike in the past, though, when he had contented himself with initiating a handful of adepts into his ideas of higher culture, now, encouraged by his successful publications, he strove for a more elevated degree of effectiveness. In his records, he wrote of wanting to "wrest the masses from state domination." That sounds as if he had wanted to pit himself against the Italian republic. In the conversations he had with Montinari about his plans, the designation "Operation Nietzsche" soon became established.[15]

Even in Lucca, as "Socrates," Colli had been full of contradictions. As a mystic, he had imbued his Chosen Few with philological exactitude; as a disdainer of politics, he had done so with political resistance. It is at this point that we encounter a further paradox: nothing caused him greater unease than the spoken word dying off and human individuals becoming isolated within written culture. Yet at the moment he himself strove for communal action, he also resorted to the strategy employed by Italian intellectuals since at least the *Risorgimento*: to win the hearts and minds of their compatriots by journalistic means. Benedetto Croce had required nothing more than a magazine and a publishing house to stand up to Mussolini; Antonio Gramsci had used his incarceration to devise the methodology of "cultural war of position"; and Palmiro Togliatti had declared the battle for hegemony part of the official party line. In spite of his martial rhetoric, even Colli once again proved himself to be an *homme de lettres* – for whom another book series would seem the adequate means of his scholarly revolt. "My plans are legion," he wrote in the letter to his schoolmate cited above, they all revolve around establishing a new educational canon, with a preference for the classics (outstanding authors into the nineteenth century) who will be newly selected and packaged. A uniform series would have to be made (Science – Art – Philosophy), universal (but with a particular cultural thrust), consisting of texts of moderate length with programmatic introductions (without a historical, philological apparatus).[16]

The opportunity arose for Colli when Paolo Boringhieri, an editor for Einaudi, purchased the rights to part of the scholarly program and, with this tangible capital, opened up his own publishing house. In the *Enciclopedia di Autori Classici*, which Colli edited together with Montinari, Gigliola Pasquinelli, and several other former *paides* for Boringhieri Editore, an eclectic series of just over a hundred philosophical, literary, scientific, and theological titles appeared between 1958 and 1965, at first glance with no recognizable principle of selection holding them together. What, to name just a few examples, do Hölderlin's *Empedokles*, the *Upanishads*, Stendhal's *A Life of Napoleon*, Robert Boyle's *The Sceptical Chymist*, Hippolyte Taine's *Titus Livius*, and Jacob Burckhardt's *Sullo studio della storia* have in common? To start, only that these were apocryphal writings in intellectual Italy around 1960; neither historical-philosophical nor Marxist nor Catholic references appeared. One clue nevertheless emerges from the fact that Nietzsche's *Schopenhauer as Educator*, in Montinari's translation and with a programmatic introduction by Colli, was published as the first volume. If Giuliana Lanata, an associate of the time, may be believed, then the series marked the attempt to spread Nietzschean thought by indirect means. With his *Enciclopedia*, she claims, Colli was setting out to do nothing other than reconstruct Nietzsche's imaginary library.[17]

In his book *Dopo Nietzsche* (*After Nietzsche*), Colli later criticized Nietzsche for having preferred the works of scientists and literati to the philosophical classics. From this attitude of refusal supposedly sprang a lack of "theoretical clarity." In 1958, however, Nietzsche's eclectic proclivities seemed particularly suited to redefine the depleted conventions of the genre. With Einaudi, Colli had often had no success with his proposed texts for translation because they had been too unphilosophical – according to the traditional understanding. This explains why, in many of his ideas, Einaudi advisor Norberto Bobbio had spotted an "illegitimate expansion of the sphere of philosophy." Before they discussed individual titles, a fundamental clarification was thus necessary: "We must come to an agreement about what we understand today, in Italy, as philosophy."[18]

With the *Enciclopedia di Autori Classici*, Colli in a sense offered his belated reply. He conceded no future to thought in its prevailing Hegelian and Marxist varieties: "Philosophy today is dead." In his eyes, there was only hope for revitalization if we manage to abandon the errant path of modernity. To this end, he considered it necessary "to dispense with the name of philosophy and the philosopher, to disguise oneself, and – as Nietzsche once did – to start again from scratch under a new name." His many anachronisms notwithstanding, he proved himself astonishingly fashionable with this scheme. Talk of the "end of philosophy" was indeed a widespread diagnosis after the war – one need only look to Heidegger or the Frankfurt School. Many of the book series and journals founded in Rome, Paris, and Frankfurt in those days also claimed to liquidate the old way of thinking, whether through stylistic innovations, transgressions in content – into literature, the humanities, or political praxis – or new media like the paperback; in all cases it was about establishing new interpretations and uses for philosophy. The New Left may have enjoyed the most success with its rebranding. In series like *La Scienza Nuova* by Edizioni Dedalo, *Théorie* by Éditions Maspero, or Frankfurt's *edition suhrkamp*, a genre – "theory" – began its victory march, gaining its identity by distinguishing itself from academic philosophy.[19]

Crossing over the Abyss

Colli succeeded with his apocryphal encyclopedia neither in establishing a new genre, nor in liberating the masses from the domination of the Italian state. The public response was – to put it gently – subdued. Critics found fault with the "mystical tones" of the series and the "magical, sacerdotal conception of the 'philosopher'" that the editor propounded in his introductions. One especially blunt reviewer even felt reminded of the "India nonsense" that had satisfied "the homespun mysticism of those dutiful members of theosophical societies fifty years ago." What seemed even more worrisome to him, however, was that Colli wanted to recommend a rereading of "the most logical among the reactionary philosophers" – by which he of course meant Nietzsche.[20]

Since his first conversations with Cesare Pavese, Colli had insisted again and again on making Nietzsche's own works available in new translations. Yet there was no apparent space for his ideas in either the antifascist Einaudi culture or the milieu of political Catholicism. That Colli now returned to his plan in the late 1950s had just as much to do with his new self-confidence as an editor as it did with the continuing crisis among the Left.[21] Above all, however, it was news from Germany and France that encouraged him to take another stab at it.

"Nietzsche has the distinction of being the only philosopher who was ever regarded as a contributing factor to a world war," wrote Eric Voegelin, the German political scientist who emigrated to the United States, in 1944. Two years later, Nietzsche in fact stood in the dock at the Nuremberg war crimes trials. To be sure, François de Menthon, the lead French prosecutor, conceded that his philosophy was not to be compared with the "brutal simplicity" of the Nazis, but his "vision of domination over the masses by absolute rulers" did distinguish him as their "forebear." The tenor of Nietzsche publications that appeared in Germany after the war tended in the same direction. Authors of leftist, liberal, or Christian-humanist derivation vied with one another to bury the mastermind of the Third Reich in execrations. One can imagine what Colli, who followed the German discussion to the extent possible, thought of such views. The spirit of reckoning, he wrote in a review for *Rivista di filosofia* in 1950, only proved "what Nietzsche himself had predicted, namely, that the Germans, with their penchant for fanaticism and slander, would never be capable of understanding his thought."[22]

Nietzsche could nevertheless be made most easily comprehensible to his contemporaries if one were to interpret him – ignoring his farewells to humankind – as a humanist with an existentialist tinge, as a thinker who would first diagnose the crisis of meaning in modern civilization, but who had also seen the precondition for free self-assertion in the vacuum of traditional values. Thus, in his famous lecture from 1947, did Thomas Mann explain how Nietzsche would have to content himself with "being called a humanist." Karl Schlechta, the philosophy professor in Darmstadt, espoused a similar view, even though for him Nietzsche's humanism amounted to nothing more than his having predicted the nihilism of scientific, technological civilization, which only now in the atomic age was revealing its full scope. That Schlechta's name is still remembered today, however, is hardly because of his rather unoriginal interpretation, but rather because of his edition of Nietzsche, published in parallel, which heralded the beginning of the postwar history of Nietzsche's editions.[23]

Montinari, who got to know Schlechta in the 1960s, regarded him as a "rueful Nazi." In the secondary literature, however, the image of an unideological scholar predominates. If one compares Schlechta's statements from the 1930s with those from the 1950s, what emerges without a doubt is the impression of a pronounced ideological malleability. A party member since 1933, since 1934 an employee of Weimar's Nietzsche Archive responsible for the never-finished historical-critical edition, Schlechta had become a professor in Darmstadt after the war, establishing with the Darmstädter Gespräche (Darmstadt Conversations) one of the most important forums for West German postwar humanism. His Nietzsche edition *Werke in drei Bände* (*Works in Three Volumes*) appeared with Hanser Verlag in 1954 and 1956. From the perspective of content, it had little new to offer. What caused a sensation, however, was Schlechta's "Philologischer Nachbericht" ("Philological Report") in the third volume, in which the editor made serious accusations against his former employer.[24]

Schlechta was neither the first nor the only person to accuse Elisabeth Förster-Nietzsche of dark deeds. Since its founding, the Nietzsche Archive had been forced to defend itself against public allegations and legal complaints, but it was Schlechta's black book that first made these circumstances known to a broader audience in their context. Supported by older testimony and his own recollections, he recounted philological wrongdoings, stretching over four decades, in which hardly any sin, from wanton negligence to unscrupulous falsifications, had gone uncommitted. It was not his fault that Nietzsche's transmission history read "like a crime novel," the author wrote for his report in justification: "Philology has frequently been thrilling." Mustering overwhelming evidence, he demonstrated that Förster-Nietzsche had suppressed and even altered unpopular letters by her brother in order to legitimate herself as a reliable trustee. What weighed even more heavily was the accusation that *The Will to Power*, the magnum opus issued posthumously from Nietzsche's papers, was a gratuitous selection, never intended by Nietzsche in this form, owing solely to his sister's "ambition for a primary work." Schlechta's own ambition, by contrast, consisted in reestablishing the "pure manuscript sequence" by presenting in chronological order the aphorisms from which Förster-Nietzsche had composed *The Will to Power*. This idea, too, had occurred to others before him. Schlechta cited Ernst Horneffer, a former coworker in the archive, who just after the turn of the century had demanded that one must "issue Nietzsche's manuscripts precisely as they are, word for word, refraining entirely from subjective ordering or combination."[25]

With his revision, Schlechta in no way intended to enhance the status of Nietzsche's *Nachlass* – the expectation that in Nietzsche's papers one might stumble upon the essence or the secret of his thought he viewed precisely as the disastrous inheritance of their prior transmission history. It was necessary to dispel the magical aura of the Weimar Nietzsche cult. For that reason, Schlechta took great pains to profane his literary legacy. When he had come to the archive in the 1930s, he had already been forced to realize that the posthumous writings contained nothing "that could surprise someone who knows everything Nietzsche published or designated for publication." Apart from that, Nietzsche's "late handwriting" could scarcely be deciphered anyway. To be sure, the plan for a complete critical edition, interrupted by the war, must one day be finalized – but Schlechta did not have high hopes for it. It was with good reason that Nietzsche had withheld "the vast bulk" of his papers. That their content would probably have to "remain unresolvable" for ever Schlechta ascertained without regret. "Nietzsche had plunged himself into the abyss of time as a sacrifice. The abyss has closed; we can only cross over it now."[26]

In West German cultural journals, Schlechta's edition was generally welcomed as a line drawn under the "Elisabeth Förster-Nietzsche Era." Walter Jens, a professor of classics at the University of Tübingen, wrote in *Texte und Zeichen* that, with the new edition of the manuscripts, his colleague in Darmstadt had finally revealed "the true Nietzsche." Schlechta's revelations merited a cover for *Der Spiegel*. Its waves even reached across the Atlantic: "Freed at last from the clutches of his sister and her racist friends," wrote the critic for *Time* magazine. By contrast, the *Merkur*, published in Munich, made its pages available to Schlechta's opponents. They had been able to overlook the trend of demonizing Nietzsche as a precursor of fascism, but to downplay him as a cultural critic and trivialize the secret of his writings was, one gets the impression, an inadmissible affront. Karl Löwith, who had received an offer to join the faculty in Heidelberg after his odyssey through Italy, Japan, and the United States, ascribed Schlechta's humanistic reading to "the post-1945 restoration in need of security." With his attempt to break the spell of Nietzsche's bequest, however, he had merely brought a "new Nietzsche legend" into the world.[27]

Rudolf Pannwitz, a follower of Stefan George, weighed in with a patently sharper tone. Modifying Nietzsche's *topos* of the "last man" in a monumental critical diagnosis, he had warned forty years earlier, toward the end of the First World War, against the advent of "postmodern man." For Pannwitz, Schlechta, too, likely numbered among this species. Only the exponent of an epoch which had lost its ability to recognize and perceive true greatness through "mercantilism, dynamism, and barbarism" could come up with the notion of redeclaring this "behemoth of rock," this "traversal of world spheres reminiscent of Gilgamesh" that Nietzsche's late work signified, the shoddy contrivance of his less well-endowed sister. For Pannwitz, Schlechta's dispatching gesture carried no weight for the very reason that, by his own admission, he had simply skated over an abundance of "unsifted material." Above all, however, he was infringing with his edition upon the principle of hermeneutic propriety: "No one has the right to publish an author whom he views like *that*."[28]

Heidegger's reaction to the new Nietzsche edition survives only indirectly. Walter Kaufmann, a German-Jewish emigré who left a lasting imprint on the American image of Nietzsche after the war, published a report in 1957 on the status of West German philosophy, based on his experiences as a Fulbright professor in Heidelberg. In this report, Heidegger, among others, made an appearance – and as the "virtuoso of concealment" at that. "He loves mystery," reads Kaufmann's skeptical assessment, which referred just as much to Heidegger's own oeuvre as it did to his relationship to Nietzsche:

> In conversation he will hint that Hegel's most profound ideas are to be found in relatively little-known drafts, antedating his first book, while the best of Nietzsche is to be found in incompletely published notes which are now inaccessible in Eastern Germany. Heidegger has photo-stats of this material hidden in a safe place: there can be no thought of publication now. Why? Because nobody knows Nietzsche's handwriting well enough.

For Kaufmann, who was beholden to the Enlightenment, these were typical Heideggerian mutterings. Like Schlechta, he accorded Nietzsche's unpublished writings no particular significance. Heidegger, however, might have been the most effective of Nietzsche's inter-preters in helping the myth of his *Nachlass* to achieve its second heyday: "What Nietzsche published himself during his creative life was always foreground," he wrote in his Nietzsche monograph from 1961. "His philosophy proper was left behind as posthumous, unpublished work."[29]

Dangerous Papers

Today, Nietzsche's *Nachlass* is incorporated into the holdings of the Goethe and Schiller Archive in Weimar, where it lies alongside that of his sister, and quite a few linear feet of files concerning the business operations of the old Nietzsche Archive. Among the most peculiar documents from the latter registry are the mailings the archive received in the months before and after the collapse of 1945: from friends and promoters signaling support, from ideological hardliners issuing final calls to persevere, and from concerned business partners wanting to settle up their most recent accounts. From today's perspective, many of the submissions read together as evidence of a disturbing normality. "None of us can presage whether German spirit will blow through these lands again anytime soon," wrote a Berlin law professor in early

1945, lamenting the loss of the Polish General Government. Philipp Reemtsma, the Hamburg cigarette manufacturer whom Elisabeth had won over in the 1920s as a patron, approved funds for another year. There was even news from former employee Karl Schlechta, who by then was teaching philosophy in Mainz after a war deployment in Italy: "For the next semester I have announced a series of Nietzsche lectures which I am greatly looking forward to. This semester was quite nice: nearly thirty-three auditors and a good seminar. The exams were less gratifying!" Half a year later, in October 1945, a request arrived in Weimar from the Hamburg branch of Steinway & Sons: "Hopefully you survived the eventful recent months intact. We would enjoy hearing from you about them. We would also like to inquire after the status of the Steinway grand piano, model 'B 211,' leased to you." Soon afterward, the archive, its accounts frozen since July, was sealed off by the Soviet Military Administration. It is thus unlikely Steinway ever received a reply.[30]

In the late 1950s, Western scholars of Nietzsche seemed to fare no differently than the piano builders. As to the whereabouts of Nietzsche's manuscripts, they groped around in the dark – or at least acted as if they did. In his report, Schlechta had summarized what he had been told "only indirectly and in many different ways." According to that, the dangerous papers had been loaded onto trucks by a German work crew in April 1946 and carted off "with an unknown destination" – not atypical for the method of the Soviet Trophy Brigades who scoured occupied territories for cultural assets. In this matter, Schlechta himself, through back channels, had contacted the Thuringian state president, whose intervention was presumably responsible for the return of the manuscripts in July 1946. Today we know that Nietzsche's *Nachlass*, packed in large wooden crates and guarded by Soviet military posts, sat on the street in front of Villa Silberblick for days before a decision was made on its future fate. According to Schlechta's report, the manuscripts were placed into interim storage on the ground floor of the villa and ultimately handed over to the Goethe and Schiller Archive in 1950, which "since the summer of 1953 has been safeguarding" them. But instead of attempting to contact the archive, for his new edition Schlechta had drawn solely on the material accessible in the West. "A more nuanced solution will be possible only when the manuscripts are accessible again," he concluded – without expressly emphasizing that he did not regard that as especially likely and perhaps not even as especially worthwhile.[31]

As little as they may otherwise have had in common, Schlechta was in agreement with Heidegger, who likewise insisted that Nietzsche's *Nachlass* was "inaccessible" in the Soviet-occupied territories. Rudolf Pannwitz also prepared the readers of *Merkur* for the eventuality that the occult writings might have to be written off as lost "in the Eastern Zone." Herbert W. Reichert, an American Germanist who compiled the *International Nietzsche Bibliography* together with Schlechta, even wanted to deter Western researchers from using the Goethe and Schiller Archive in the event that it opened its stacks to them; to fall prey to an act of communist "cultural propaganda" could scarcely have been in keeping with Nietzsche's wishes.[32]

On the other hand, would Nietzsche have been pleased to have fallen into the clutches of cold warriors? If one looks at the *Nachlass* debates of the late 1950s, anticommunism is the least common denominator. With reference to the Soviet embargo and the illegibility of his manuscripts, Nietzsche was declared inaccessible on two accounts at once. Whether worry about the half-life of one's own interpretations or a tendency for mystification had priority, bemoaning the absent manuscripts may have been the real Nietzsche legend of this period.

The Italian Job

Colli wrote in July 1958 to the Einaudi editor Luciano Foà,

> [T]o date a complete critical edition of Nietzsche's works is lacking, and not only in a philological sense, but also in a much more fundamental one. Indeed, we must assume that the Nietzsche we know – posthumous or otherwise – comprises scarcely more than half of the original material in manuscript. No more precise estimate can be made about the extent of the unpublished materials, however, since the manuscripts are housed in the "Nietzsche Archive" in Weimar and have not been examined by anyone since the war.

In order to solve the "riddle" that, as ever, surrounded Nietzsche, "and to which the revelations à la Schlechta can in no way do justice," the once-in-a-lifetime opportunity presented itself to Einaudi to undertake a "complete, definitive Nietzsche edition in the original." Should the publisher not be interested in such an enterprise, Colli's old project of a new Italian translation could still be considered as an alternative.[33]

It was not solely the German debate that had attracted Colli's attention. Independent of Schlechta, French Germanist Richard Roos had given a similarly withering appraisal of Elisabeth Förster-Nietzsche's editions that same year. It is obvious why Colli's ears perked up: the multitude of "undeciphered manuscripts" under discussion in the various articles must have been an endlessly enticing prospect for the *filologo*. From the first, he had ascribed a special importance to Nietzsche's unpublished works. Aside from the "exoteric depiction intent on comprehensibility to the layperson," he believed he could discern in his work "an esoteric, clandestine, very personal deepening of his own thought." Nietzsche's scribblings were thus the opposite of mere preparatory studies. In his private notes, as yet uncorrupted by any intention for publication, he must have come especially close to the fiery core of his Dionysian experience. In his published works, there were hints at this everywhere: "Do people not write books precisely to conceal what they are keeping to themselves?," it reads, for instance, in *Beyond Good and Evil* – for Colli an unmistakable clue that there was something else lurking beyond the printed words.[34]

Like Heidegger, he thus regarded Nietzsche's books published during his lifetime as superficial. But unlike Heidegger, who did not want the secret of Nietzsche's manuscripts violated, he argued for returning to the sources. In his letter to Foà, Colli also did not fail to highlight the incalculability of the political situation. The difficulties facing their plan were "enormous," their access to the Weimar archival holdings blocked by "ideological, political obstacles." As "foreigners aiming to take responsibility for the edition of a great German author," they would have to reckon with deep suspicion in Germany. But, on the other hand, precisely as foreigners, it might also be added, they would find themselves in an extremely advantageous position: while Heidegger, Schlechta, and the other West German Nietzsche scholars were caught up in the logic of the Cold War, they were able to operate free from political sensitivities.[35]

Furthermore, it is at this point we stumble anew on that ambivalent, even contradictory, relationship to philology that had been expressed in Colli's spiritual exercises with his *paides*. The fact that he found Nietzsche a mystically illuminated thinker did not prevent him from pushing for philological enlightenment. Perhaps, in yet another respect, a characteristically Italian unselfconsciousness manifested itself here: unlike in Germany or France, philology was never condemned as vacuous scholarship. The craft of textual criticism was part of a long national tradition there that hearkened back to those heroic Italian "philologist-poets" of the Renaissance, admired even by Nietzsche, whose ethos of critical precision had always been regarded as a role model for modern, anti-academic intellectuals. Even an intellect so beyond suspicion of the "freemasonry of useless erudition" as Antonio Gramsci indulged in philological studies in his *Prison Notebooks* for that reason. Political intellectuals like Pier Paolo Pasolini or Adriano Sofri were also deeply committed to philological immersion into detail. What Colli's *"mentalità di filologo"* expressed was therefore not only a personal idiosyncrasy, but also a cultural bearing that, until now, has garnered little attention in the history of intellectuals, focused solely on the French and German variants.[36]

In the end, though, there was a personal angle to Colli's eagerness to scope out the situation on site, too. As he related to Foà in his letter, now – in the summer of 1958 – he had an associate at his disposal "particularly suited to this task": "He is a first-rate expert in German language and literature, has traveled frequently to Germany, especially to East Germany, and is well versed in editorial problems."[37]

Montinari, to whom he was referring here, had meanwhile settled into his new life. He was translating, acquiring suitable titles, and handling copyright matters – with the significant difference that this work no longer pertained to the Marxist classics, but to Colli's encyclopedia of the Counter-Enlightenment. The affair with Gigliola Gianfrancesco seems not to have lasted long, however, as disclosed by the letters that this notoriously fickle man was soon writing again to other women. In one of them from 1960, two years after returning to his *pedagogo*, he took preliminary stock of things, employing the ponderous style of his intermittent statements of accounts:

> I, too, am essentially back at the beginning after more than ten years have elapsed since my entrance into practical life. I cannot issue positive pronouncements about the things with which I occupied myself up until around two years ago. Today I sense that I am at the start of an actual journey, although the external and internal hindrances are numerous. I think I have finally figured out who I want to be. I speak not as one who knows exactly what to do, but as one who can only render a very negative judgment on all of present-day society (and here I also include the present-day "Left"). The academic wasteland and the lack of "culture" in our cultural institutions are bleak; people are living outwardly, constantly after the newest and most original ideas – in the best case. I speak like this because for more than ten years I led exactly this life (even if I was saved by reticence and doubt).[38]

Negotiations with Einaudi, meanwhile, were slow to proceed. To make a large Nietzsche edition based on the Weimar manuscripts would mean treating the ideologist of the reactionary bourgeoisie on equal footing with Gramsci – for the flagship of progressive Italy, still an outrageous sacrilege. At best, they could imagine publishing a modest Italian translation on the basis of extant editions. Still, however, the new prospects seemed not to have left the book publishers completely unimpressed, for in November 1960, after quite a few letters back and forth, Luciano Foà signaled that they were willing to bear the costs for local reconnaissance.[39]

4

OVER THE WALL AND INTO THE DESERT
Weimar, 1961

Dear Giorgio, first, something personal. I've met very friendly people here. They have not only made available to me all the material that, as you know, is stored at the Goethe and Schiller Archive, but have also taken care to find me a much better place to stay than I had managed to myself. I am now living in the villa . . . of Nietzsche! That's where I'm writing you now. I have a fantastic room with a veranda and a view over Weimar and into the garden where the ailing Nietzsche must have gone for walks. It is very quiet here. The villa is constructed in the "Bayreuth style," on a hill somewhat outside Weimar. It is the ideal place to work. I was moved in a very peculiar, ineffable way when I held a manuscript of Nietzsche's in my hand for the first time, and again when I crossed the threshold of this house. It doesn't matter that everything having to do with Nietzsche has disappeared; the site is sacred anyway. This trip to Weimar is perhaps the most important event of my life.[1]

Thus reads the first of countless letters Montinari wrote to Colli from Weimar in subsequent years. He may not have sautéed a cross as he had in 1943, nor burned a copy of *The Will to Power*, but of all his epiphanic experiences, this one nevertheless appears to have been the most consequential. For his excursion to the GDR, he had planned only two weeks. Yet, before his death, he would not find his way out of the labyrinth of Nietzsche's writings he entered in April 1961. The East German Gesellschaft für kulturelle Verbindungen mit dem Ausland (Society for Cultural Relations with Foreign Countries), with which he had dealt in his role as director of the Centro Thomas Mann, had been helpful in organizing a research permit.[2] To his surprise, the Goethe and Schiller Archive then granted him free access to Nietzsche's manuscripts. The assertions by West German Nietzscheologists seem to have proven unfounded – not a trace of embargo, surveillance, or ideological finger-wagging.

No Suspicious Traces

Two years after Montinari's first trip to Weimar, in 1963, an essay by Walter Benjamin appeared with edition suhrkamp that would later rank among West German '68ers' favorite texts. "The Work of Art in the Age of Mechanical Reproduction," Benjamin's prolegomena to a revolutionary cultural politics, originally drafted in the 1930s, argues that the category of the "original" in art has become meaningless due to the possibilities of technical replication and the accumulation in modern society of the "sense for all that is the same in the world." Still, Benjamin did not outline a narrative of decline. Together with the aura, he wrote, the work of art also loses its class aspect. In the age of reproducibility, he thus saw opportunities for emancipated reception, for the politicization and democratization of art: in short, for demolishing global bourgeois reality.[3]

Viewed from Benjamin's perspective, editorial philology is a hopelessly reactionary discipline. Admittedly, it was also caught up in the wake of new technologies of reproduction. Without the possibility of duplicating manuscripts and thus making them independent of their, in some cases, far-flung repositories, few of the grand historical-critical editions of the nineteenth and twentieth centuries would ever have seen the light of day.[4] One could illustrate that point well, using as examples Colli and Montinari, whose hunger for microfilm was insatiable. Counter to Benjamin's hypothesis – and this is crucial – literary manuscripts were not, however, robbed of their aura through photomechanical reproducibility. The reverence that overcame Montinari when, for the first time, he leaned over a page inscribed by Nietzsche did, to be sure, have a great deal to do with his enthusiastic disposition; comparable experiences, often upon first contact with unpublished manuscripts, however, are practically a hallmark of modern editorial philology.

Norbert von Hellingrath, for instance, launched his renowned edition of Hölderlin after stumbling upon late, scarcely decipherable Hölderlin manuscripts in Stuttgart's Landesbibliothek. "[T]here I sit," he recorded from the euphoric depths of editorial labor in 1914, "and every new word by Hölderlin that I tease from the pages comes alive in me such that I tremble." Not just the editor, but his contemporaries, too, were bent on glimpsing in Hölderlin's enigmatic hieroglyphs the spirit of the poet himself at work. In the cultural atmosphere of the *fin de siècle*, scribblings, fragments, remnants, were regarded as the royal path to literary genius. Perhaps one must correct Benjamin to the effect that the cult of authenticity, which he viewed as a premodern form of art appreciation, in reality constituted a modern reaction to the experience of comprehensive reproduction. Elisabeth Förster-Nietzsche could hardly have chosen a better moment to valorize her brother's *Nachlass*. Without the aura that the handwritten, the unfinished, the unpublished, took on at the time, in the incipient age of the typewriter, *The Will to Power* would probably never have become one of the most influential philosophical books of the twentieth century.[5]

The magic of the handwritten manuscript was capable of surviving even war and fascism unscathed. One example more closely linked to Montinari is the philological initiation of Kafka editor Gerhard Neumann, who in his autobiographical reminiscences recalled sitting for the first time before Kafka's original manuscripts in the Bodleian Library at Oxford in the 1970s: "[T]he icy cold in the venerable reading room, carefully leafing through the precious pages of Kafka's octavo notebooks (which he had carried with him in his jacket pocket and written on in pencil in the Alchimistengäßchen on Prague's Hradschin), lead traces that threatened to fade a bit more with the turn of every page." In Benjaminian terminology, a magical experience of presence; for the budding editorial philologist, the "experience of a state of exception." Had Nietzsche had something similar in mind when he wrote that the "experience" was "the obligatory qualification for a philologist"?[6]

Compared to Kafka's sparse literary remains, the Nietzsche *Nachlass* the archivists placed at Montinari's disposal in Weimar consisted of an almost unfathomable abundance of material: fair copies and first printings of books published by Nietzsche himself; the lecture manuscripts and philological treatises from his time as a professor in Basel; the portfolios full of loose pages with ideas, concepts, and excerpts; as well as the notebooks he had used to record his streams of thought. In order to load onto trucks the avalanche of paper, the scope of which outweighed his published oeuvre many times over, the Russians had needed more than a hundred large wooden crates. Under Elisabeth Förster-Nietzsche's aegis, everything had already been ordered, catalogued, and furnished with those call numbers that pepper the pages of the volumes of commentary in the Colli–Montinari edition like a secret code.[7]

"It is a desert that opens up before the reader's eyes," read Karl Schlechta's cautionary words to future users. In his letters to Colli, Montinari instead gave the impression of having happened upon a gold mine. "We could do it all in a diligent, new, definitive way," he wrote, full of enthusiasm. His greatest worry concerned whether there were competing editorial projects, but he was assured no other interested parties had materialized as yet, aside from a professor from Leuven. Schlechta, too, wished to examine the manuscripts, though he was not willing to come to the GDR to do so. All in all, therefore, a favorable opportunity – but only "if we manage to seize it at the right time."[8]

The problem lay not in persuading Colli. The problem lay, as ever, in the ideological qualms of the Einaudi publishing house. In Turin, the pair were now known by the moniker "Nietzsche Boys" – and with growing weariness at that, it turns out, for when after Montinari's return Colli prodded them to consider a large Nietzsche edition just one more time, the publisher finally withdrew from the project for good.[9]

The loss of their business partner did not deter Montinari from traveling to Weimar a second time in August 1961 – this time, though, with the nervousness of a prospector returning to his claim, keeping careful watch for suspicious tracks. To his relief, however, the director of the Goethe and Schiller Archive, Karl-Heinz Hahn, informed him that everything had remained quiet in the interim. Only the Belgian professor had been in touch, "but he is not the sort to be afraid of, Hahn thinks, considering we have too great a head start, and in any case, this is an academic who needs at least ten years for anything."[10]

At this point, Montinari still seemed to believe they would arrive at their aim faster themselves. In his letters to Colli, he expressed his "irrepressible will to be finished," but was simultaneously quite aware that to complete work on Nietzsche's first notebooks alone "a great deal of time" would be necessary. Sometimes he required days to transcribe a single page. "Being able to read German handwriting doesn't mean much. You have to learn how to read Nietzsche. That is the core of the issue." At least as large a problem as that was a result of their dependence on support from the East German authorities. "That they had confidence in Colli and Montinari is incomprehensible," Wolfgang Harich later wrote. Indeed, that they would leave a German author, and an enemy of the state at that, to a couple of Italians possessing no proven expertise at all, whose knowledge of German was not even beyond all doubt, could not have been foreseen.[11]

When Helmut Holtzhauer, the director of the Nationale Forschungs- und Gedenkstätten der klassischen deutschen Literatur (National Research Centers and Memorial Sites of Classical German Literature), to which the Goethe and Schiller Archive also belonged, invited Montinari on an excursion to Wartburg Castle, the latter initially perceived it as a vexatious obligation: "You can believe me that I didn't like leaving my manuscripts to go look at this fortress." But earning the goodwill of the director proved to be a turning point. Holtzhauer was not only a communist and a decorated resistance fighter who had served eight years in prison under Hitler, but also a music enthusiast, a Goethe connoisseur, a humanist – or, in other words, a member of the educated classes. His journals, kept for over two decades in a stylistic shorthand, offer insights typical of his milieu into the life of a man who over time – and with increasing distance from political reality – withdrew deeper and deeper into the realm of the mind and the fine arts.[12]

Lacking ideological reservations about Nietzsche, Holtzhauer became something of an unofficial sponsor of the editorial project. He helped procure visas, guaranteed access to the collections, and shielded the Italians from potential competitors. It turned out to be helpful that he was, for his part, as was inevitable for an educated middle-class German, a lover of Italy. When Colli came to Weimar for the first time in 1962, he was met at the train station by a limousine from the Nationale Forschungs- und Gedenkstätten – "as though I were some important professor." At the formal dinner the director hosted at the Hotel Elephant, he realized to his relief that none of those present were bothered by his poor German. "Everyone is unbelievably friendly," he wrote to Anna Maria. "It is enough for them that these Italians have appeared to showcase Germany's literary treasures." In the microcosm of Weimar society, culture obviously rated more highly than politics.[13]

The Air in Weimar

In 1965, after traveling through both German states, Israeli journalist Amos Elon painted a bleak portrait. In the West, even if the unease caused by the eerily present past was amplified by ostentatious prosperity, he marveled at the accomplishments of the Economic Miracle all the same. By contrast, his notes from the East lack all ambiguity: "A traveler's first impression of the DDR is one of oppressive, universal shabbiness. It seems as if the war had ended only the day before yesterday. [. . .] Large fields of rubble covered with garbage and overgrown with weeds peep out behind red, wooden, placard-covered Potemkin walls that read: OUR STRENGTH FOR SOCIALISM. IT SECURES PEACE AND PROSPERITY," and: "Nowhere do so many people appear so depleted and worn down as in this joyless country."[14]

In Montinari's letters to Colli, one searches in vain for observations of this kind. Not even once did he find it worth mentioning that the vestiges of the Buchenwald concentration camp were located on the hills he so enjoyed letting his eyes wander over from Nietzsche's former room. As on earlier visits, he felt comfortable in the GDR from the outset. As ever, he was convinced that it represented the better system. Such political avowals, however, no longer made up the core of his relationship to actually existing socialism. "The austere and plain atmosphere here does me well," he wrote to Colli during his second stay.

> Besides, I'm very fond of the climate: cool with a bit of sun and some rain now and again. Italy seems more and more like an African country to me. Imagine: my stomach troubles have disappeared although I eat quite normally without taking any sort of precautionary measures. I think the air in Germany, and in Weimar in particular, is made for me.

Nietzsche, who famously viewed his homeland as a series of "scenes of disaster" for his bodily functions, would have rolled over in his grave. While searching for the appropriate climate, he had fled from Thuringia to Italy. His Italian editor took the reverse course.[15]

In his accounts from the early 1950s, Montinari had glimpsed everywhere in the GDR nothing but the future, unlike in the morally corrupted Federal Republic. Ten years later, the reasons for his appreciation seem to have flipped to their opposite: what he could not emphasize often enough in his correspondence with Colli were the "tranquility" and the "earnestness" of Weimar. Although he himself was initially amazed that solitude became a need for him, he luxuriated in the feeling of being in a place lost to time. "My life takes place here amid great quiet and absent outside events" – written on August 21, 1961, one week after the construction of the Berlin Wall! Careful not to endanger their always fragile consensus, he imposed political restraint on himself vis-à-vis Colli. There is, however, no reason to doubt the authenticity of his escapism. Even according to the unofficial collaborator from the Ministry for State Security who had been observing him since 1964, Montinari avoided "every sort of political involvement."[16]

"And the shouting of today, the clamor of wars and revolutions shall be a mere murmur to you!," Nietzsche had claimed in *The Joyful Science*. After years of politicization, Montinari seemed to take this of all maxims to heart in socialist daily life. In the archive, one has the impression he perceived current events only as distant background noise. Even after the end of his career in the party, he remained a reader of newspapers, having the *Unità* sent to Weimar, reading the *Neues Deutschland* as well, and engaging in political discussions with Helmut Holtzhauer, but what connected them more deeply were their conversations about nineteenth-century German intellectual history. What Montinari thought of Hans Mayer's desertion, Ulbricht's reform policies, or later the Prague Spring has left no traces in either his correspondence or his *Nachlass*. "Philology is, namely, that venerable art that requires of its admirers one thing above all else: to go aside, to take time, to become quiet," reads the foreword from Nietzsche's *Dawn*. In this sense, the GDR turned out to be the philological provinces; Montinari's new home seemed to be located less in the State of Workers and Farmers than in a past lost to reality, its wall of time protecting cultural heritage from the profanation to which it was helplessly subject in Western societies.[17]

This was even more true for Colli, who did sit in Florence at the microfilm Montinari had obtained, but who visited his partner in Weimar once a year after 1962. Hardly anything sprang to his mind about actually existing socialism except that it constituted the punishment of the Germans for the war. Although neither the climate nor the cuisine suited him and he subsisted on spaghetti brought from home, he promptly transfigured Weimar into a mythical site of remembrance. "The first impression is peculiar and gorgeous," he wrote Anna Maria. "Everything is 'Geist' here, and every place brings to life a reading experience from my youth." Incredulous, he listed just how many big names were crammed together in close quarters: Schopenhauer, Schiller, Lucas Cranach, Herder, Liszt . . . "The places where a great man lived or died have the same power as music," he noted down after his visit to the Goethe-Haus. Days spent in the archive exerted a similarly intense effect. He noticed the "odd calm" and the "distance from all things" that came over him while working with Nietzsche's manuscripts: "My life takes on a new dimension here, a greater depth." For the first time in years, he even found a poetic inspiration.[18]

With the car Holtzhauer placed at their disposal, along with a driver, the two Italians went on excursions through Thuringia and Saxony, where further epiphanies awaited Colli. Only in the yawning void of downtown Dresden did he comprehend the magnitude of destruction the war had wreaked. A standing-room-only performance of the St. Matthew Passion in Leipzig's Thomaskirche on Good Friday 1963 became a "religious experience" for the atheist. In Naumburg, on the

The view from Colli's room in the Hotel Elephant: "The church in the middle is Herder's, where he preached and wrote about history and other things. On the horizon the hill of Buchenwald."

other hand, grand disappointment awaited: "not a trace" of Nietzsche, who after all had spent a portion of his childhood there. Even in his birthplace, Röcken, no one had any use for Nietzsche, though there, to Colli, "everything [seems] as it was before": the "plain little church," the parsonage, the duck pond, and Nietzsche's grave, which vaguely reminded him of Schopenhauer's. "The more one is exposed to drab, everyday life in the DDR," Amon Elon, the Israeli journalist, wrote in his previously cited travelogue, "the more pleasant it is to flee into remote periods of the past." One might get the notion he had read Colli's letters to arrive at such a conclusion.[19]

The Craft of Reading

Although Montinari commanded extensive editorial experience as a former editor at Edizioni Rinascità, he came off like an amateur in Weimar. Despite unequivocally finding the extant editions to be insufficient, he was nonetheless uncertain about the method they themselves had to employ to edit Nietzsche's oeuvre into a definitive form. Even so, an obvious place to begin would have been *The Will to Power*, the *corpus delicti* of Nietzsche's reception. On the basis of the sources identified in the appendix of the *Großoktavausgabe* (large octavo edition), Karl Schlechta had put the fragments selected by Elisabeth Förster-Nietzsche into their original chronological order, thus voiding the post-hoc classification scheme. Since he had restricted himself to organizing the material published by Nietzsche's sister, however, his edition also fell short in reestablishing the "manuscript sequence" from which the aphorisms had been taken.[20]

Montinari spent his weeks decoding, transcribing, and establishing the chronology of the various notebooks in which Nietzsche had collected material for his "*Umwertungsschrift*," or "revaluation text." Delio Cantimori, whom he consulted frequently on philological questions during this period, provided the decisive catchword. He was excited, he wrote, to get to see "the result of the *recensio* of the manuscript 'Will to Power.'" The term refers to the Latinism-laden jargon of editorial philology, which Montinari began autodidactically working his way into. At this point, in order to be able to keep following him, a few remarks about the practice of textual criticism are imperative.[21]

"The eighth of April 1777, when Friedrich August Wolf devised for himself the name stud. philol., is the birthday of philology," Nietzsche recorded in his notebooks for the never-published fifth *Unfashionable Observation*, "We Philologists." An academic discipline by this name has in fact existed only since the late eighteenth century. While older philologists (among them the famous Italian Renaissance humanists) had relied on their divinatory abilities (which is to say, on their innate sense of language and their familiarity with ancient authors) in order to "heal" their texts from errors in transmission or "corruptions," German professors like the one Nietzsche mentioned, Friedrich August Wolf, or his colleague in Berlin, Karl Lachmann, claimed to make their discipline just as exact as the mathematical sciences by establishing as the new standard the method of the systematic *recensio*. Performing a recension means not only scouring a received text for blatant or hidden errors, but also "collating" it, or comparing it critically, with all available variants, right down to the first edition or the oldest accessible manuscript, in order to reconstruct its entire transmission history – which of course assigns greater value to the older, more original "textual witnesses." In this way, not only can the points be identified at which deviations, mutations, and errors have crept in and propagated themselves in subsequent editions, but ideally one will even succeed in reconstructing an "archetype," an *Urtext* identical to the author's intentions that need not even have existed, but that as a kind of ideal original forms the basis of all later versions corrupted over time. Thus, even within textual criticism, one can discern the trend toward temporalization so typical for many sciences of the nineteenth century. Like comparative anatomists, linguists, or, later, evolutionary biologists, philologists evinced a special predilection for family trees, so-called *stemmata codicum*, in which the widely ramified offspring of more or less distant archetypes could be represented synoptically. Karl Lachmann in particular, the doyen of German editorial philology, was later rebuked for hubris, for with his methodology, he claimed not only to reconstruct the author's intentions, but also – in his own words – "to give [the work] a more perfect form than the one in which the author brought it into the world."[22]

Now, Montinari's intention was to show that Nietzsche precisely did *not* bring a work into the world bearing the title *The Will to Power*, and in other respects as well, he faced different problems than the German philologists of the nineteenth century, who had developed their methods while dealing with ancient and medieval codices. But Cantimori could still quite rightly speak of a *recensio*, for unlike his predecessors – whom he would later dub "philological nonentities" – Montinari based his reconstruction of Nietzsche's revaluation text, for the first time, on the cumulative available printed and handwritten materials. The philologically ironclad result of his probe, not drafted until years later, reads like this: when Nietzsche lost his mind, he had not been planning a work with the title *The Will to Power* for a long while. The passages of his notes he viewed as worthy of publication were incorporated into his final books, *Twilight of the Idols* and *The Antichrist*. Everything else, Montinari was convinced, one might then publish – if at all – only in its authentic context.[23]

Deconstructing the alleged magnum opus was only the beginning. The longer Montinari tinkered with Nietzsche's manuscripts, the clearer it became to him that they must proceed in the same way with the entire *Nachlass*. "One thing seems certain to me," he wrote Colli in August 1961.

The manuscripts must be completely deciphered and transcribed and examined page by page, which is to say ordered chronologically. For example: yesterday I prepared a sort of diagram with all the aphorisms from *Dawn* by going through the manuscripts containing them in order. Two things came to light while I did this: (1) The genesis of *Dawn*, (2) The *exact* chronology of the individual manuscripts. A thorough analysis of all the material, with readings and transcriptions, could lead to even more accurate philological results. If this is important for the draft manuscripts of a work published by N. himself, then even more so for the pile of unused manuscripts. That means reading and transcribing everything will make us aware of a thought being elabo- rated from a journal to a notebook, from that notebook to another. All this has never been done before![24]

While Colli – like Heidegger or the disciples of the George School – bet he would hit upon the unmediated expression of Nietzsche's Dionysian inspiration in the archive, Montinari arrived at the notion of being able to watch the philosopher gradually generate his thoughts in his manuscripts, as in a workshop – which were not the same thing. Montinari was neither the first nor the last editor to speak about wanting to observe his author at work – perhaps a basic voyeuristic impulse of textual criticism is manifest in this image. As early as Karl Lachmann, one can gather that the philologist must "look into the writer's mental workshop and wholly reproduce his original endeavor." Even Wilhelm Dilthey, who advocated for archiving the *Nachlässe* of authors, dreamed of gaining access to their "workshops." For Montinari's contemporary Walter Kaufmann, Nietzsche's notebooks constituted a "gigantic workshop full of sketches, drafts, aborted attempts, and unfinished dreams."[25]

Perhaps the most ambitious attempt to illustrate the entire genetic process of a literary work dates back to the Tübingen philologist Friedrich Beißner. In his historical-critical edition of Hölderlin begun in 1943, in the middle of the war, he had documented the complete preliminary studies and phases of revision from the poet's *Nachlass*, in chronological order, in a labyrinthine and convoluted "appendix of stages." Beißner's motto was to resolve the "spatial disorder" of the handwritten manuscripts into a "temporal order" – naturally without losing sight of which result Hölderlin himself was after with his revisions.[26]

It makes sense that Montinari would orient himself toward German philologists. Comparing published with unpublished variants convinced him of the fact that, in Nietzsche's texts, "not one image, not one word, not even one punctuation mark in lieu of another" was random. This made the Nietzsche Archive's unilateral editorial policy all the more scandalous. The only appropriate response to this transmission history had to be to reconstruct Nietzsche's oeuvre from *his* perspective, to compile a version that mapped out *his* trains of thought – and the Lachmanns and Beißners provided the suitable tools for just such an edition.[27]

At the request of Helmut Holtzhauer, Montinari set about articulating the guiding principles of the new edition in the summer of 1962:

the works published by Nietzsche himself were to be issued on the basis of their first printings, while taking into account the preliminary stages, and the unpublished texts were to be issued in full, for the first time and in the order they had been written down – which, due to Nietzsche's habit of writing in his notebooks from both ends, would require an elaborate reconstruction. Another note that has survived in Montinari's own *Nachlass* must be cited in order to understand the claim to certainty connected with this conception: "Anyone who reads Nietzsche's notebooks in their chronological sequence will gain a precise picture of his creative work: everything lies clearly and logically before their eyes, no doubt is possible about the intentions expressed in Nietzsche's plans." Several years later, Montinari couched his self-image as an editor in the plainest of terms: *Che cosa ha veramente detto Nietzsche* – "what Nietzsche really said" – is the title of his only Nietzsche monograph.[28]

Nietzsche Is a Disease

Notwithstanding how very inspiring the work was for him, to exchange Florence for Weimar was no easy step for Montinari. During the initial years, his enthusiasm was surpassed only by his despair. While Colli now had a family of seven, Montinari was still a bachelor in his mid-thirties, oscillating back and forth between Germany and Italy, between different plans for life, different beliefs, different affairs with women. In his letters to Colli, mention is made of an "alarming void." He felt "exhausted and lost within," his life seeming to him "backwards and terribly precarious." After his break with Marxism, he had at first let himself fall back into their Graecophile role play, accepting the older man as generator of ideas, teacher, and mentor. But to the extent that "Operation Nietzsche" metamorphosed into his personal cause, so too did his need grow to emancipate himself from his *pedagogo*. "There are several things we have to clear up, less with respect to 'worldview' than to what I need to 'become the person I am,'" he intimated in August 1961, in an allusion to Nietzsche. His dealings with the self-assured Colli reinforced his sense of having no perspective of his own: "I often feel shapeless, gray, boneless." He lamented his "undisciplined, flaccid, lazy, languid character" and dreamed of "constancy" and "inner balance." Over long weekends in Weimar, he tried to compensate for these deficits in his own way, by taking stock, giving account, and – as he had done on previous occasions – engaging in systematic self-exploration: "To lend consistency to my thoughts, I have begun writing everything down in a notebook. It is clear that I must have my own opinion about everything that matters to us (Nietzsche, scholarship, politics, etc.)."[29]

In a recollection of his friend, Cesare Cases traced an arc into the sixteenth century, when Lucca had been a nexus of the central Italian Reformation for two decades. Having addressed himself to the Protestants of his hometown in his *tesi di laurea*, Montinari embodied for Cases the legacy of this uninterrupted tradition. The extent to which the Reformation continued shaping Lucca's cultural climate after the leading heretics had gone into exile is a question that cannot be answered in a few sentences. But given that Cases was right that we must in fact imagine Montinari as a closeted Protestant, then his anti-Catholic affect and moral rigor, his textual literalism, and his penchant for self-examination fit together like puzzle pieces to form a coherent whole that lends his orientation toward philology a quasi-religious character.[30]

"I will find out how to save my soul yet," he wrote Colli in October 1963. He was fully aware of the spiritual dimension of his decipherment work. And indeed, when read in context, his letters and diaries – in which philological observations mingle with self-diagnoses – almost amount to something akin to a work of pietistic confessional literature. In the beginning was the experience of awakening that overtook Montinari in the face of Nietzsche's writings. What followed were the obligatory crises, contestations, and doubts, interrupted by moments of euphoric certainty, which also manifested in his painfully ambivalent relationship to Nietzsche; for Montinari, grappling with his author was a battle to be waged anew each day. As a "finicky aesthete," as a misanthrope and reactionary, Nietzsche could abruptly become insufferable to him – though only to enthrall him all the more intensely again the next moment.[31]

One could write a whole book about how Nietzsche was read and how these readings in turn became a *topos* in literature and philosophy, reading him having always appeared to be more than just an intellectual activity: the experience of a "blissful intoxication," as the *Lebensreform* proponent Emil Gött had confided to his diary just before the turn of the twentieth century; a difficult "art," as Thomas Mann wrote after the Second World War; or pure "intensity," as Jean-François Lyotard was to declare in the 1970s – in every case an act of liberation, of subversion and transgression, that shifted the boundaries between philosophy and poetry, reason and madness, reading and life. Nor is Montinari an exception to this rule. "Nietzsche is neither a poetic genius nor a philosopher, neither a 'moralist' nor a psychologist," he wrote toward the end of 1963. "Nietzsche is a disease. Every word, every concept, every experiment of his evokes a personal response within me. Nietzsche is a problem not yet solved – and I, too, am a problem not yet solved. As soon as I decide to engage with my disease, I engage with his – and vice versa."[32]

Only one thing would help: completing the Herculean labor. Ever the assiduous pupil, Montinari documented his workload in his letters to Colli: "Working in the archive looks like this: seven hours a day, sandwiches and tea for lunch (I bought a Thermos in Milan, but you can get one here now, too!)." – "Today I did not even take a twenty-minute lunchbreak." – "Today I managed sixteen pages! All of this is a huge strain on me, but it is a strain I take on gladly, I'd even say: 'with fanaticism.'" Entering the reading room was pleasure and agony and a daily drill that gave his life stability. "In a state of depression," he informed Colli, from the low point of one of his many crises. "The only spark of inspiration comes from work, from Nietzsche." Over time, his sense grew that this work suited him: "Nietzsche is proving to be a great test for me. I do not know how to explain to you that this work is becoming more and more *my* work precisely because it is so agonizing." No redemption without suffering – even in this respect Montinari followed the pietistic model.[33]

In his letters to Colli, Montinari's spiritual needs can be observed gradually converging with his philological ideas. As far back as 1954, when his first doubts about his aptitude as a communist intellectual had arisen amid the tedium of his military service in Bari, he had wondered whether the "search for truth" were not a far more fitting task for him than politics. Ten years later, politics had shifted to the background. In its stead, the search for truth took on another quality. During his East German exile, Montinari discovered that novel certainty associated with the principle of fidelity to the text. He was "on the hunt for the real Nietzsche," he informed Colli in 1962, still without any particular fervor. Over time, however, he developed a downright enthusiasm for the *Urtext*. He was driven by a "raging passion for the truth," one letter from the following year reads. It will not have escaped Colli that an allusion to Nietzsche was also contained therein.[34]

As we know, Nietzsche is the philosopher who questioned the "value of the truth." In this regard, he even surpassed so radical a critic of bourgeois society as Karl Marx. The provocation began in ascribing a "value" to truth in the first place, truth being tantamount – in the self-understanding of a nineteenth century so faithful to science – to the ideals of objectivity, to disinterest, or to what Nietzsche-reader Max Weber would later call "value freedom." But ever since the whole dubiousness of the desire for knowledge had become clear to him through his engagement with the figure of Socrates, Nietzsche never again stopped attacking this optimistic epistemology as a fallacy. "What within us wants to get at the truth?," went the question he constantly posed, and his answer aimed at debunking the "will to truth" as an expression of the same morality – Christian-ascetic and hostile to life – of which it usually pretended to be the enlightened counter-principle. The false choice could only be avoided if one were to relinquish truth itself as a regulative principle. "Nothing is true, everything is permitted," was thus Nietzsche's notorious rallying cry of transgression, and it comes as no surprise that young Mussolini is said to have liked this passage.[35]

How, though, did Mussolini deal with the other passages – those in which Nietzsche professed a "passion of knowledge" that previous philosophers had lacked? For instead of ending with the negation of Socratic culture, he took it so far to the extreme that it flipped into the affirmation of an even more radical will to truth. Concealed behind this lay Nietzsche's grand narrative of decadence and nihilism, which – in spite of his diatribes against the modern philosophy of history – marked him as a genuinely modern thinker. Just as Marx had predicted that bourgeois class domination would crumble from its inherent contradictions, Nietzsche diagnosed the "self-sublation" of the Platonic-Christian regime of truth – for "all great things perish through themselves." In the final analysis, the ethos of truthfulness would be forced to turn on itself and convict the "will to truth" of its inhospitable logic. All this declaimed in a tone of urgency: for unlike Marx, who banked on the long-term advance of productive forces, Nietzsche regarded this turning point as having already arrived – and in the form of his own person, to boot. He was "simultaneously *décadent* and *beginning*," he wrote in his self-portrait *Ecce homo*. With his obsessive intellectual integrity and his willingness to surrender every hard-fought conviction, this descendant of a long line of Protestant clerics saw himself as both the consummation of and the triumph over that "two-thousand-year training in truth" for which Christianity was responsible.[36]

The Knight of the Woeful Figure

Montinari's transformation into a philologist had many reasons: the ideological crisis of the late 1950s; the aura of the manuscripts in the Goethe and Schiller Archive; the increasing familiarity with an author who encouraged him in his fidelity to the text. His last doubts about the nature of his mission may, however, have been dispelled only by his encounter with Erich Podach.

It would be nice to know what hazards of fortune had induced Podach, a German-Hungarian Jew who had become a communist during the First World War and after the Second an honorary professor for systematic cultural studies at the University of Stuttgart, to devote his life's work to, of all people, Nietzsche. Since the 1920s, he had endeavored to prove that Nietzsche had been nothing more than a mentally unstable ideological writer. "Podach's position is more or less as follows," Montinari wrote Colli after meeting the independent scholar in the archive during his third sojourn in Weimar in early 1962:

> Nietzsche is not a serious philosopher. That is true especially in his late unpublished writings, which reveal the desperate attempt to say something without his being capable of doing so, and which confine

themselves to destroying everything that had ever been said before him. Politically, Nietzsche is an insufferable dilettante and of course a dyed-in-the-wool reactionary; ultimately, he is a comedian. Moreover, Nietzscheans are a despicable breed, not just the coarse ones, but the cultivated ones, too, for instance the "Georgiasts," as he calls them: [Ernst] Bertram, Karl Reinhardt, Kurt Hildebrandt, and even [Edgar] Salin. All of them people who would not have had a problem with Hitler.[37]

Following Karl Schlechta's revelations, Podach had been the only one to have submitted a request to the Goethe and Schiller Archive to examine the material personally, instead of joining in the renewed whispering about Nietzsche's *Nachlass* – which was certainly also due to the fact that he as an old communist harbored no political reservations about the GDR. "His heart beats on the left," Montinari wrote. "Today he remains aloof from all parties, but he has a political past that resembles mine, just that his is much nicer: he was in Moscow, met Lenin in 1921, etc." What is even more spectacular to him, however, was that in the 1920s Podach had met Lou Andreas-Salomé and the widow of Franz Overbeck, characters from Nietzsche's personal entourage. As a veteran of the old ideological battles, he embodied the continuity of a legendary past amid the prosaic present of the archive's daily routine.[38]

Over the course of these battles, Podach must have learned tough lessons about suspicion. He found himself surrounded on all sides by adversaries. For him, Karl Schlechta was nothing but a former accomplice of Förster-Nietzsche who aimed to distract from his own complicity with his accusations. The others, like Heidegger or Löwith, who spread the fiction of the *Nachlass* kept under lock and key by the communists were, by contrast, primarily concerned with the longevity of their own interpretations. "Here in Germany, interest in the central Nietzsche problems is unfortunately low," Podach wrote Colli. "People only bother with interpretations that hang in the air." To undertake a historical-critical edition himself, he lacked more than just the financial means. The "oeuvre-analytical study" *Ein Blick in Notizbücher Nietzsches* (*A Glimpse into Nietzsche's Notebooks*) that he published in 1963 is an eclectic work, in part philologically factual, in part fiercely tendentious, that, aside from transcriptions of portions of the revaluation manuscripts, contains a whole host of peculiar theories, polemical potshots, and the rudiments of a psychopathological reading of Nietzsche. "With this book, he declares war on all the big names of Western Nietzscheology," Montinari wrote. Podach was not just the only one among the Nietzsche scholars who deserved respect – "He is also the only one in Germany who can help us."[39]

This had all the more significance since Colli and Montinari were now under contract with a publisher. Like Paolo Boringhieri before him, Luciano Foà, Colli's most important contact at Einaudi since Pavese's death, had gone into business for himself: in 1962, he joined forces with the office machine entrepreneur Roberto Olivetti, taking with him as seed capital the rights to an Italian Nietzsche edition the Turinese publisher had spurned. It was nevertheless beyond dispute that the risk of such a venture could not possibly be borne solely by Adelphi Edizioni. The editors had long since decided that a German-language edition should appear concurrently with the Italian one, but Nietzsche's reputation in both the GDR and the FRG was too dubious for the search for a German publisher to seem promising. Instead, in April 1962, Foà and Colli managed to spark the interest of Gallimard in Paris in a French Nietzsche edition. At the time, though, Nietzsche was not an easy-to-place author in France either, for which reason the summer months elapsed in protracted negotiations about details.[40]

In the meantime, Podach was already picturing their future collaboration. He felt called to contribute to the edition and reveled in the idea of snubbing his opponents with the news "that an international brigade is setting to work with fiery zeal." Montinari's initial enthusiasm, by contrast, did not last long. "Although I am learning a lot from this man and although we are politically aligned," he wrote, "our conversation is very trying for me." Podach's battle against imaginary enemies bordered on paranoia. In the hyperactivity of his monologues, he tended to lose his false teeth. In the poignancy of his shattered state, he demonstrated what it meant to relinquish the objectivity of editorial work and instead be consumed in the Cold War of partisanship. The letter in which Montinari outlined for Podach the incompatibility of their different approaches thus marked a crucial moment for Montinari himself: for the first time, he spelled out his new self-understanding as a philologist. He and Colli, he wrote, neither identified with a particular faction, nor did they pursue the objective of asserting a particular viewpoint with their edition. Their intention was merely "to form a sober, historically contextualized opinion grounded in the facts, that in essence virtually ignores the quarrels of the anti- and pro-Nietzscheans."[41]

The Politics of Facts

Basing an opinion on "facts" in order to overcome the dispute among the parties – the history of an entire discipline could be reconstructed from this half-sentence. Textual criticism may not have been elevated to the rank of an academic science by German professors until the nineteenth century, but many of its achievements nevertheless date back at least to the humanists of the Italian Renaissance. Toward the end of the fifteenth century, for instance, Angelo Poliziano advocated for emending manuscripts not on the basis of divination, but by systematic comparison. Not long after, Piero Valeriano appended a critical apparatus to his Virgil edition. And Giannantonio Campano, who supervised the first Roman book printers, evinced a keen awareness for the difference between text and interpretation when he contended in the foreword to his edition of Livy that he had never been "a curious interpreter," but had confined himself to "correcting mistakes by the scribes."[42]

In sketches for his fifth *Unfashionable Observation*, Nietzsche extolled the "assailing active element" of the old "poet-philologists," which for him stood in the greatest possible contrast to the profes- sorial bearing of the "philologist-scholars" in his own epoch. As a matter of fact, the advances made by *ars critica* in the early modern period had less to do with insular erudition than with the flaring up of religious and political conflicts – which comes as no surprise, given the political relevance possessed by the authority on the written tradition in a Christian society shaped by dynastic claims to power. While the Italian humanist Lorenzo Valla demonstrated through philological means that the "Donation of Constantine," the decree from which the popes derived the legitimacy of the Papal States, was a forgery, in the sixteenth century the French jurist and historian Jean du Tillet published a collection of historical documents to undergird the house of Valois's claim to the French crown. It makes sense why we would later speak of the "historical-critical method": in cases such as these, criticism of the written sources and a determination of historical facts amounted to almost the same thing.[43]

The true hour had come for the philologists, however, only when Christian Europe disintegrated into two inimical denominations. Much is true about Nietzsche's observation that an enhanced intellectual and linguistic sensibility numbered among the consequences of religious wars. It had taken the "subtler quarrels of the sects," he writes in *The Joyful Science,* to familiarize believers with the notion "that the 'eternal salvation of the soul' depends upon the small differences among concepts." Admittedly, even scholars of the Middle Ages had known that the Bible had originally been written not in the Latin of the Vulgate, but in Hebrew and Greek. Yet only with the scriptural literalism of the Protestants did the magnitude of theological danger arising from such problems of historical transmission increase. If, as the principle of *sola scriptura* purported, all truth proceeded from Holy Scripture, then doubts about its wording must bear on the foundations of faith. Thus the stage was set for a huge philological clash: in the second half of the sixteenth century, the Protestant Hebraists Louis Cappel and Johannes Buxtorf became embroiled in a debate about when vowel markings had been introduced into the Hebrew *Urtext* of the Old Testament. In 1678, realizing the explosive power of such disputes, the Oratorian Richard Simon published his *Histoire critique du Vieux Testament,* a history of the transmission of the Old Testament from the oldest Hebrew versions through those in Greek to the most recent Latin editions, in which he showed that mutations, deviations, and errors had crept in at every stage. That presented him, a Catholic, with the opportunity to refute the scriptural fixation of the Protestants as an absurdity and make the case for the necessity of an ecclesiastical hierarchy.[44]

Even Pierre Bayle's *Dictionnaire historique et critique,* the landmark of the historic-critical method in the late seventeenth century, has a sectarian background. Ernst Cassirer described Bayle, a Huguenot who converted to and from Catholicism and later fled to the more tolerant Netherlands, as the "Galileo" of history: as the one who had provided a methodological and theoretical foundation for the new "concept of the factual," which gained plausibility in the course of philological and political debates. At first blush, Bayle's *Dictionnaire* of 1696 is nothing more than a lexicon of historical persons – King David has an entry, as does Tacitus and the French philologist Joseph Scaliger – a who's who of the European educational canon. Upon further inspection, however, it turns out to be an apologia for a new kind of certitude, as its author not only compiled countless historical facts, but also used his exuberant footnotes to document the methodological rigor with which he, in each individual instance, had sifted through, compared, and adjudged the available documents with respect to their credibility, admitting only that which had doubtless been the case according to evidence from the historical record.[45]

With his "*vérités de fait*," Bayle took up an epistemological fallback position. The political refugee had experienced the explosive power of philosophical and theological truths first-hand. It is not for nothing that the "dispute between the parties" so frequently comes up in the digressions smuggled into his footnotes: the background against which he developed his epistemology of facticity was religious civil war. In contrast to the opinions and dogmata that had unsteadied the seventeenth-century intellectual public, the facts he wanted to leverage had the quality of being "common to all men." They formed the foundation of a divided world people still had to be able to agree upon, even when the consensus of a divided worldview had shattered. Getting mixed up in the laborious verification of historical facts was thus no end in itself for Bayle, nor a pedantic exercise, but rather a political school of sangfroid: "Now is it nothing to correct the unfortunate tendency we have to make rash judgments? Is it nothing to learn not to assent lightly to what we see in print? Is it not the very essence of prudence not to accord belief too readily?"[46]

After everything that has been said, it must come as a surprise that Nietzsche of all people harbored a special fondness for Bayle. Nietzsche is, after all, notorious for his claim that there were no facts, nothing which was the case, only perspectival interpretations controlled by the will to power. "Facts especially do not exist, only interpretations."

– *"A meaning must always be inserted first, so that there can be 'facts'"*
– "In truth *interpretation is a means itself of becoming master over something."* Such passages, many more of which may be found in his published and unpublished writings, earned Nietzsche the rebuke of having paved the road into the so-called post-factual age. Still, it is not that simple: for every negation of objective truth, for every passage in which he repudiates the fact – or the "text," as he also liked saying as a philologist – in favor of its exegesis, an instance may be found for the contrary assertion, according to which nothing mattered for cognition so much as differentiating between fact – or text – and interpretation. In *The Antichrist*, for example, his polemic against Christianity, Nietzsche seems to relate the whole infamy of theologians to their *"ineptitude for philology"*: "By philology should be understood here, in a very general sense, the art of reading well – recognizing facts *without* falsifying them through interpretation, *without* losing caution, patience, finesse in the drive for comprehension. Philology as *ephexis* [i.e. wariness, PF] in interpretation: whether concerning books, newspaper columns, destinies or weather events." Pierre Bayle had had this very thing in mind when he had warned against the risks of hasty judgments.[47]

The Germanist Hendrik Birus made an elegant suggestion for resolving Nietzsche's inconsistent relationship to facts. Where he rejected each possibility for factual truth, he spoke as an epistemologist who, inspired by Schopenhauer and Kant, sketched out the plans for his own transcendental philosophy. Where, on the contrary, he insisted upon facticity, on precise reading, on the categorical distinction between text and interpretation, he spoke as a cultural critic who had purloined the "art of reading well" from his discipline, ancient philology, to make it a tool for a new *"historical philosophizing"* which drew the most far-reaching conclusions from the most incidental details of cultural history. When Nietzsche wrote that "[a]ll of science attained continuity and steadiness only when the art of reading correctly, that is, philology, had reached its peak," this may therefore be understood as a statement about his own joyful science as well – which, with its combination of quick and slow thinking, of essayistic finesse and academic thoroughness, has lost nothing of its fascination to this day.[48]

Down with the Philosophers!

Here we are once again able to turn to Montinari, who recognized in Nietzsche's historical-critical philosophy the paragon of his own mission. "*Human*[, *All Too Human*] in particular is the book in which I would feel like underlining almost everything," he informed Colli, who had especially little use for the very title with which Nietzsche had renounced Wagner and, at least temporarily, transformed himself into an Enlightenment thinker: a manifesto of unreserved striving for knowledge, an apologia of the "small, unpretentious truths" only available at the price of grand convictions. "Convictions are more dangerous enemies of truth than are lies"; if Montinari counted this aphorism from *Human, All Too Human* among his favorite passages, then it was only because he saw in it the ethics of his own *Bildungsroman*.[49] In his resolution to ignore the "quarrels of the anti- and pro-Nietzscheans" and draw upon only naked "facts" during his deciphering work, a distant echo reverberated. As with the philologists and the historians of the confessional age, Montinari's orientation toward facts can also only be understood as the vanishing point of his political disenchantment at the conclusion of the twentieth century's wars of opinion.

It had been the "end of the period of metaphysical certainties," he later recalled in an interview with *il manifesto*, that had convinced him "that the only antidote to overly adventuresome speculations is historical and philological labor"[50] – an end which spans an entire decade. It had essentially begun in 1948, when the communists lost the first parliamentary elections in Italy. It had cast shadows over 1953, when Montinari had witnessed the uprising in East Berlin. Three years later, in the *annus horribilis* for Western European leftists, it had finally run its course. Like many of his contemporaries, Montinari could have become a militant liberal after 1956, or he could have joined one of the New Left groups. That he remained loyal to the party in spite of everything, seeking new certainty not in the heights of theory but on the terrain of philological facts, had just as much to do with the aura of Nietzsche's manuscripts as it did with the method of his political initiation. In the late 1940s, his academic teacher Delio Cantimori had acquainted him with a communism distinguished by its hostility to theory and by its historical sense of reality. There was no path leading from this communism either to the lifestyle experiments or to the speculative fantasies of the New Left. All the more, it led to rigidity in textual criticism; one only had to be guided by Cantimori's example.

Already during the 1930s, over the course of his increasing distance from fascism, the professor had metamorphosed from an idealist in the vein of Gentile to a historical materialist who preferred working in the archive over philosophical speculating. Yet not until the 1950s, when communism had lost its revolutionary intensity and the ideological fronts in the Cold War had consolidated, did service to historical facts become his final undertaking. "In this new epoch, historical scholarship must make a conscious effort to return to bibliography, erudition, and philology; it is the only sure thing. As was the case before, scholarly history arises from controversy even today. It is the only usable weapon." Cantimori had noted this shortly after the unsuccessful elections of 1948. As he had in the 1930s, he returned to the early modern wars of religion, even in the changed political landscape. If he identified once more with the heretics and sectarian refugees of the sixteenth and seventeenth centuries, then he did so less because of their political radicalism than because many of them had been meticulous historiographers and philologists. For Pierre Bayle, the virtuoso of the historical-critical method, he felt a special affection.[51]

The year 1956 marked a drastic turning point for Cantimori. He found himself forced to question not only his loyalty to the Communist Party, but also the balance of his life as a political intellectual altogether. "My greatest mistakes," we read in his personal notes from this period:

> (1) believing I understood something about politics; (2) believing the fascists had been the ones who carried out the revolution; (3) hanging out among the communists; (4) not breaking with the sterile moralism à la Rousseau and Mazzini; (5) joining the PCI; (6) interrupting my studies to translate Marx, etc. Retreating into research is the only remedy. To bring a chaotic, aimless life to a tidy end.

If his resolution from 1948 still exuded confidence about attaining a new, objective perspective in the afterlife of ideologies, in these lines he gives the impression of a man confessing his failure to himself. He sarcastically noted his increasing alcohol consumption – as if he had to compensate for his ideological sobriety with other intoxicants. In 1957, he renounced his fealty to the PCI. "It isn't that my convictions have changed," he wrote, "but I no longer understand certain things, and that is why I can no longer act on behalf of any party."[52]

Dating from the same period are diagnoses from which it emerges that Cantimori regarded the era of the modern state – and thus of European history – as definitively over. To be sure, his reaction to his epochal disappointment consisted precisely in a meek retreat onto the terrain of historical facts. Nevertheless, he was still unable to resist entirely the temptation, in a sweeping gesture, to elevate the sinking of his political ambitions to the level of an occurrence with historical-philosophical dimensions. After the war, like many of the radicals whom he had esteemed in the 1930s – figures like Hendrik de Man, Ernst Jünger, or Carl Schmitt – Cantimori also began toying with motifs of *posthistoire*, the sort of temporal self-positioning that for a generation of political intellectuals represents the processing of trauma. After the hope of being able to "make" history had turned out to be hubris, the notion that the historical movement as a whole had petrified into crystalline brittleness exerted a comforting effect. But while de Man faced his personal *posthistoire* in a mountain cabin in the Alps, and Jünger and Schmitt retreated to the sylvan solitude of the West German Central Uplands, the urbane Italian Cantimori found his final refuge in the Biblioteca Nazionale in Florence, where, without entertaining further grand plans for publication, he idled in a timeless present amid the sources for his underground history of heretics. After the loss of ideological horizons, belief in work provided ultimate support.[53]

Even his letters to Montinari are shot through with the melancholy of this Protestant ethic: "What is crucial is that we work and that, to a greater or lesser degree, we somehow continue pulling the cart of our labor onward," he advised the younger man – encouraging him not to linger on interpretive questions, but to concentrate entirely on recon-structing Nietzsche's wording. "Down with the philosophers, long live the philologists!" was Cantimori's maxim, which also contains the quintessence of his own experience as a political intellectual. Over the final years of his life, he fancied himself a craftsman – unmolested by ideological pretensions – who wanted nothing more than to pursue his honest day's work: "What holds true for the work of a lathe operator, for instance, of a carpenter, stonemason, etc.: the job is either done well or done poorly. Political, ideological preconditions etc. have no meaning. That is equally true for the work of the historian."[54]

The extent to which Montinari was shaped by his role model can be gleaned from the fact that after Cantimori's death he adopted the self-image of the honest craftsman as his intellectual legacy. When in the late 1960s Colli reproached him for overdoing things with his philological rigor, he replied that he aspired to follow all the rules of the art: "as would a good cobbler who makes good shoes." For the older man, who positioned himself as ever in the domain of the pre-Socratic sages, this disclosure could not have contained much to identify with. In ancient Greece, after all, the "lowbrow" *banausos* represented a social class of artisans excluded from any sort of enlightenment. On the contrary, Montinari seems to have finally found the role that accorded with him. Even in the 1980s, as a Fellow at West Berlin's Wissenschaftskolleg (Institute for Advanced Study), he would style himself as an outsider in the select circle of tenured professors when insisting he was "a philologist, a hard worker, essentially nothing more than a lackey."[55]

Many things resonate in this understatement: the class attitude of the social climber; the proletarian sympathies of the communist; and an anti-intellectualism typical of the old Left. Mostly what it contains, however, is an answer to a century-old problem: searching for a way to opt out of the tense realm of ideologies, Montinari – like Bayle, like Cantimori – exchanged the large bills of ideological convictions for the small change of textual literalism.

His metamorphosis into a philologist was largely complete when he received a letter from a young French philosopher in November 1963. "From July 3 to 7, 1964, the Seventh International Philosophical Colloquium will take place at the Royaumont cultural center," Gilles Deleuze wrote. "This year's topic is Nietzsche. Martial Gueroult, professor at the Collège de France and chairman of the committee, requests I inform you that he would be both delighted and honored were you to accept the invitation to participate in this colloquium."[56]

5

WAITING FOR FOUCAULT
Cerisy-la-Salle, 1972

The Nietzscheanism of the second half of the century origi-
nated in France in the 1960s. While West German expositors
had scarcely more than moderately existential interpretations
to offer, in Paris Nietzsche was made into the pioneer of a new
philosophy of difference. It was not the first time that his proponents
there thought they recognized in him a kindred spirit – which had
a lot to do with the fact that Nietzsche, in turn, was influenced so
heavily by French authors. As early as the turn of the century, when
the first translations and, shortly thereafter, the first *Œuvres complètes*
had appeared in print with avant-garde publisher Mercure de France,
many French readers had gotten the impression they were dealing with
a pan-European or even French writer – so un-German did Nietzsche's
aphoristic style and his nearly unbridled anti-German feelings seem to
them. And had he not himself predicted that he would be understood
more "in Paris and New York" than in "Europe's flatland, Germany"?[1]

Georges Bataille and his co-conspirators from the secret society
Acéphale could also have invoked this prophecy in their desire to
remedy the injustice perpetrated against Nietzsche by the National
Socialists – by claiming him for themselves as the guarantor of a
radical moral freedom. Bataille's Dionysian saturnalia were so arcane
that only a handful of his contemporaries had heard anything at all
about them. Yet he wielded all the greater an influence on the French
Nietzsche renaissance of the postwar period. Of the scholars who

descended on Royaumont in 1964, almost all were shaped in some fashion or another by Bataille: Pierre Klossowski and Jean Wahl, who numbered among the founding members of Acéphale, but also Gilles Deleuze, who at eighteen years of age in 1943 – over the summer in which Colli had gathered his Chosen Few around him in Lucca – had been embroiled in his first discussions about Nietzsche by Bataille and Klossowski at the salon hosted by leftwing Catholic and Jules Verne devotee Marcel Moré.[2]

Alone against the Nietzsche Mafia

Deleuze's invitation had an electrifying effect on Montinari. Finally, the long-awaited opportunity had presented itself to showcase their edition to an international audience of experts. Colli, on the other hand, thought they had more important things to do than waste their time on academic debates. "Please excuse me," he wrote Montinari, who insisted on contriving a strategy for their appearance, "I do not attach to Royaumont the importance you do" – particularly as he suspected they would not be received with open arms. The name Heidegger may not have appeared on the list of presenters, but it did include Rudolf Boehm, the professor from Leuven who had been circling over Weimar like a hungry vulture for years, and Karl Löwith, alongside Heidegger and Jaspers *the* Nietzsche authority in Germany. Only recently, in an article in the *Neue Rundschau*, Löwith had likened the proposition of yet another complete edition of Nietzsche to robbing the dead. Clearly, he wanted to discredit their edition in the German publishing sector. One might think Colli had been infected by Erich Podach's paranoia. As his letters show, in no way did he believe that "guru Karl" was acting on his own behalf, but rather that it was only the "first phase of the attack" that the academic establishment was scheming against them.[3]

Montinari nevertheless insisted on accepting the invitation. Only when they "state the facts," he wrote, and demonstrate the deficiencies of the existing editions would they succeed in thwarting "Löwith's maneuver" and winning over the "bigwigs of Nietzscheology" to their side. In the end, Colli permitted him to draft a lecture in German in both their names. "But it ought to be short and not take up too much of your time." Above all, it was important for them not to lose sight of their actual goal: "Our concern can only be about these two outcomes: (1) discouraging Boehm with respect to his publication; (2) making a good impression on Löwith so he stops putting pressure on our potential publishers." Colli regarded as slim the chances of achieving even just one of these aims.[4]

As described at the beginning of this book, the conference in fact began less than promisingly. Colli and Montinari were greeted by the Nietzsche celebrities with open suspicion on the very journey there. What's more, the organizers had scheduled Montinari's lecture for Sunday morning – in other words, the most thankless time slot of the entire conference. Using numerous textual examples, he elaborated why a new Nietzsche edition was "not only of philological interest today." Although they were *small* omissions, misreadings, twisted meanings, he presented, he felt justified in drawing far-reaching inferences. He established the untenability of the previous record, expressly emphasized the "careful" archiving by the competent authorities in the GDR, and held out the prospect of reconstructing the authentic text. He counseled the philosophers, just as Nietzsche had the theologians of his day, to pause their interpretation in the meantime.[5]

Montinari's lecture was followed by the first part of the accompanying cultural program, which included a concert by the Juilliard Quartet, with works by Mozart, Debussy, and Schubert, and an excursion to Chantilly. What worlds of difference from the nocturnal rituals Bataille and his conspirators had performed in Nietzsche's name! If Royaumont is recalled as the primal scene of a wild new manner of thinking, then that is certainly not because the customs of academic conference proceedings had been subverted. On the contrary: conventions like these contributed to Nietzsche's metamorphosis from a political writer espousing a worldview to a philosopher of the academy. In addition, however, his compromised legacy had to be shifted to the realm of the metaphorical and metaphysical. As Thomas Mann had declared already in 1947, he who takes Nietzsche literally is lost. In this vein, Walter Kaufmann's remark that Nietzsche's books were "easier to read but harder to understand than those of almost any other thinker" amounts to the same thing. And even the genius of Heidegger's reading consisted in transporting Nietzsche's ideas into that nebulous sphere where his own thought was at home. If one were looking for a generic motto for the interpretation of Nietzsche after the war, then it would be not to fall into the trap of his obvious, literal meaning. "[N]othing clumsy and straightforward is admissible, every kind of artfulness, irony, reserve is required in reading him." It was with these words that Mann had characterized the new "art" of reading Nietzsche.[6]

The French philosophers in Royaumont who were laying out the baselines of their fluid thought availed themselves of this art as well. Gilles Deleuze cautioned against understanding Nietzsche in an all too obvious way, against mistaking the "will to power" for "wanting to dominate," or the "strong" for the politically "powerful," or the "eternal return" for the monotonous "return of the same." Pierre Klossowski, who personified the continuity of bohemian interwar culture, took the same tack when he discounted the notion of Nietzsche's aggressive individualism. His tragic truth had first come to light at the moment of his mental breakdown, when – signing his letters of madness as both Christ *and* Dionysus – he had confirmed the loss of his personal identity and withdrawn from monotheistic civilization's imperative of unity. On the final day of the conference, Michel Foucault helped such wide-ranging readings onto a stable footing when presenting his theory of interpretation. Invoking Nietzsche's reflections on the relationship between text and exegesis, he sketched the contours of a boundless hermeneutics that was no longer tied to any *Urtext*: "There is nothing absolutely primary to interpret, for after all everything is already interpretation."[7]

No wonder Colli and Montinari found this intellectual atmosphere uncomfortable. The "world without being, without unity, without identity," of which Deleuze spoke, ran counter to their intellectual bearing. "I care just as little about Klossowski as you do," Colli wrote on a subsequent occasion to his friend. And if their letters mention the "great Foucault" or the "ineffable Gilles," then they do so mostly at an ironic, if not sarcastic, remove. The theory of exuberant interpretation in particular had to make a mockery of their endeavors. If indeed all attempts to reconstruct the authentic Nietzsche were rendered moot, then not only was their project of a historical-critical edition doomed to failure, but neither was it possible even to raise a principled objection to the way in which his sister misused his legacy.[8]

Deleuze later remarked that his generation was no longer concerned with acquitting Nietzsche of the charge of fascism; Bataille and Klossowski had already done so for them. Colli and Montinari's fidelity to the text, by contrast, was driven by the need, finally, to give Nietzsche a chance to speak for himself before his oeuvre was once more authorized for interpretation. What lurked behind their alienation from the French Nietzscheologists was much less an episte-mological than an ethical difference.[9]

Against Interpretation

Even if one is not inclined to concur with his radical conclusions, Foucault exhibited an astonishing sensibility for the spirit of the times in his mapping of the interpretive process. He was not just making the case for nullifying the regulative authority of the *Urtext*, but also identifying the question of exegesis as the key problem facing the intellectual situation of the age. In the late nineteenth century already, the German philosopher Wilhelm Dilthey had prophesied that, in the future, the business of philosophers would be to interpret the classics. Only in the imitative climate of the postwar period, however – when speculations about the end of philosophy were added to the agenda of intellectual self-assurances, together with the diagnosis of the "end of history" – did the hour come for hermeneutics. The decisive factor for this was Nietzsche's philosophy of interpretation, from which Heidegger had meanwhile expropriated a foundation for fundamental ontology; among the characteristics of the *Dasein* he had defined as the mode of human existence was the obligation to relate to the world always already in an exegetic way. *Truth and Method*, the "philo-sophical hermeneutics" published in 1960 by Heidegger's student Hans Georg Gadamer, was circulated like a manifesto of the new humanities at German universities in the initial years after its issuance. For disci-plines anxious to resume their interrupted traditions and relearn their cultural heritage, it afforded them a welcome organon. Might the art of exegesis not even be able to take on the role of a new fundamental reflection that would render philosophy in its conventional form obsolete? New professorships, new journals, and new institutions like the research group "Poetics and Hermeneutics" or the "Department of Hermeneutics" founded at the Free University in West Berlin in the 1960s by Jacob Taubes, the scholar of Jewish studies and one of the German participants at the Royaumont colloquium, testified to how much was expected of the new paradigm, across all disciplines. From the Royaumont transcripts, it is evident that similar discussions had taken place in France, too. Following Foucault's lecture, one of the French audience members wanted to know whether the interpretive techniques he had described were not suitable for taking over philosophy's "line of succession."[10]

The victory march of hermeneutics also elicited fierce counter-reactions on the other side. Amid the intellectual climate of the postwar period, it was at once the great bearer of hope and the emblem of that climate's reactionary spirit. It was at Royaumont, after all, that Jean Wahl floated the theory about the present being "sick from interpretations" – a thought which German philosopher Herbert Schnädelbach took up in the 1980s with his diagnosis of "*morbus hermeneuticus*." Foucault himself, who appeared to regard the unleashing of exegesis in 1964 as a cognitive necessity of the modern age, had been battling the hermeneutic "systems of discursive multiplication" since the 1970s with his clean-up operations in discourse analysis. And even Jacob Taubes wondered, toward the late 1960s, whether hermeneutics was "not entrenched in the Counter-Enlightenment, body and soul." No one, however, expressed an aversion to interpretation as early and as firmly as American critic Susan Sontag, who wrote her famous essay "Against Interpretation" in 1964, the same year the Nietzsche scholars convened in Royaumont. Like Foucault, Sontag noted that her age was marked by an unprecedented "itch to interpret," but she drew opposing conclusions from this observation. Whereas Foucault had glimpsed an inflation of meaning, she diagnosed the loss of immediacy. In turns of phrase that reveal how strongly she then was influenced by Nietzsche's second *Unfashionable Observation*, she exposed the proliferation of exegesis as a symptom of an overly intellectual era closed off to aesthetic experience and argued for a return to sensual encounters.[11]

Had Colli been aware of Sontag's essay at the time, he would doubtless have agreed with her. "In truth, Nietzsche must not be interpreted in any way," he wrote in the text announcing the complete Italian edition. "We must simply lend him our ears." Colli would certainly have agreed with another of Sontag's observations as well, namely that interpretation constituted a "radical strategy" to tailor unfashionable works to the standards of a later-born readership by foisting on them a "true" or "latent" meaning that deviated from the wording. Was that not exactly the operation that the Nietzscheologists of the postwar period were perpetrating against Nietzsche? Regarding Kafka, yet another author who attracted twentieth-century exegetes "like leeches," Sontag noted that he had "been subjected to a mass ravishment" by "armies of interpreters." Such drastic phrasings were alien to the pair of Italian philologists, but in this matter – and with respect to Nietzsche – they doubtless espoused a similar view. To judge from their circumspect commentary, the French philosophers seemed to their minds like rapists.[12]

Watching TV in Reinhardsbrunn

In spite of all the unease, Colli and Montinari's trip to Royaumont had to be marked a success. To be sure, they did not succeed in persuading the philosophers to cease interpreting. But Foucault and Deleuze promised their collaboration as co-editors of the Gallimard edition. And Karl Löwith of all people offered to help them search for a German publisher.[13]

After his return to the GDR, Montinari's life fell back into the rhythm of the deciphered pages, of the small triumphs and fits of despair – before things soon took a wonderful turn. In this respect, too, his story follows the genre conventions of pietistic, revivalist literature. The very fact that he wrote Colli that he had arrived in Weimar "as if I had returned home" set a new tone. When Colli paid him his yearly visit in August 1964, he was amazed the reputation his friend now enjoyed in town society. Mazzino had become a *"mezzo padrone,"* a "little boss," he wrote in his report to his wife. At the celebration that took place on the Frauenplan for Goethe's 215th birthday, Montinari had to shake innumerable hands and was interviewed by GDR television.[14]

His connection with Sigrid Oloff, a librarian at the Goethe and Schiller Archive who, like him, boarded at the Villa Silberblick, contributed to his integration into Weimar society. In the past, Montinari's love affairs had invariably resulted in euphoria and desperation, existential crises, and, not least, a huge loss of time. To Colli's surprise, however, his new sweetheart seemed to exercise a salutary influence on his associate. "What is missing this time is the torturous, sentimental trait that otherwise accompanies Mazzino's amorous relationships." In October – at which point Colli had returned to Italy – Montinari hinted at marriage plans: "Giorgio, I am happy. I find peace at Sigrid's side. My knots and entanglements are loosening, my restlessness is subsiding." While quite of few of his old comrades were starting to experiment with new kinds of relational models at this time, Montinari set his course for the port of bourgeois marriage – a development the *pedagogo* gave his blessing, posthaste: "I am sure you now have the maturity to contemplate marriage in its fullest sense. I think your life will undergo a radical change."[15]

The party withholding its blessing, however, was the relevant ministry. "It seems we need a permit from the GDR authorities," Montinari wrote, "because Sigrid would be eligible to leave the country if she became an Italian citizen. Unfortunately we don't know any exact details." What followed were protracted visits to government offices in the capital. Montinari cursed the policy of the Italian government, the refusal of which to recognize the GDR as a state made his position even more complicated. Yet his loyalty to socialism was also severely put to the test. In his letters from the winter of 1964–5, he inveighed against "petty bureaucrats who don't want to take on any responsibility" and reported relapses into black melancholy: "Sometimes I tell myself that it is impossible to be happy." He fell far behind the stipulated quota with his transcriptions. He was supposed to have been in Florence by then to work with Colli on the philological appendix. When the information came to light in April that he had to relocate his place of residence to the GDR permanently to receive the marriage permit, Colli lost his patience: "In your last letter you inform me that you are willing to stay in Weimar for an unforeseeable period of time and that it does not matter to you how you will support yourself. That leaves me speechless." What was to become of their edition and of their friendship if, on top of it all, Montinari was forced to take East German citizenship? What if he gave up his freedom in favor of his marriage?[16]

Thanks to the intervention of Karl Löwith, things at least finally started moving in their search for a German publisher. All previous attempts had failed not only because of the reservations of the publishing industry, but also because of Montinari's intransigence. Beck Verlag? "Affiliated with the National Socialist Nietzsche cult – forever." Kröner? "Whenever I remember that they tacitly continue to print the *Will to Power*, I get boiling mad." In August 1964, shortly after his return from France, Montinari's joy had been all the greater when Siegfried Unseld had gotten in touch with Colli to signal his interest in a licensed German edition for Insel Verlag. It was not about "questions of national prestige," Walter Boehlich, the editor in charge, had assured them. But "beyond a small, admittedly reliable circle of libraries and cognoscenti," Unseld did not expect big sales opportunities. Nietzsche almost ended up in the milieu of Suhrkamp culture, but the offer of 150,000 Deutschmarks had not been enough for Colli.[17]

Now, though, in the spring of 1965, while Montinari was in danger of being swallowed up by the GDR, he was in discussions with De Gruyter Verlag, located in West Berlin. At De Gruyter, too, they were reluctant to buy the rights to a German Nietzsche edition that followed in the wake of a parallel publication in a foreign language. "We will have to convince De Gruyter," Montinari wrote, "that the edition represents something completely different, the significance of which is not diminished by the existence of an Italian and French edition." At some point, Löwith, by then a militant supporter of their undertaking, seems to have stepped in with the remark that it would be a "national disgrace" if the negotations fell through. Perhaps that was instrumental in mobilizing the Deutsche Forschungsgemeinschaft (German Research Foundation), whose financial commitment tipped the scales such that, in the end, a contract materialized.[18]

The turning point in Montinari's personal affairs moved into view, however, only when he rallied his party friends from the PCI, which conducted its shadow diplomacy in cases like these for want of official channels. At the beginning of June, the situation seemed as good as hopeless. "You have to be patient and can't have any illusions," Montinari wrote. All the more surprising, then, that the couple were permitted to marry in July, after the bridegroom had shifted his official place of residence to Weimar, and to spend their subsequent honeymoon at Schloss Reinhardsbrunn in the Thuringian Forest: "Apartment with living room and bedroom, bathroom, television(!), radio: 60 Marks a day," Montinari reported, not without pride. That they opted for Reinhardsbrunn nevertheless had nothing to do with a particular preference for the charm of real socialist luxury enclaves. The compromise to which the functionaries had agreed stipulated that Sigrid Montinari must not leave the GDR until further notice, despite her marriage to an Italian.[19]

In September, she gave birth to a son. When triplets followed in August 1966, eleven months later, Walter Ulbricht sent a congratulatory telegram. It was at this point at the latest that Montinari was a well-known personage in Weimar. With his cigars, his little Fiat, and his stable of children, he must have cut a striking figure in the East German town.[20] The citizens of Weimar were in the dark about one key aspect, however: the fact that he was living in their city in order to edit a certain Nietzsche was a well-kept secret.

The Ostracized Thinker

At the time, Helmut Holtzhauer had granted him free rein only under one condition: that his work, as Montinari expressed it in one of his letters to the foreign branch of the PCI, be "a purely private" affair. Conversely, this limitation points to the fact that there was no place for Nietzsche within the public sphere in the GDR until the 1980s. The journalistic coverage by German émigrés from the East and Soviet cultural officials which had accompanied the closure of the Nietzsche Archive in the late 1940s had portrayed the "intellectual author of fascism" as the archenemy of socialism. Unlike in the Western zones of occupation, where the mood after the war had been similar, if not in terminology, then still in substance, this verdict became the line of official cultural policy in the GDR. With *The Destruction of Reason*, Lukács had supplied a theoretical basis for the short circuit from Nietzsche to Hitler. According to Wolfgang Harich, its reviewer for the *Deutsche Zeitschrift für Philosophie*, the book, which Montinari had read in East Berlin in 1954, contained "the perhaps most profound and persuasive critique of Nietzsche that was ever written." In Ernst Bloch and Hans Mayer, Nietzsche's last prominent advocates left for the West in the early 1960s. Since that time, competing interpretations no longer existed.[21]

It was for this reason that if Nietzsche's subsequent reception history played out at all, then it did so in secret: no publications, no debate, no politics of memory. When Montinari first set foot in the Villa Silberblick in 1961, he was forced to realize that "everything having to do with Nietzsche" had disappeared. On their excursions together, Colli later marveled that there were no visible traces of any kind, aside from Nietzsche's gravestone, either in Naumburg or in Röcken. To the locals, Nietzsche seemed to be a stranger. Not until 1982 were his gravesite and birth house placed under historical landmark protection.[22]

In this regard, Heidegger's insinuation that Nietzsche was being kept under lock and key by the communists did possess a kernel of truth: for citizens of the GDR, the dangerous trove of writings at the Goethe and Schiller Archive were indeed inaccessible. The Nietzsche researchers Montinari encountered in the reading room over the years came from Switzerland, Japan, and even Australia – but no East German scholar was ever among them. Like Radeberger pilsner or Köstritzer *Schwarzbier*, Nietzsche's *Nachlass* was treated as an export article reserved – if not always in exchange for hard currency – for non-socialist foreign countries.[23]

With his work, Montinari was thus subject to a kind of unofficial pledge to secrecy in Weimar. In addition, he had been under surveillance by an employee of the Ministry for State Security since 1964. The informant's reports paint the picture of an ascetic philologist who focused his complete concentration on his activity in the archive: "Montinari is personally very unassuming, not at all amenable to the temptations of the 'Economic Miracle.' All luxury leaves him unmoved, he only wants to work." To the unofficial collaborator, Montinari's communist convictions were expressed in these virtues. While he did not commit himself to "historical and dialectical materialism," he did act out his political beliefs "on a practical level," visit the May Day parades, read the right newspapers, and show up at employee meetings "out of genuine interest." Aside from his achievements in the Italian class struggle, Montinari's character traits were mentioned in particular: "I am of the opinion that any sorts of duplicity or dishonesty are impossible with him." With respect to Nietzsche, no worrying interpretations were to be expected from him, for "Montinari does not interpret, he just edits." He had an inherently positive attitude toward the GDR: "Montinari stresses again and again that a philology of Nitzsche [sic] is authentically possible under the conditions the GDR has established, whereas until the end of the war, the *Nachlass*, Nitzsche's manuscripts, were in the hands of either purely fascist people or those under very strong Nazi influence who concocted a Nitzsche in their same vein."[24]

The praise of socialist cultural politics that the confidential informant conveyed with obvious satisfaction suddenly flips into a revisionist reading here. Evidently, it had escaped him that the theory that Nietzsche was tampered with contradicted Lukács's orthodox line. "In any case, it is good," he continued for the record, "that a writer who has been abused by the Nazis and has renown throughout the world is being presented free of distortions, omissions, and forgeries, purely in a philological sense." It was clear he had made Montinari's standpoint his own.[25]

In essence, the file "Gießhübler" reveals at least as much about the informant as it does about his target. First and foremost, one can take from it a gloomy portrait of the career academic as an unofficial collaborator. A literary scholar at the Nationale Forschungs- und Gedenkstätten and a staunch leftist who had come into contact with the later political refugee Hans Mayer and the "counter-revolutionary" Wolfgang Harich during his literary studies in Leipzig, and who had himself been subsequently expelled from the SED due to "revisionist conduct," Hans-Heinrich Reuter, or "Gießhübler" – the Fontane specialist had taken his code name from *Effi Briest* – exhibited particularly favorable attributes for an informant: essentially "a positive GDR citizen," as his recruitment file noted, but with sufficient preexisting political encumbrances to be susceptible to blackmail at any time.[26]

His scholarly ambitions handed the Stasi additional leverage. Especially in Germany, where graduates spent years, if not decades, waiting for a professorship, academic careers had always been precarious situations. German socialism seems not to have made an exception to this rule. As if dangling a carrot, the Stasi beckoned with the prospect of promotion, or a professorship, or a prestigious position in the capital: "The IMS [unofficial collaborator for security] was told that such a possibility would be considered in due course," appears repeatedly throughout the meeting reports. Moreover, "Gießhübler," whose targets included not only visiting foreign scholars, but also Helmut Holtzhauer and Karl-Heinz Hahn, the director of the archive, was in turn under observation by another unofficial collaborator. As his file shows, the Stasi had already installed a dense network of informants at the Nationale Forschungs- und Gedenkstätten in the 1960s.[27]

Nietzsche's Dirty Secret

The contract with De Gruyter, which finally materialized in December 1965 after protracted negotiations, signaled a turning point for Montinari. "Only with the German edition does my work of all these years take on meaning," he wrote to Cantimori. That was not just because, in strictest terms, one could only speak of the "genuine Nietzsche" in the German original, but it also had to do with the fact that Montinari no longer deemed the critical apparatuses of the Italian and French editions adequate. The reconstruction of the "preliminary stages" – the aspiration to render the genesis of Nietzsche's work comprehensible from the first drafts to the fully formulated aphorisms – corresponded to the standard of editorial philology set since the nineteenth century. But it had since become clear to Montinari that a further factor had to be considered in Nietzsche's case: "The big problem is Nietzsche's 'sources,'" he wrote to Cantimori – a problem that had been on his mind for some time already, but that only now, in the second half of the 1960s, became his primary concern.[28]

Nietzsche underscored time and again how important it was for him to be liberated from the fetters of written scholarship. Because of his bad eyesight, it reads in *Ecce homo*, he had been forced to bow out from "bookworming" as well as philology. "We do not belong to those who only get ideas among books, or occasioned by books," one reads in *The Joyful Science*. As became ever clearer to Montinari with time, however, this had little to do with the truth. Not only had Nietzsche remained a ravenous reader until the end of his productive life, but even more so than with other philosophers, his thought depended on what he was reading. Upon close examination of the fourth *Unfashionable Observation*, "Richard Wagner in Bayreuth," Montinari had made his first spectacular find: the text was assembled together in large part from Wagner quotations. "I took all the works of Wagner (nine volumes) from the library," he wrote to Colli, "and found a large quantity of quotations. 'Wagner in Bayreuth' is full of them." What Wagner himself had regarded as the homage of a kindred spirit – "Wherever did you get this knowledge of me?" – had thus in reality been an encoded provocation prior to Nietzsche's public break with the composer a short while later.[29]

Based on bountiful evidentiary material, including Nietzsche's excerpts as well as the underlinings and marginalia in his books, Montinari embarked on a forensic search that would keep him busy for the rest of his life: "Nietzsche's borrowings from books he read overshoot all predictions. Did I tell you that I found two aphorisms from *The Will to Power* attributed to Nietzsche that are nothing more than the translation of two passages from Tolstoy and Renan? We must be on our guard." One does not need a great deal of imagination to conceive of how time-consuming this search was. Hiding behind every word of Nietzsche's might be a concealed allusion. "Worked for seven hours yesterday and found *one* quotation," Montinari reported. "The quotes by Burckhardt on the Greeks are – at least for now – impossible to find." Once again, he believed he would "suffocate" in work. On the other hand, he was very proud of his "philological perspicacity" and felt he was on the scent of something "sensational."[30]

With his new apparatus, Montinari did indeed enter philologically uncharted territory, seeing as how his reconstruction of Nietzsche's sources signified nothing less than a redefinition of the concept of the "preliminary stage." To be able to comprehend the evolution of the works of an author like Nietzsche, so his discovery went, it was not enough to document the revising of drafts and the honing of phrasings; what he was reading and how he adapted what he read as his own also figured into it. One might also put it differently: instead of drawing upon the abundance of his Dionysian inspiration, Nietzsche had tacitly borrowed quite a few – or even many – of his ideas from other authors. Montinari was aware that this finding raised the question of Nietzsche's originality. "The montage in 'Wagner in Bayreuth,'" he assured Colli, "does not negate the fact of Nietzsche's greatness." While it was possible to pinpoint what prompted his thought, Nietzsche himself nevertheless remained "the formative, regulative, evaluative principle of these impulses." As a practitioner of philology, Montinari had little interest in distilling from his discovery a theory of authorship or of the concept of the work. Where he did show interest, however, he appeared eager to declare the fruits of Nietzsche's reading as his own accomplishment as well: "Nietzsche's reading of other authors – documented in (mostly) hidden quotations in his writings, in excerpts in the *Nachlass*, in marginalia, underlinings, and other traces of his reading in volumes from his library – is a constituent of his oeuvre. It therefore belongs in the text, while simultaneously pointing beyond the text."[31]

Colli, who saw in Nietzsche an intuitive thinker, found such attempts at definition pedantic. In the past, too, they would fight about the scope of the apparatuses, but only when Montinari began with his study of the source materials did their argument take on a categorical dimension. It was not just about the fact that Montinari's "philological lunacy" led to further delays; on top of it all, Colli accused his partner of "scientific overzealousness." "What is the point of it all? To honor Nietzsche's memory? I don't think so. For you to feel like an excellent scholar? To please readers like Wolfgang Müller-Lauter?" Montinari's confession of wanting to pursue an academic career after his return intensified their mutual estrangement. Although Colli himself had been teaching in Pisa for years, he still viewed the university as the negation of a philosophical existence. "You must always consider the fact," he reminded the younger man, "that in our whole endeavor, two elements are central for me, namely 'honoring' Nietzsche and furthering his impact on the present." It was for that reason that he did not want to be responsible for an edition that Nietzsche himself would not have liked. What's more, he wanted to appeal to readers "who are neither idiots nor pedants." An apparatus that documented what Nietzsche was reading in addition to the customary preliminary stages, however, was in danger not only of becoming "hypertrophic"; in the web of his cross-references, he was also obliterating Nietzsche. "In the past, our quest to destroy the intoxication and the myth surrounding Nietzsche was near and dear to your heart. Beware of lapsing into the opposite approach, which in my view is by no means any better."[32]

Death of an Author

In June 1967, as the student protests escalated in West Berlin, the first volume of the French edition, long awaited and repeatedly delayed, was published in Paris: *Le gai savoir*, including the unpublished fragments from 1881 and 1882, in a new translation from the German by Pierre Klossowski. Colli noted with satisfaction that the starting shot of the French edition was accompanied by a massive press response. In their jointly written introduction and in interviews in *Figaro* and *Le Monde*, the prominent co-editors, Deleuze and Foucault, did not shy away from arousing great expectations: they promised unpublished material and new findings, and in contrast to Habermas in Frankfurt, who reiterated how antiquated Nietzsche was, they brought him into the discussion as a highly topical thinker.[33]

In *The Order of Things*, the book that had made him famous in France the year before, Foucault had configured the episteme of the present to begin with Nietzsche. With the watchword of the eternal return, Nietzsche had "burned" the "promises of the dialectic," which is to say, the idea of a continuous, progressing history, and with the death of God and the annunciation of the *Übermensch*, he had anticipated the diagnosis of humankind's disappearance. With the realization that words did not constitute tools of impartial knowledge, but rather an opaque reality *sui generis*, however, he had, above all, initiated a "radical reflection upon language" – a tradition in which

Foucault located his own thought. He cited Nietzsche's famous apprehension from *Twilight of the Idols*: "[W]e shall never rid ourselves of God, since we still believe in grammar." Nietzsche, he wrote, arrived at this radical epistemological stance through his linguistic studies. "Many experts," Foucault explained in *Figaro*, would have a hard time "with Nietzsche's philological beginnings." For him, on the other hand, Nietzsche's academic profession represented the key to his thought. In Foucault's function as co-editor, he had even advocated for including Nietzsche's early philological writings in the French edition as well – an initiative that had foundered on the fact that the publisher saw no interested parties for these works.[34]

Claude Gallimard was mistaken here, for if the French edition elicited an exceptional response, then it did so because Nietzsche returned in France as a visionary theorist of a new language. The "core problem" of Nietzsche's philosophy, Foucault elaborated in *Le Monde*, can be found "reproduced in the discursive form itself." As a result, unexpectedly, a kind of preestablished harmony existed between between Colli and Montinari's intention to publish Nietzsche in authentic form and the Paris poststructuralists' interpretations. The fact, for instance, that Nietzsche had failed in writing his final magnum opus, leaving behind instead only scattered fragments, loses all biographical coincidence in these readings and transforms into a symptom of the "downfall of the book" per se – an event to which the French thinkers ascribed the greatest importance. If, as Jacques Derrida, Maurice Blanchot, Roland Barthes, and Philippe Lacoue-Labarthe repeated in almost monotonous unanimity, philosophy in its conventional form had been bound to the form of the book, then the inability to write books – or at least to finish them – revealed that, with Nietzsche, something else has superseded them. "If the world of Nietzsche," Maurice Blanchot wrote in 1969, "is not handed over to us in a book, and even less in the book imposed upon him by an infatuation with culture and known by the title *The Will to Power*, it is because he calls us outside this language." To penetrate into this realm beyond philosophical discourse, which Blanchot identified with Nietzsche's "fragmentary writing," was the objective of his own mode of writing. Deleuze, too, made the case for allowing oneself to be seduced by Nietzsche into new "modes of expression." The Strasbourg philosophers Philippe

Lacoue-Labarthe and Jean-Luc Nancy demonstrated that Nietzsche's *"désœuvrement,"* his failure in book form, had begun long before *The Will to Power*. Nietzsche's "most significant philosophical insight," one German reader later wrote, summarizing the French discussion, had been the "retraction of the idea of the work." What constituted his actual legacy was thus not his transgression in content, but his transgression in form.[35]

"It looks," Colli wrote in early 1967, "as if the 'Nietzsche fever' in France is more intense than ever." The timing for the publication of the first volume seemed to be ideal. The editors nonetheless soon discovered that their edition had met with embittered resistance. The first portent of imminent unpleasantries was a letter to the editor in *Le Monde* that at first glance appeared fairly harmless. The philosopher Jean Beaufret took the liberty of politely pointing out an oversight: the allegedly "unpublished" fragments that *Le Monde* printed as teasers for the new edition had been included in the Kröner edition of *The Will to Power* and, moreover, had existed in French translation since the 1930s. With his correction, Beaufret laid bare more than an embarrassing error; he questioned the raison d'être of the new edition, for even in the editors' afterword in *Le gai savoir*, there was sweeping talk of "unpublished" (instead of "posthumous") fragments. And if the editors seemed not to know whether and which of the textual passages had appeared elsewhere, their claim about going beyond the current standard of transmission history would become preposterous. We need not be paranoid to surmise that what was asserting itself here was the long arm of Heidegger, who in Beaufret had found his man in France. "By adding a few aphorisms, notes, and additional drafts, they will not alter our understanding of Nietzsche," Jean-Michel Palmier, yet another Heideggerian, wrote in *Le Monde* a short while later. "Colli and Montinari's undertaking is not nearly as new as has been claimed."[36]

At Gallimard, where multiple postponements of the publication date had already generated poor morale, the blunder with the "unpublished" fragments led to recriminations. For Colli and Montinari, there was no doubt about whose failure the error could be attributed to. Since their meeting in Royaumont, Colli wrote Dionys Mascolo, the editor in charge, the two co-editors had never been heard from again, nor had they responded to any of their queries about the trans-lation. "I must confess, the volume was produced in too great a rush and without clear responsibilities," Mascolo conceded; Deleuze had been frequently ill, and Foucault had been residing in Tunisia since 1966. When Foucault finally stepped down fully from his editorial role in April 1968, he explicitly did not want this move to be seen as an expression of criticism or a lack of interest. "But," Mascolo informed Colli, "should he not agree with this or that point, it's scarcely possible for him to exert influence from such a great distance." Furthermore, because he had recently been caught in the crossfire of public criticism, Foucault thought "it would be better for the edition if it was not burdened with his name."[37]

The real reasons for Foucault's withdrawal only became apparent a year later. In order to understand what was really going on, we must return once more to Montinari's editorial guidelines for his and Colli's edition in 1962. Along with the basic principle of publishing Nietzsche's notebooks in their entirety and in chronological order, he had put on record at the time all that should *not* be taken into consideration:

> Everything that cannot be regarded as Nietzsche's own expression (i.e. insofar as it reveals nothing about his thought and personality) and that could be viewed as pure repetition will be excluded from our edition. Consequently, personal memos and notes of merely extrinsic or incidental substance (e.g. intimations of financial matters, such as payments, bills, cost estimates, notes about the scheduling of lectures, about railway timetables, about inns, etc.) will be omitted; the same goes for paraphrases and excerpts from books by other authors.[38]

This passage showed up in almost unaltered form in the editorial afterword which had revealed a vulnerability for Jean Beaufret, and which now, not a full year after his abdication as a responsible co-editor, served Foucault as the target of his attack. In February 1969, in his famous lecture "What Is an Author?" given before the Société française de philosophie, he endeavored to deconstruct the categories of authorship and work: "When undertaking the publication of Nietzsche's works, for example, where should one stop?" he asked.

Surely everything must be published, but what is "everything"? Everything that Nietzsche himself published, certainly. And what about the rough drafts for his works? Obviously. The plans for his aphorisms? Yes. The deleted passages and the notes at the bottom of the page? Yes. What if, within a workbook filled with aphorisms, one finds a reference, the notation of a meeting or of an address, or a laundry list: is it a work, or not? Why not? And so on, ad infinitum. How can one define a work amid the millions of traces left by someone after his death? A theory of the work does not exist, and the empirical task of those who naïvely undertake the editing of works often suffers in the absence of such a theory.[39]

This was unmistakably addressed to Colli and Montinari, whose difficulties in meeting their stipulated submission deadlines Foucault almost spitefully seemed to allude to in his last sentence. Against the project of allowing Nietzsche himself to have his say and restoring his oeuvre to him, purged of all post hoc overpainting, he counterposed another "ethical principle" that boiled down to freeing the interplay of signs from the compulsion to identify the author, which went hand in hand with the ideology of the bourgeois individual.[40] The irony is that Foucault owed his knowledge of Nietzsche's wild *écriture*, the "millions of traces" the philosopher had left behind after his death, to his collaboration with the two Italians on their edition. Is the debacle Colli and Montinari experienced in France to be labeled a betrayal, an ennoblement, or simply a dialectic? What made their edition so adaptable, on the one hand, was, on the other hand, what provided the means to its own repudiation. All the philological problems they had encountered over the course of the 1960s were posed as fundamental philosophical questions by their French readers – but only to prove that their efforts to find the voice of an author in the chaos of Nietzsche's scribblings, and to define the boundaries of a work, distorted him hardly any less than his prior editors had done.

Montinari's study of the source material had a special role to play in this dialectic. As described above, he expressly did not want the discovery that Nietzsche owed many of his ideas less to flashes of intuition than to reading other authors to be seen as relativizing his originality. For the French, by contrast, the very concept of originality was part of an obsolete vocabulary. In 1967, Julia Kristeva developed her theory of "intertextuality," according to which "any text" represented the "absorption and transformation of another." In his well-known essay from the same year, Roland Barthes drew upon this idea when he wrote that the "death of the Author" was synonymous with the "birth of the reader," because the reception of already circulating discourses was concealed behind every literary production: "The text is a tissue of quotations drawn from the innumerable centres of culture." While Kristeva and Barthes primarily had in mind the modern novel from Cervantes to Michel Butor, it was not long before their theories found their paradigmatic exemplar in Nietzsche the montage artist.[41]

In 1971, the previously mentioned Strasbourg philosophers Philippe Lacoue-Labarthe and Jean-Luc Nancy issued a French translation of Nietzsche's little-known philological writings on rhetoric – among them a lecture manuscript from the winter semester of 1872–3, sketches for a planned book entitled *Über den Kampf von Kunst und Erkenntnis* (*On the Struggle of Art and Knowledge*), as well as its short, incomplete introduction, "Ueber Wahrheit und Lüge im aussermoralischen Sinne" ("On Truth and Lie in an Extra-Moral Sense"). In these texts, written after *The Birth of Tragedy* but never published during his lifetime, Nietzsche had first registered that fundamental skepticism regarding truth that would become the trademark of the new French thought: "What then is truth? A mobile army of metaphors, metonymies, anthropomorphisms, in short, a sum of human relations which have been poetically and rhetorically intensified, transferred, decorated and which, after lengthy use, seem firm, canonical, and binding to a people." Probably no other dictum of Nietzsche's was quoted in subsequent years as frequently as this passage from "On Truth and Lie." What for Lacoue-Labarthe and Nancy was more crucial than recognizing the specious character of truth and the tropic nature of language, however, was the discovery that this recognition was reflected in the form of Nietzsche's texts. After having failed to condense his research on rhetoric into a book, Nietzsche had moved away not only from a systematic mode of writing, but also from the pretension of identifying his text with his authorial voice. Through painstaking studies of source material, redolent of Montinari's forensic search, Lacoue-Labarthe and Nancy established that Nietzsche had borrowed his theses on the figurative character of language, down to the way they were phrased, from the works of long-forgotten contemporaneous linguists. Once again, he turned out to be a tinkerer playing with the set pieces of nineteenth-century culture. Had Nietzsche himself not written that he felt "frequently like the scribblings which an unknown force draws across the paper to try out a new quill"? Even if, as Heidegger had claimed, he was supposed to be the last thinker of the metaphysical era, his anticipation of subjectless writing showed that he had already escaped the illusions of logocentrism.[42]

"Taking these contexts seriously," the aforementioned Kafka editor Gerhard Neumann wrote in view of the French debate, "can terrify the editor who regarded himself as a levelheaded craftsman." This did not initially seem to be the case for the craftsman Montinari. Even before the publication of *Le gai savoir*, he had suspected the French would instigate a "war," but some time would elapse before the philological consequences of the new philosophical spirit of the age became clear to him. He spent the year 1967–8 translating *Thus Spoke Zarathustra* into Italian and preparing notes for the apparatus of the German edition, a labor that filled him with particular satisfaction in light of multitudinous "sublime decipherings." "The days pass by, and I immerse myself more and more not just in the apparatus, [. . .] but also in the ideas and the world of Zarathustra," he wrote Colli in May 1967 – only to report a year and a half later that he had just reemerged "from the visions and unceasing raptures in the third Zarathustra." The interim had witnessed the police shooting of student protestor Benno Ohnesorg, May '68, and the Prague Spring. These political occurrences, however, seemed to register only distantly with Montinari. In his letters from West Berlin, where at the time he stayed regularly to confer with De Gruyter, there is talk of opulent lunches at the Europa-Center and forays into the nightlife of Charlottenburg, while one searches in vain for references to the rebelling students.[43]

In 1969 in the embargoed holdings of the old Nietzsche Archive, Montinari stumbled upon an unknown chapter from *Ecce homo* in which Nietzsche had written about his sister in a way one can only describe as an execration: "[T]o believe myself related to such a *canaille* would be a profanation of my divinity." This spectacular finding provided final proof of the extent to which Nietzsche's texts had been manipulated by Elisabeth. "Our edition will really mark a turning point," Montinari predicted to his partner in a euphoric mood. While his deciphering work in Weimar was gradually coming to a close, he concocted future editorial projects – among them an edition of "Nietzsche's conversations" and an annotated catalog of "Nietzsche's reading material," to include all literature he had consulted, together with markings and marginalia. At this point, Colli and he had signed another contract with De Gruyter for a complete edition of Nietzsche's correspondence. Montinari wrote his partner that he was possessed by "the demon of philology" – "which surely won't meet with your approval."[44]

Since their rift over the boundaries of textual criticism, Colli had increasingly withdrawn from the operational work. While Montinari reported on other "miracles of deciphering" over the course of 1969, he committed to paper the sum of his philosophical reflections after decades of thinking about doing so. "It makes me happy finally to be a philosopher," he wrote upon the publication of *Filosofia dell'espressione*, "that's what it always came down to. Unfortunately, I'm afraid my book will be as good as incomprehensible for everyone else." His concern was not entirely unfounded: Montinari enlightened the De Gruyter editor, who thought the book had something to do with Expressionism, that the title concealed a concept of a dualistic metaphysics – and although he himself had been familiar with Colli's ideas since he was fifteen, he also feared that the book would leave him out of his depth. "When I get a hold of it, I think you'll have to wait a bit before you find out whether I understood it."[45]

Simultaneously, Montinari was preparing for his return to Italy. He managed both to secure a teaching position at the Department of German Studies at the Sapienza in Rome, and to persuade his PCI friends to intervene once more in his favor. In January 1970, Sigrid Montinari submitted her application for expatriation. In their Weimar surroundings, husband and wife forced themselves to observe absolute silence. Montinari wanted to stave off the moment, he wrote, at which people "will no longer see me as 'one of us.'" With success, apparently: in early 1970 still, IMS Gießhübler, who had been surveilling him for six years, went on record that the Italian's imminent departure was not expected. Ten months later, the Montinaris moved to Italy. Gießhübler's final report suggests that he felt hoodwinked by his subject:

> Before Prof. M. left our republic with his entire family in late October of this year, he was invited once more by the IMS to his apartment. Here he was able to ascertain that in Prof. M. we are dealing with someone who expressed a negative attitude toward all political-ideological questions. He rejected the entire socialist system of government. Prof. M. had never been as open and honest with the IMS about his true political disposition.

The informant also thought he knew what this change of heart could be ascribed to: "He views this basic attitude of Prof. Montinari as directly related to the Nitsche [sic] research carried out now for years."[46]

Quote Unquote

While Montinari's informant did in fact find his way back to the orthodox position of Lukács at long last, in France Nietzsche's transformation into a radical philosopher of language was running its course. With *Humain, trop humain* and *Aurore*, the next volumes of the Gallimard edition were published, while the disastrous editorial afterword from *Le gai savoir* gave rise to an unending chain of addenda, corrections, and justifications. "This error has shaken the prestige of our edition, not just in France," Colli wrote to his publisher. Montinari, for whom the German edition constituted the state of the art, was himself of the opinion that the French edition was "poorly made."[47] In July 1972, while he was staying in Weimar to conduct further archival research and Colli was occupied with other matters, the tale of their reception culminated in a showdown that has taken its rightful place in the annals of French intellectual history.

Under the programmatic title *Nietzsche aujourd'hui?* (*Nietzsche Today?*), the second large-scale stocktaking of French Nietzscheanism took place that summer in Cerisy-la-Salle, in Normandy, and the scope of the convention alone revealed how much the German thinker had grown in significance since the mid-1960s. With the exception of Foucault, who was teaching as a visiting professor at the University of Buffalo, nearly all the big names of French contemporary philosophy were represented, and for the first time, with Sarah Kofman and Sylviane Agacinski, women figured among the presenters. The papers, which appeared in print the following year, add up to a thousand pages. It was the tone, however, that marked the actual difference from the *Colloque de Royaumont*. Social interactions had become more informal, the debate more direct, and the language less professorial. As can be inferred from the minutes of the discussions, part and parcel of the self-understanding of the new Nietzschean leftists was to question the rules of cultured academic discourse.

Thus, in his lecture on the Dionysian nature of capitalism, Jean-François Lyotard showed reverence to the "men of profusion," among whom he included "pop [artists]," "hippies and yippies," and "madmen." "More Nietzschean than Nietzsche's *readers*," the professor explained. "One hour of their lives offers more intensity [. . .] than three hundred thousand words of a professional philosopher." Even Deleuze, who described academic philosophers as "bureaucrats of pure reason," delegitimized himself and his peers in his talk entitled "Nomadic Thought" from rendering judgment about Nietzsche's topicality. That question had to be answered by "young musicians," "young painters, young film makers." "Those of us here today are, for the most part, already too old." It was in Deleuze's remarks from this period that can best be gleaned the counter-revolutionary aspirations tied to obliterating humankind and subject, author and book, from the arsenal of cultural meaning-making. While in 1967 Roland Barthes was still describing the "removal of the Author" – the attempt to deprive the act of personalizing literary discourse of its self-evidence – as a Brechtian alienation effect, Deleuze was already showing interest in its immediate political effects: "When we become the least bit fluid, when we slip away from the assignable Self, when there is no longer any person on whom God can exercise his power or by whom He can be replaced, the police lose it." And while Barthes had voiced the conviction that it was illusory to want to escape cultural codes *entirely* – "a code cannot be destroyed, only 'played off'" – Deleuze now, in Cerisy, was using Nietzsche to invoke the utopia of an "absolute encoding." For him, too, this encoding proceeded from a linguistic event: "[Nietzsche] seizes on German to build a war-machine which will get something through that will be uncodable in German." He, too, found it necessary to shatter the old forms of thought. He did not content himself, however, with tracking down Nietzsche's revolutionary gesture in his writing: "It is not at the level of the text that we must fight." The micrology of exact reading thus had a merely subordinate significance for Deleuze. To unleash Nietzsche's forces, it was instead necessary to establish a relationship with an "extra-textual practice."[48]

That was unmistakably directed at Jacques Derrida, whose lecture entitled "The Question of Style" culminated in a close reading of a single, ostensibly trivial sentence. Eschewing each and every convention of academic philosophy, his virtuosic commentary on a few fragments from *The Joyful Science* in the Gallimard edition was many things: the attempt to outdo Heidegger's interpretation of Nietzsche using Heidegger; proof that within the texts of the notoriously misogynist Nietzsche there simultaneously existed the affirmation of a feminine element that transgressed all conceptions of essence, identity, and truth; and, last but not least, a resounding slap in the face for Colli and Montinari which overshadowed all the indignities the pair had had to endure since 1967. Derrida skewered a fragment that Montinari had included among the unpublished pieces from *Le gai savoir*; Nietzsche had written "*ich habe meinen Regenschirm vergessen*" – "I have forgotten my umbrella," within quotation marks – in one of his notebooks.

In his painstaking interrogation, Derrida demonstrated the absurdity inherent in wishing to ascribe this sentence – as his "impulsive" readers from Italy did – to an authorial subject named Nietzsche: "Maybe a citation. It might have been a sample picked up somewhere [. . .]. We never will know *for sure* what Nietzsche wanted to say or do when he noted these words, nor even that he actually *wanted* anything." Naturally, at this point, Derrida, too, returned to the ill-fated editorial afterword. In the editors' assertion that they had incorporated only Nietzsche's "own" texts, he claimed to recognize "a monument to hermeneutic somnambulism. In blithest complacency their every word obscures so well a veritable beehive of critical questions." His point was not that the forgotten umbrella violated the criterion of

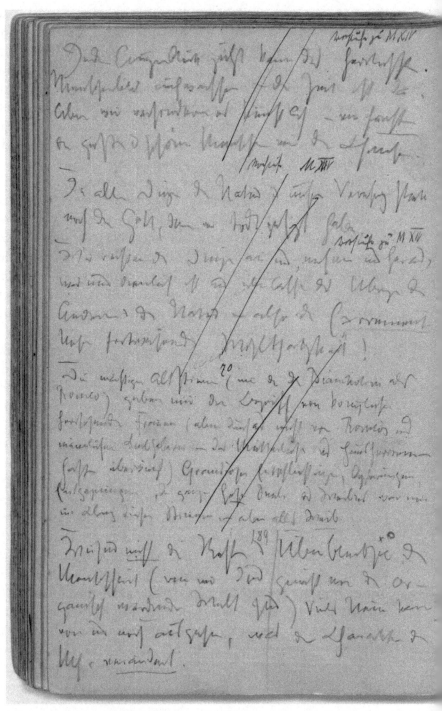

"ich habe meinen Regenschirm vergessen" – *"I forgot my umbrella"* (below right).
A description of fact? A thought? A quotation?

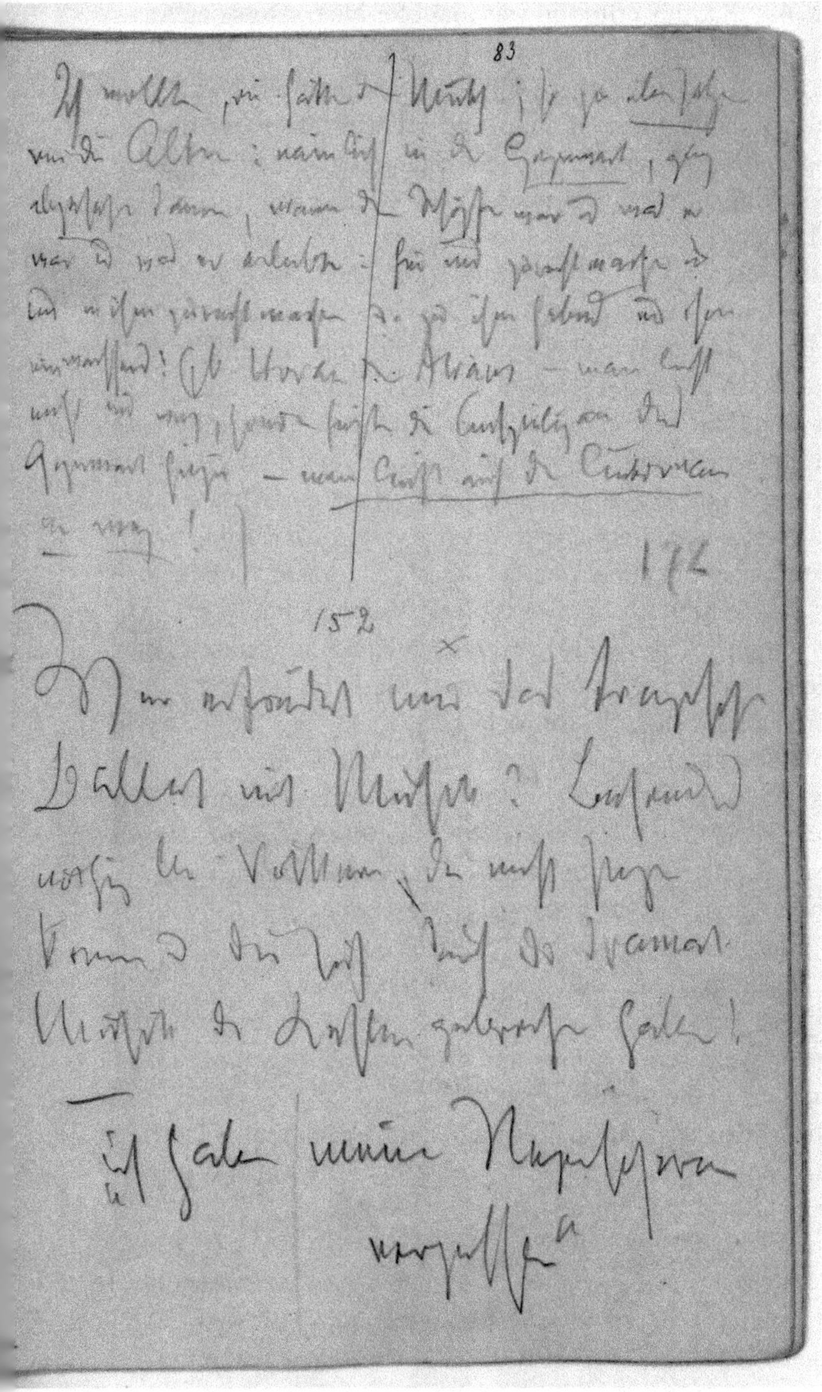

"one's own," but that this criterion was inapt for Nietzsche's oeuvre as a whole: "[T]he totality of Nietzsche's text, in some monstrous way, might well be of the type 'I have forgotten my umbrella.'" And this finding could be generalized once more as well: Derrida closed his talk by insisting upon erecting an "epochal regime of quotation marks" over all those difficult signifiers related to Western phallogocentrism like "truth," "unity," "meaning," and so on. Bearing in mind the stellar rise of written, gestural, and spoken quotation marks since the 1980s, one might conclude that at least the academic world in the Western hemisphere has, to a great extent, complied with this demand.[49]

In Colli and Montinari's absence, it fell to Richard Roos, the French Germanist who had made public Nietzsche's sister's adulterations at the same time as Schlechta, to defend the cause of philology. In his talk "Règles pour une lecture philologique de Nietzsche" ("Rules for a Philological Reading of Nietzsche"), which is still worth reading today, he opened up the entire panorama of Nietzsche's transmission history – from his Nazification, through his "pleasure in juggling fragments," to the temptation to varnish his reactionary ideas in aesthetics and metaphoricity – in order to derive from it the necessity of a literal, patient reading as Nietzsche himself had called for: "Who, aside from the philologist, still reads like this today? Who today shows the written text the respect which compels him to extinguish himself in the presence of the text?" Roos's insistence that the Nietzsche edition contribute to reconstructing the genesis of the texts, to identifying the sources, and to clarifying the historical context could have come from Montinari himself. And although he made recourse to the disparaged entities of "meaning" and "authorship," the philosophers might have let him get away with his paean to philology – if he had not gotten the idea toward the end to glorify his line of work, full of pathos, as "an ascetic discipline in the service of truth."[50]

In the subsequent discussion, Bernard Pautrat, a student of Derrida who was among the organizers of the conference, flew at this provocation like a bull seeing red:

> You're telling us: here's a text, it has its truth, you even said *the* truth; by working on this text, can we *really* find out what the *real* Nietzsche *really* wanted to say. . . . Do you actually believe that there is a truth of

the text and that you can proceed objectively and neutrally, without ideological assumptions or political intentions?

At this, Roos, polemical in turn, apologized for not having ostentatiously put the word "truth" in quotation marks "as you do here every time there is a disagreement about the usage of a term." This sounds as though the French Nietzscheans had already been using air quotes in 1972 to distance themselves from big signifiers. The debate ended with Pautrat accusing Roos, with his philology, of wanting to establish a "police machine" – flanked by its sister disciplines psychiatry and pedagogy – that would possess a single function: to guarantee the power of the norm and to subject Nietzsche, yet again, to the coercion of the social order: "What I'm asserting against you is the right, if not to nomadism, then at least to vandalism. You will never manage to prove to me that Nietzsche himself didn't respond like a vandal to the texts he read."[51]

It is unsurprising that Roos attracted the ire of the leftist Nietzscheans with his call for a philological reading beholden to the author's intentions and to the truth. After the fading of the great utopias, the subversive reader as poacher embodied the last pale imitation of the revolutionary subject – a figure who responded to the loss of political hopes exactly like Montinari's craftsman. Three years later, in an interview quoted already in the introduction to this book, Michel Foucault, the theorist of disciplinary power, declared just how little use his generation had for a philology that felt itself bound to the literal truth: "The only valid tribute to thought such as Nietzsche's is precisely to use it, to deform it, to make it groan and protest. And if commentators then say that I am being faithful or unfaithful to Nietzsche, that is of absolutely no interest."[52]

6

BURN AFTER READING
Berlin, 1985

66 **I** am aware that I will move from a socialist state with a logical, steady, forward-looking evolution to a capitalist society full of unrest, in which a strong communist party is nevertheless the leading force in opposing the existing conditions," Sigrid Montinari had written in her application for expatriation. "It will be the personal objective of my husband as well as myself to employ our knowledge and appreciation of the great advantages of this socialist state of the GDR to deepen the connections and understanding between Italy and the GDR, especially in the field of culture."[1]

As blatant as her use of official jargon here may have been, her depiction was consistent with the Italian situation: the country she migrated to with her husband and children in October 1970 was in fact riven by great unrest. In the "Hot Autumn" of the previous year, striking workers from the Fiat factory had declared their solidarity with students from the University of Turin. A short while later, the first of those bombs exploded from which the 1970s in Italy derived their moniker *anni di piombo* (years of lead). Just as the Montinaris settled near the Collis outside Florence, the Red Brigades let their voices be heard, à la the West German Red Army Faction, in their first flyers. The political climate resembled in multiple regards that of the Federal Republic of Germany – except that the Red Brigades were operating with a much more deeply layered interior of supporters and sympathizers, that the Italian state enjoyed far less backing among its citizens overall, and that aside from terrorism of the Left there was also a terrorism of the Right.[2]

One cannot avoid the impression that in 1970 Montinari was returning not just to his homeland, but also to the past. In parallel with his slowly ascendant university career, he found his way back to political party work in Florence after years of isolation among Nietzsche's papers. Life in the GDR had admittedly alienated him from actually existing socialism, but not at all from the Left per se, and the moment was ripe to become involved with the PCI, which experienced its second golden age in the 1970s under its new party chief, Enrico Berlinguer. Montinari numbered among the adherents to the *compromesso storico* (Historical Compromise), the strategic pact with the Christian-Democratic minority government, by means of which Berlinguer, like his predecessor Togliatti, aimed to commit his party to a parliamentary course supportive of the state. Montinari passed harsh judgment on the "nihilism" of the radical Left. "We, too, have our terrorists," he declared at a party convention in November 1977, shortly after the events of the German Autumn,

> perhaps a bit less intellectual and bit more small-time, but just as dangerous and fanatical as those in West Germany. We, too, have our *K-Gruppen* [communist groups], as they are called there, which is to say, the various pseudo-revolutionary circles; we, too, have declassed petty bourgeois, bored with the daily political struggle, who cultivate the myth of the guerrilla; we, too, have reactionary forces for whom there cannot be enough terror in Italy, since they are pursuing the strategy of escalation against the advancement of democratic forces.

And Italy, one might add, suffered its political catastrophe as well when Aldo Moro, party leader of Democrazia Cristiana and architect of the Historical Compromise, was abducted six months later by the Red Brigades and executed before the eyes of the Italian public.[3]

Anarchy of Atoms

For Montinari, the situation was complicated by the fact that radicals of all stripes invoked Nietzsche more and more frequently during this time. Nietzsche was not only the avowed favorite author of a neofascist *brigatista* like Giancarlo Esposti, who died in a gunfight with the Carabinieri in 1974; in the late 1970s, he was also increasingly cited by the "nihilistic" Left. In 1978, shortly after the Moro kidnapping, Montinari, like many other observers of the political spectrum, detected a "shift in the ideological tone": hardly a day went by then when Nietzsche's name did not appear "in the leftist press." With their edition, Colli and he had wanted to contribute to safeguarding their author from ideological cooptation. Instead, they were forced to watch as he fell victim to a renewed politicization, though under reverse circumstances. The "Nietzscheanization of the Left," the ramifications of which are still palpable in the culture wars of this new century, made itself felt in the 1970s not only in France, but also in Italy. Deleuze had spoken about divesting oneself of "the assignable Self." The new revolt, Triest Germanist Claudio Magris wrote, was directed against the "thousand-year-old idea of the rational and unitary subject" and thus against the condition for the possibility of conventional leftist liberation movements themselves. For the Nietzschean Left, the tyranny of unity itself was still manifested in the wantonness of the revolutionary individual. Instead of joining the game of representation played by political interests, this Left thus aimed at releasing "centrifugal and anarchist energies" and dissolving every identity "in the sea of impulses."[4]

The leitmotif of this new movement, the apotheosis of difference, the affirmation of the many, the critique of all forms and notions of unity, had been diagnosed by Nietzsche himself as early as the *fin de siècle*. His late text *The Case of Wagner* contains a small symptomatology of "*décadence*" that reads like a prophecy of the postmodern Left:

> The word becomes sovereign and leaps from the sentence, the sentence spreads out and obscures the meaning of the page, the page gains life at the expense of the whole – the whole is no longer a whole. But that is symbolic for every style of *décadence*: every time anarchy of atoms, disintegration of the will, "freedom of the individual," morally speaking – broadened into a political theory, "*equal* rights for all."[5]

In the "anarchy of atoms," Montinari the old leftist saw a reactionary phenomenon. He noted with unease the *Zarathustra* graffiti that appeared on the walls of Italian university buildings during the "autonomous" protests of 1977. For this communist schooled in Gramsci, they represented "a new Nietzsche myth that lumps together elements of conservative ideology with those of leftist theory." He diagnosed a politically ambivalent syncretism circulating among the channels of the mass media which questioned the cultural hegemony of the PCI.[6]

Even Colli, who was tracking the completion of their edition from somewhat of a distance, had to have quibbled with reencountering the Great Unfashionable One as a fashionable author. That did not, however, prevent him from enjoying, with almost childlike glee, the public attention he received as Nietzsche's "rediscoverer." To his own surprise, he found giving television interviews a "pleasant diversion." He even granted the national public broadcaster RAI access to his family home in the Florentine hills. It was in this spirit that *Dopo Nietzsche* (*After Nietzsche*) came about, a book in which he condensed his decade-long meditations on Nietzsche into polished aphorisms. Aside from the afterwords he contributed to the volumes of the Italian edition, it is his most approachable work.[7]

This was unable to alleviate his chronic shortage of money, however. "Massive financial problems," one reads among the diary entries written in his stenographic style from 1976. The situation forced him to become involved in another monumental editorial project: *La Sapienza greca* (*Greek Wisdom*), an annotated edition – running to eleven planned volumes – of the surviving fragments of the pre-Socratics. Deliberately ignoring Derrida's criticism of "phonocentrism," he returned to the oral origins of Western thought. "Heart and mind are still young," he noted, perhaps to encourage himself. It is said that Colli in his later years preferred to communicate in Ancient Greek. The first two volumes of *La Sapienza greca* had just appeared in print when, two years later, in January 1979, he died of an aneurysm at the age of sixty-one. Until the end, he had only contempt for the leftist Nietzscheanism emerging from France.[8]

Colli amid the landscape of his longing, Cape Sounion, 1962

The Red Brigades of Textual Criticism

For Montinari, who was left deeply unsettled by Colli's death, French thought would become a serious threat only when its influence was asserted in the field of editorial philology. One obvious point in time was the Frankfurt Book Fair of 1975, where, with great fanfare, the small leftwing-radical publisher Roter Stern presented the project of a new Hölderlin edition that claimed to render all extant editions – and the Stuttgart edition by Friedrich Beißner in particular – superfluous.[9]

The long-haired Hölderlin editors must have seemed to Montinari – who as a regular visitor to the Frankfurt fair may have been among the public – like the Red Brigades of textual criticism solely due to their apodictic tone. Dietrich Sattler, the initiator of the scheme and a graphic designer with no philological training, was not afraid to evoke echoes of the Reformation when he compared the existing editions with the power apparatus of the Catholic Church; his comrades-in-arms, by contrast, with the Protestant heretics who had "taken possession of the word" in order to steal Hölderlin "by hook or by crook" from the philological "high priests" and return him to his rightful readers: "The time when one class of brokers preemptively relieved those without a voice of that alone which is human, thinking it an undue burden, is conspicuously approaching its end," read his prediction. With some delay, the spirit of anti-authoritarian revolt seemed to have arrived in editorial philology as well.

The Frankfurt editors' premise suggested that Hölderlin himself had been a revolutionary whose madness expressed the final resistance against the "preeminence of circumstances," and whose incomprehensibility resulted from the "difficulty of casting off constraint and norms." In order to salvage his exemplary act of rebellion for the present, therefore, every form of "textual selection" had to cease; everything had to be published – notably the late, unfinished works marked by so-called delusion – with maximal completeness, authenticity, and accessibility. What Sattler went on to outline was the process today called "text-genetic editing," which in his portrayal looked like a revolt against Old European privileges; what was to be documented was no longer the progression of the "preliminary stages" leading to the completed work, but rather the writing process in all its richness of variation. Through meticulous decipherment, Beißner had wrested formally elaborate poems from the nearly illegible, continually overwritten palimpsests of Hölderlin's late works. But "was it ever about poems?," Sattler provocatively questioned. He argued for forgoing the "straitjacket of a postclassical idol of form" and editing the alien folios as "labyrinths of possibility" for divergent readings, among which none was to be regarded as definitive. That implied the leveling of difference between final result and variant, between fragment and preliminary stage, and the abolishment of space between the text and its apparatus.

As Beißner had done, the Frankfurt editors intended to juxtapose the temporal layers of the textual genesis in a "phase analysis" comparable to his appendix of stages. Yet in addition to the chronological principle, their edition included a topographical one. Their most evident innovation consisted in working for the first time extensively with facsimiles, a technique that had been both the great temptation

and the bane of editorial philology since the spread of the first photomechanical processes in the nineteenth century. To refrain from resolving
the "spatial disorder" in the handwritten manuscripts to a "temporal
order" was, as Bernard Cerquiglini put it, equivalent to a "farewell
to thought" for the exponents of the field. It is indisputable that this
defensive position had much to do with professional self-affirmation. In
this respect, Sattler absolutely struck a nerve with his counter-revolutionary rhetoric. With his facsimiles, he not only wanted to deliver
on his promise of complete authenticity, but also wanted to empower
readers in one and the same *coup de main*: "Consistently providing
images of all manuscripts important for appraisal, in facsimile and in
a typographically differentiated transcription, makes the users of the
Frankfurt edition largely independent of the editors."[10]

In the newspaper arts pages, unanimous enthusiasm prevailed: "An
individual, an autodidact even, takes on the entire crew – internally
at odds with one another – of Hölderlin scholars." Even renowned
Hölderlin specialists voiced their approval. Despite turning out to
be anything but easy to read, the first volumes were even a popular
success. Much of what Sattler accomplished should also have been
congenial to Montinari. After all, he, too, had gotten into philology
as a dilettante and leftist, and he, too, was ultimately dealing with an
author whose amorphous late works had been illicitly brought "into
line" by his previous editors. On the other hand, he employed the exact
same traditional editorial methods on which the Frankfurt editors
declared war. When Sattler issued the threat of making the Stuttgart
edition "more obsolete" "with each volume" of the Frankfurt one,
then the same was also true in principle for Montinari's own edition.
Mainly, however, Montinari had to have been disconcerted by Sattler's
political rhetoric. With his rejection of the "madness of normality,"
with his affirmation of "anarchy" and "resistance," he sounded just
like those "declassed petty bourgeois" who endangered the Historical
Compromise in Italy.[11]

Did the new leftist Nietzscheanism now also have the last word in
editorial philology? With their exhaustive typographic transcriptions,
the Frankfurt editors seemed to orient themselves toward a thinker
like Michel Foucault, who had called for treating the "millions of traces
left by someone after his death" equitably, if at all. Unlike Foucault,

they showed no reluctance in speaking about Hölderlin's "intentions," but these intentions had little else to do with the aims of a traditional author. First and foremost, the author was no longer primarily viewed by his text-genetic editors as the creator of a work, but rather more like a kind of writing animal. His role seemed to be limited to having left traces on paper. Had Hölderlin in his later years even wanted to continue writing and publishing poems? Did not his folios, as Sattler thought, instead constitute the "record of an individual's self-affirmation" uncoupled from any intent to publish?[12]

Such novel, radical questions also necessarily made a Nietzsche philologist take notice. "I know no deeper distinction in the overall optics of an artist than this," Nietzsche had written in the fifth book of *The Joyful Science*: "whether he looks at his budding artwork (at 'himself' –) with the eyes of a witness or whether he 'has forgotten the world.'" From this entry, it is not, however, evident to which sort of artist he himself felt he corresponded – those who leave behind an oeuvre or those who leave behind only writing. On the one hand, a distinct desire to have an impact was signaled by his predilection for constantly inventing new titles for unwritten books. On the other hand, just as many pronouncements may be found that attested to his disinterest in potential readers. "Mihi ipsi scripsi" – "I wrote it for myself" – was the motto he had selected for himself, perhaps also to prevent disappointments, while working on *Zarathustra*. The same ambivalence emerged from the fact that he had addressed the book to "everyone and to no one." "How could I write for readers? . . . Rather I make notations, for myself," can be read in a notebook from the late 1880s. The question of Nietzsche's audience was further complicated by the fact that he was convinced he was ahead of his age by a generation, if not by several.[13]

Dietrich Sattler claimed that Montinari endeavored to win him over to edit Nietzsche's late notebooks at the Frankfurt Book Fair in "1975 or 1976." If Montinari had realized that this very material from which Elisabeth Förster-Nietzsche had composed *The Will to Power* demanded a more radical philological methodology, then he kept this knowledge to himself for ten years. Luciano Zagari, a Germanist from Naples who met him at the Wissenschaftskolleg in the 1980s, is not the only person to recall what "radical criticism" Montinari leveled against Sattler's process; he regarded the editing of Hölderlin's late work as an "unending work in progress" to be an anachronism that would transform the poet into a modernist. Mostly, however, the mistrust of his guild toward the facsimile seemed to him to have become ingrained. Forgoing a rectified text for reading and instead unfurling the complete chaos of the manuscripts meant surrendering a cryptic author like Hölderlin entirely to illegibility. "It would be naïve to assume that the reader unfamiliar with Hölderlin's manner, by reading or even understanding, could cut through the jungle of ink marks written in, over, and beneath one another," Rolf Michaelis, the chief literary critic for *Die Zeit*, wrote in 1975. In leafing through the Frankfurt edition's labyrinths of text, which are engulfed in gray fog, you understand what he means. Without a doubt, Montinari would have agreed with this verdict. Instead of making authors like Hölderlin – or Nietzsche – more accessible, technical reproduction, in his view, contributed to their continued mystification.[14]

Nietzsche in Paperback

Of the around forty planned volumes of Colli and Montinari's own edition, just about half were in print by the end of the 1970s. In order not to miss out on Nietzsche's new popularity, De Gruyter forestalled the slow grinding of the editorial mill in 1980 with a fifteen-volume *Kritische Studienausgabe* (Critical Study Edition) in Deutscher Taschenbuch Verlag. In 1976, the *Süddeutsche Zeitung* had written that the new Nietzsche edition was passing the public by almost unnoticed, but the following year, *Merkur* printed the first laudatory review. Just in time for the publication of the paperback edition, which was accompanied by new biographies, anthologies, and a special volume of the *Rowohlt Literaturmagazin*, cultural critics ultimately declared "Nietzsche's rediscovery" in West Germany as well. "The vastness of his repositories of insight was even greater than had at times been assumed," wrote the *Deutsches Allgemeines Sonntagsblatt*. After years of delay, Claudio Magris noted, the "flag of a wild autonomy" was now hoisted in Nietzsche's homeland, too. To make "leftists" and "Greens," "*Stadtindianer* [urban hippies]" and "nomads" aware of the man with whom they were really dealing, Rudolf Augstein spelled out Nietzsche's commonalities with Hitler in *Der Spiegel*: the dream of being an artist; constantly puttering about with diets; the drive to hypostatize their personal failures into a "global conflagration" . . . Augstein regarded the Parisian Nietzscheans, whose works were also more and more present on the German book market, as a new generation of destroyers of Reason. He preferred to align himself with the writings of "Nietzsche's student" Giorgio Colli, whose meditation *Dopo Nietzsche* he praised as a "strict and stern" reading of the dangerous thinker.[15]

What role did the new edition play, though? What part did it have in the Nietzsche renaissance? German critics also struggled with such questions as had plagued Colli and Montinari in France since the late 1960s. Certainly, the "tiresome dispute about Nietzsche's alleged magnum opus" could finally be regarded as settled. Add to this the correction of major misreadings, which resulted in the meaning of many a textual passage virtually flipping to its opposite. And the abundance of unknown fragments, too, constituted a great editorial achievement. In spite of everything, a completely different author did not emerge from all of this. A new image of Nietzsche should not be expected, Montinari had confided humbly to *Der Spiegel* upon the publication of their first volumes. At most, the Nietzsche of the new edition would make a less inscrutable impression: "The brilliant sorceror holding the key to a new era for humankind in his hand was a fallacy," the *Süddeutsche Zeitung* wrote. "What comes into focus is a bourgeois pastor's son, a brilliant straggler of the Romantic epoch who wages a desperate, neurotic battle against the forces of his own past (Christianity, Wagner, Schopenhauer)."[16] Erich Podach had arrived at a similar conclusion in his day.

We must not, however, measure the significance of the *Studienausgabe* only according to the novelties of its contents. What matters with Nietzsche's rediscovery are ultimately not just the texts, but also – to borrow a concept from literary theorist Gérard Genette – the paratexts. It makes a difference that his oeuvre has been available since 1980 in a paperback edition, edited by two Italian antifascists, the minimalist white of which neutralizes the circumstances of his sinister reception history. Within the intellectual history of West Germany, the

Studienausgabe represents the counterpart to Suhrkamp's edition of Hegel; only through Nietzsche's actual transformation into a successful softcover author – in the late phase of the "paperback revolution" – did he fully step out of the shadows of National Socialism and become the next big thing during the long summer of theory.[17]

For Montinari, however, this unexpected valuation was bound up in a huge misapprehension. It was not enough that the "autonomous" Left coopted his favorite author; on top of that, his edition became the vehicle for a reading that bore out Nietzsche's French interpreters. This was due to the fact that it shifted the work's center of gravity – again – to the unpublished fragments. Spanning nearly 5,000 pages, these fragments – from the young professor's excerpts to the last notes of madness – were featured like an ongoing "intellectual diary" kept for over two decades. Walter Kaufmann had once warned against mistaking the "drafts, abandoned attempts, and unfinished dreams" in Nietzsche's notebooks for an "ultimate position." But Nietzsche's new readers did not care about that. Far from regarding his scribblings as definitive, they were fascinated precisely by their ephemeral provisionality. Here, in this string of pearls of unredacted fragments, they discovered the valuable raw material for a mode of thought regulated neither by any intended exploitation, nor by any intervention on the part of publishers – a mode of thought which, if one is to believe the French philosophers, developed its characteristic explosive force precisely in its transgression of genres. "Not Nietzsche's findings, but how he ended up at them, the stages of his 'generation of thoughts,' the paths of concepts and metaphors to which the edition and its corresponding interpretations draw attention," Henning Ritter, a journalist and private scholar, wrote in the *Frankfurter Allgemeine Zeitung*. One might also say that Nietzsche's legacy was converted into another state of matter: if Elisabeth Förster-Nietzsche had strategically elevated her brother's *Nachlass* to an *oeuvre*, then Colli and Montinari leveled it out into a continuous *text*. Amid this "dust cloud" of discursive events, the books published by Nietzsche during his lifetime hardly constituted anything more than random concretions.[18]

The research into the source material on which Montinari was increasingly focusing during the 1980s bore out this reading substantially. In a series of articles, Henning Ritter homed in on the "philological style of the reading of Nietzsche" then becoming predominant within the context of the new edition. Through the search for his reading material, the apprehension of Nietzsche had "changed profoundly." The "proclaimer of the strongest words and of final, unparalleled thoughts" had turned into a "medium of reception" that had combined together the set pieces of nineteenth-century European culture as a *bricolage* – a "good European," one "toying with thoughts," a "Nietzsche for readers," denazified, but at the same time deprived of any agenda of his own. Roland Barthes had defined the text as a "tissue of quotations"; Derrida had wanted to add imaginary quotation marks around the totality of Nietzsche's sentences. Montinari's students converted these philosophical ideas into philological research. If attempts had been made in the first half of the twentieth century to reduce Nietzsche's thought to a single concept at any price, then their aim consisted in resolving its ponderous signs in the labyrinth of references. "The closer you look at a text by 'Nietzsche,' the more Nietzsche as author vanishes," wrote Nietzsche philologist Glenn Most – note that he himself put "Nietzsche" in quotation marks.[19]

In the 1980s, while the deconstruction of the author Nietzsche advanced, Montinari made futile attempts to exorcize the spirits he had summoned. He issued reminders that he merely wanted to illuminate the historical context of Nietzsche's thought with his studies. He argued for recognizing Nietzsche's montage technique as a fully fledged creative feat. Suspicion of fostering fresh mystification nevertheless lent his success an aftertaste of vanity. "I'm sleeping poorly, waking up three to four times, thinking the blackest thoughts," he wrote Anna Maria, Colli's widow, in 1981; "everything comes undone and leaves behind a feeling of failure." Nietzsche had returned, not as the guarantor of freedom, but as a postmodern subject. "Our edition," Montinari wrote, "has played an integral part in this return."[20]

The Great Conspiracy

Nietzsche's comeback in the West was noted on the other side of the Iron Curtain as well. Heinz Malorny, a research associate at East Berlin's Zentralinstitut für Philosophie (Central Institute for

Philosophy), discerned a climate "of nihilistic destruction and pseudo-revolutionary, anarchist subversion" in late 1970s West Germany. "The wave of sex in film and literature, pop and Beat, the layabouts, hippies, and *Provos*, the drug abuse, or the streamlined models of cars are manifestations of the contemporary 'rebirth' of Dionysus," he wrote, still more at the height of the 1960s in his terminology, while *Christiane F.: Autobiography of a Girl of the Streets and Heroin Addict* topped the bestseller lists in West Germany. The Nietzschean *Zeitgeist* could not surprise an observer versed in the philosophy of history; it had to be regarded as the ideology of a "bourgeoisie in the terminal stages of its dominance." Not a peep about the fact that a subtle thaw was taking place in the GDR as well, where practically nothing had been published on Nietzsche since the days of Georg Lukács: the first dissertations were being written; the first editions were being under-taken; plans on hold for decades for a Nietzsche documentation site at Villa Silberblick were being dusted off. An ecumenical conference at Magdeburg's Sebastianum in 1982 was devoted to the question of "why many people today, especially among the younger generation, are turning to the long-blackballed philosopher." Even the Ministry for State Security, which kept a watchful eye on new Nietzsche activities, recommended "doing more in this area in the near future and not ceding the field here solely to bourgeois ideology and its propaganda." Kurt Hager, in charge of cultural affairs for the Politburo, took the same line when arguing three years later for viewing this enemy of the working class in the future as part of the national heritage.[21]

It was amid this climate that Montinari, together with his old acquaintance Karl-Heinz Hahn, director of the Goethe and Schiller Archive, issued a large-format facsimile edition of Nietzsche's fair copy of *Ecce homo* with Edition Leipzig in 1985. So as not to endanger progress on the edition, he had never let his good GDR contacts slide. He paid regular visits to the Weimar holdings into the 1980s. Concomitantly, he rose to be the doyen of international Nietzsche studies. He edited the influential journal *Nietzsche-Studien*, mediated between East and West German scholars, and in the final years of his life enjoyed the privilege of a sort of standing invitation to West Berlin's Wissenschaftskolleg. "Quite gradually, without his noticing it, particularly without his wanting it, power fell into his hands," wrote

Cesare Cases in his obituary. "A signal from him was enough, and the GDR would approve travel, the FRG would disburse grants, and publishers would donate *Studienausgaben*."[22]

With its lavish reproductions and a sales price of 290 East German Marks, *Ecce homo* – the first and last of Nietzsche's works ever to have been published in the GDR – was technically envisaged for export. A search for a response in West Germany will turn up nothing, though. The book's both brief and turbulent reception history played out domestically. In December 1985, shortly after it had been distributed, Wolfgang Harich stumbled upon *Ecce homo* in a bookstore display window on Berlin's Friedrichstrasse. He pressed the staff to remove the volume from the display, sparked a brawl, was forced to retreat without having achieved his aim, and filed charges with the police at the nearest station. The officers were annoyed, in that the incriminated book was not Western literature – a factor that of course for Harich constituted the actual scandal. On the evening of the same day, he drafted a petition to Willi Stoph, the Chairman of the Council of Ministers: "I would hereby like to request as a matter of urgency that you actively counter the endeavors currently underway to bring about a 'renaissance' of the legacy of Friedrich Nietzsche in the German Democratic Republic." What followed was a multi-page excommunication, culminating in the assertion that Nietzsche was "the most reactionary, most misanthropic figure there has ever been over the entire development of global culture from ancient times to the present day."[23]

It was not the first petition Harich sent on the matter of Nietzsche, but following the incident on Friedrichstrasse, the tempo of his interventions increased. In 1956, the junior researcher had wrecked his brilliant career by seeking to win over the Soviet ambassador for the establishment of an all-German, demilitarized state – an insane coup, inspired by the Stalin Note, which would have effectively involved depriving Walter Ulbricht of power. As mentioned above, one member of Harich's entourage at the time was also the young literary scholar Hans-Heinrich Reuter, who would later become active as IMS Gießhübler. After many years of detention in Bautzen, Harich, paranoid, ideologically "chastened," and suffering from a heart condition, was sidelined as a reviewer at a publishing house. But even in his subaltern position, he insisted upon playing the role of the ideological grouch who viewed it as his task to defend pure doctrine – single-handedly, if necessary – against "spineless liberals" and other lax compromisers. Just like Georg Lukács, his intellectual idol, Harich had been an ardent Nietzsche fan as a young man. In the 1980s, however, he may have been the last German who still thought the author of *Zarathustra* capable of bringing about the downfall of socialism solely by means of the continued impact of his writings.

That Nietzsche was now allowed to be printed by a publicly owned publisher confirmed Harich's worst fears. In a cascade of letters to various cultural functionaries, and even to Erich Honecker personally, he demanded the "merciless public damnation of Nietzsche '*ex cathedra*,'" suggested setting up a working group to compile an "anti-Nietzsche anthology," and did not shy away from denouncing those responsible in his eyes for the East German "Nietzsche renaissance." All the while, he returned to the "philological legend" again and again, "which purports that Nietzsche, an honorable humanist per se, had only been distorted into a reactionary by his evil fascist sister and that the new edition, by Colli and Montinari, finally allowed that false view to be corrected." The luxury edition of *Ecce homo* was such an affront for him not least because Montinari the "Nietzsche brother" was behind it once again. When Harich was forced to take note of the fact in October 1987 that the book was still being offered for sale in the Club der Kulturschaffenden "Johannes R. Becher" (Club of Creative Artists "Johannes R. Becher"), he resigned from the cultural association.[24]

What are we to think of the Nietzsche debate that broke a decades-long public silence in the final days of the GDR? Because it was at least as much about Lukács as it was about Nietzsche, it seems like an ideological rearguard action. In 1986, the East Berlin historian of philosophy Heinz Pepperle published an article in the journal *Sinn und Form* in which he defended Lukács's reading of Nietzsche – though, in a balancing act typical of the era, not without also advocating for "nuanced appraisals." It is odd that the bone of contention this time also stems from Montinari. When it came to Nietzsche, there was evidently no way around the Italian in the GDR. To wit: Pepperle responded – with a seven-year delay – to an essay published in 1979 in which Montinari had come to the defense of his author against the symmetrical misreadings of Alfred Baeumler and Georg Lukács. It was only as a result of posthumous overpainting by the reactionary and the Stalinist, his line of argument went, following Thomas Mann, that Nietzsche had been transformed into a "strapping National Socialist," indeed into a political author at all. "It doesn't get more ludicrous than that," read Pepperle's verdict – from a socialist perspective, the equal treatment of Baeumler and Lukács alone was a provocation.[25] But his relativizing comments fell short of establishing ideological clarity. With his cautious revision of Nietzsche's image, he instead brought an already alert Wolfgang Harich to the scene.

In his retort, which he was permitted to publish in *Sinn und Form* in 1987, Harich wound up for another wide-ranging swing at Nietzsche the fascist, the anti-Semite, and the misogynist – a thirty-page oblit-eration in comparison to which even Lukács's old condemnations come off as relatively mellow. "Not to regard the man as quotable," Harich wrote, "ought to rank among the basic rules of mental hygiene." His belief that Nietzsche, as spiritual father, had been even "worse" than his executor Hitler is particularly telling – and reveals quite a bit about his own hubris as an intellectual. Once more he settled the score with the "philological legend," according to which Nietzsche had been transformed into a reactionary only after his death. It was not Elisabeth Förster-Nietzsche and her associates, he claimed, but Colli and Montinari, his exonerating witnesses, who had committed the real "crime."[26]

Amid the climate of the late 1980s, Harich largely stands alone with his rigorism. Of the other articles appearing in *Sinn und Form*, just about no one cast his lot with him. At the Tenth Writers' Congress of the GDR, Hermann Kant went so far as to compare him with Pol Pot – before Manfred Buhr, director of the Zentralinstitut für Philosophie, declared the debate over with an oracular decree in 1988. Convinced he was silenced by a concerted action, Harich, after taking on Nietzsche himself, then took on the Nietzsche lobby. In August 1989, he completed a 300-page fictional discourse in the style of Lessing's "Dialogues for Freemasons" which exposed the clandestine powers that perpetuated Nietzsche's influence. At the center of *Nietzsche und seine Brüder* (*Nietzsche and His Brothers*) is the great scandal of East German cultural politics: instead of turning the stroke of historical luck to good account and causing the toxic papers to vanish once and for all, the GDR played Nietzsche's *Nachlass* into the hands of that pair of Italians. Harich held the highest cultural commissioner, Kurt Hager, personally responsible for this. "The least one ought to have expected of GDR cultural policy would have been its thwarting of any attempt at 'reprocessing.'" Yet it did not stop there. In the 1980s, to conceal his major failure, Hager had purportedly found himself forced to relativize Nietzsche's dangerousness and set his "renaissance" in motion. Harich's speculations about an alternative course of history reveal how closely he stood to the West German antinuclear power movement, which was as strongly concerned with the long-term containment of dangerous radioactive byproducts as he was with that of Nietzsche's thought: "Wolfgang Harich: What should we have done with that Nietzsche waste? Burn it? Paul Falck: There would have been other options: permanently dispose of it in some mine, preferably in the Urals."[27]

Three months after completing his manuscript, Harich was blindsided by the fall of the Berlin Wall. It can be inferred from an appendix written retrospectively that he held Nietzsche's disastrous return responsible for this event as well, thus ultimately amplifying Colli and Montinari's impact to the level of world history: with their edition, they had not only contributed to the "refascization" of late-capitalist society, but had also, quite in passing, conquered socialism.[28]

Philology Degree Zero

Montinari was unable to experience his exaltation into an agent of this epochal fracture. Toward the end of November 1986, shortly after Heinz Pepperle had initiated the Nietzsche debate, he died of a heart attack at age fifty-eight while – as befitting his position as a philologist – arranging his library. His belated academic career had just reached its zenith with the Friedrich Gundolf Prize of the German Academy for Language and Literature and an appointment to the Scuola Normale in Pisa. Italian newspapers mourned the death of the "communist who loved Nietzsche," the "most famous Italian philologist," and the "last patriarch" of his field. "One of the most fascinating, diplomatic, and consistent scholarly lives in the second half of the twentieth century has come to an end," wrote Frank Schirrmacher in the *Frankfurter Allgemeine Zeitung*. And even *Der Spiegel*, the editor of which would still much rather have undone Nietzsche's return, paid its respects to the Nietzsche philologist in a brief obituary.[29]

The question concerning all the necrologies was what Montinari's death meant for the *Kritische Gesamtausgabe*. Work on the actual text may have been largely complete, but of the eight planned volumes of commentary that would contain the full material of the "preliminary stages" along with the critical apparatus, only the first three had been published, and the Italian and French editions were also awaiting their own completion. Was the project not tailored to the patriarch to such an extent anyway that, as Schirrmacher feared, it must remain a "tragic fragment"?[30] Montinari's students managed to distribute his workload to various working groups all the same. Unable to adhere to his editorial principles from the 1960s, however, they opened the floodgates in a methodological sense. The discipline's state of the art was now constituted by the text-genetic documentation of "writing processes" in the style of the Frankfurt Hölderlin edition. In 1991, Wolfram Groddeck, who had collaborated with Sattler in the 1970s and later joined Montinari, published Nietzsche's *Dionysus Dithyrambs* in an almost 900-page text-genetic edition with facsimiles and diplomatic transcriptions that aimed to make the genesis of the slender poetic cycle comprehensible "from the first notation to the definitive fair copy" at every stage.

Precisely because of its necessary scope, Groddeck explicitly wanted his technique to be seen not as an "alternative," but as a "complement" to the *Kritische Gesamtausgabe*. Nevertheless, after Montinari's death, the edition could not escape the pull of the new paradigm for ever. To be sure, the Italian editors had transformed Nietzsche's unscrupulous sister's fictive *work* into a homogeneous *text* – but what if, on the other hand, the late Nietzsche's *writing* refused to be translated into a linear printed image? Once stoked, the desire to read Nietzsche literally seemed impossible to satisfy. In 1994, for the philosopher's

150th birthday, as the long-awaited memorial site was inaugurated at Villa Silberblick, Groddeck announced a new text-genetic subdivision – in lieu of the still-pending volumes of commentary – which aimed to establish a "topographic" preparation of Nietzsche's late notes after 1885 using the technique that hearkened back to Sattler. We must not miss the subtext of this change in course: here of all places, in the thicket of the "revaluation writings," for the sake of which Colli and Montinari had once begun their project, their successors saw their edition as inadequate. "The basis for the planned new edition of the 'late Nietzsche' consists in the transcription of Nietzsche's complete notations, in the spatial arrangement of the manuscripts – with all slips of the pen, deletions, and corrections – and no longer in the rectified form of linear texts."[31]

When the first volumes of the ninth subdivision were published with an accompanying CD-ROM seven years later, one of the reviewers wrote of being confronted with the "solidified lava of a volcano." Thanks to the high-resolution facsimiles and the hyper-diplomatic transcriptions that distinguished among five different fonts and seven different font colors, the old, voyeuristic philological dream of infiltrating the author's workshop seemed to have been fulfilled – it was unclear, however, what was left of the author. Nietzsche's flurry of signifiers not only refused to be put into any context of meaning; it could no longer be properly cited, nor, in this *closest* of readings, could one still speak much of "reading" either. "Who is supposed to read all these notations – and, most importantly, how?," asked Ulrich Raulff in the *Süddeutsche Zeitung* with unabashed perplexity. Maybe, though, the act of reading was still part of the old phonocentric regime. If one follows the Basel Germanist Hubert Thüring, then Nietzsche's lava was about a "happening" that had to be "seen and described" – which still left unanswered, however, the question of the "who." In any case, the editors could scarcely have bargained for inspired readers with their pricey volumes. A quarter-century after the deconstructed Hölderlin had promised liberation from the fetters of meaning, the deconstructed Nietzsche seemed to be relevant still only for a professional academic readership.[32]

In his day, Dietrich Sattler had dramatized the text-genetic method as the insurrection of layfolk against the clergy of editors. Although the anti-authoritarian gesture was but a distant memory, with the new subdivision of volumes Colli and Montinari also lost the monopoly they had maintained on the *Nachlass* even after their deaths. Comparing their version with the facsimiled manuscripts makes clear that Derrida's pejorative remark about the editors' "somnambulism" absolutely contained a kernel of truth. Some of their editorial decisions come across as astonishingly gratuitous. For this reason, the new editors also accused their predecessors of having composed "phantom texts" and aligned them more closely with the old Nietzsche philology. According to Montinari's student Rüdiger Schmidt-Grépály, his teacher's edition was a "Hegelianized" version, even. Measured against their own aspirations, the unanimous judgment went, Colli and Montinari had to be regarded as having failed. "The completion of their volumes of commentary can in no way be predicted," Schmidt-Grépaly declared, "and this new edition has already begun. And it will now definitely be the last one."[33]

The Ring of Being

He should have known better. A hundred years after the first edition of *The Will to Power* was published, and forty years after Colli and Montinari had reached their decision to edit Nietzsche "once and for all," it ought to have been clear to him that the last edition could be expected only when the last reading had driven all competing interpretations from the field. Following the turn of the millennium, however, there can be no question of such a *plenitudo temporum*. Rather, Nietzsche's reception history seems headed for yet another paradigm shift, coinciding with the loss of interpretive sovereignty on the part of French, leftist Nietzscheanism. The first swan songs to the "jargon of inauthenticity" were being published. The extremism of the close reading, which had been so characteristic of the intellectual climate, seemed, as the *Merkur* observed, suddenly "strangely passé." Franco Moretti, an Italian Marxist who taught comparative literature at Stanford University, suggested switching over to distant reading instead. In the context where the "secular theology" of a Derrida or Paul de Man would represent the new orthodoxy, he preached the

	Salz	40, I links	für ein Eckzimmer u. Waldstr
	Zucker		Gustav-Adolf. Zugang
	Eier	29, I	44, III 20 Mark

Ich selber bin 100 Mal radikaler als W. oder

Sch., deshalb bleiben es doch meine verehrtesten

Lehrer: ob ich schon jetzt zu meiner Erholung

u. Erquickung ganz andere Musik nöthig habe als

die W.'s, u, beim Lesen Sch.'s, jetzt leicht

unwillig w mich langweile, oder verdrießlich werde.

Des Falschen u. Oberflächlichen ist zu Viel darin.

M. „Unzeitgemäßen" sind für bedeuten

für mich Versprechungen: was sie für Andere sind,

weiß ich nicht. Glauben Sie, daß ich längst nicht

mehr leben würde, wenn ich diesen Versprechungen

nur um Einen Schritt breit ausgewichen wäre!

Viell. kommt noch ein Mensch, der entdeckt, daß von

M. A. an ich nichts gethan habe als meine

Versprechen erfüllen. Das, was ich freilich jetzt die

Wahrheit nenne, ist etwas ganz Furchtbares u. Ab-

stoßendes: und ich habe viel Kunst nöthig, um

schrittweise die M. zu einer völligen Umdrehung

ihrer höchsten Werthschätzungen zu überreden.

86 Theresienstr.

2-6: KGW VII 4/2, 641, Anm. 195 (irrtümlich als
Fußnote 196 gedruckt)
8-44: KGB III 3, 75, Be Nr. 617

8: W.] > Wagner
10: Sch.] > Schopenhauer
18: unwillig] ¿
20: Falschen] ¿
40: viell ¿

What remained of The Will to Power: *the 9th subdivision of the* Kritische Gesamtausgabe

194   N VII 2

Hellwald, Naturgeschichte des Menschen.   2

Hermann Müller   4

{ über Pflanzen.   6

Burmeister   8

Van Hasselt   Dr Fritsch.   A Versmann   10

Hans v. Bartels.   12

Der Wille zur Macht.   14

Zahnbürste: Backhaus   16

Versuch   Grimm. Str.   18

Brandeis – von der Mark   14.   20

einer neuen Auslegung   22

alles Geschehens.   24

Skortleben (Baron Gauerstädt)   26

bei Weissenfels   28

Von   30

Veit & Co   32

(Credner)   34

Friedrich Nietzsche.   36

Johannisg. 6   38

I

Rolle   40

Kleiderbürste   42

via Nazionale 34. I.   44

2-8: KGW VII 39[21]
14-36: KGW VII 39[1]
16-44: KGW VII 4[2], 641, Anm. 196 (irrtümlich
als Fußnote 195 gedruckt)

10: A] ?
12: Hans v.] ¿
26: Gauerstädt] Vk

technique of statistically detecting literary patterns in order to find our way out of the textual meditation of Deconstruction. To the extent that the boom of French theory was going bust, the second great Nietzsche wave of the twentieth century was also at an ebb. The planes that flew into the World Trade Center on the precise publication date for the first volumes of the ninth subdivision also supplied the symbol for the end of an intellectual era.[34]

It was another Italian leftist who in 2002 called to mind a largely forgotten Nietzsche. In his thousand-plus-page study *Nietzsche, the Aristocratic Rebel*, Domenico Losurdo, an intellectual historian at the University of Urbino and a member of the Rifondazione Comunista, the successor organization to the PCI, painted a picture of a philosopher "*totus politicus*," of a thinker who had devoted the entirety of his oeuvre to the battle against the political, social, and ideational consequences of the French Revolution. As the master thinker of the counter-revolution, Losurdo's Nietzsche absolutely bears similarities to Georg Lukács's "pioneer of fascism": a reactionary, a habitual anti-Semite, and a scorner of democracy. Instead of relating him like Lukács – anachronistically – to his supposed enforcers in the twentieth century, however, Losurdo spelled out, strictly in terms of intellectual history, how deeply the self-proclaimed "Unfashionable One" was influenced by contemporaneous debates about abolitionism, the workers' movement, and eugenics.

Losurdo laid the blame for the suppression of this political frame of reference for Nietzsche's thought on the postwar period – when, since the 1960s, a "hermeneutics of innocence" had been setting the tone, continuing to displace into metaphoric and metaphysical realms his most inscrutable statements on the coming aristocracy or the eradication of the weak – on the "philosopher-priests of the Nietzsche cult" as much as he did on the edition of his two compatriots Colli and Montinari. Retroactively lending plausibility to Wolfgang Harich's excommunications, he documented both the removal of infelicitous passages from the apparatus of variants as well as the propensity of the Italian translation to depoliticize. Just like Harich, he spoke of the emergence of a "philological legend" according to which only Elisabeth's forgery had made her brother congenial to Mussolini and Hitler. Mostly, however, he criticized the editorial decision by which "all the philosopher's notes are published in the same way and accorded the same weight." Through this leveling, Colli and Montinari had not only done the history of ideas the questionable service of making Nietzsche's political monstrosities vanish in "a mass of details," but had also, moreover, surrendered him to that "postmodern Left" which had attributed more significance to his scribblings than to his annihilation fantasies. The *Kritische Gesamtausgabe* as the condition for the possibility of the French Nietzsche: Losurdo was the first one to set up this equation in these terms after the turn of the millennium. By this point at the latest, Colli and Montinari seem to have landed on all sides of the fence: while some would criticize their adherence to the transcendental signifieds of hermeneutics, others accused them of a postmodern shattering of meaning.[35]

Should we describe the following, for-now final chapter in the never-ending story of the Nietzsche edition as a return to the point of departure? In 2013, in a curious parallel action – nearly half of the ninth subdivision was then in print, largely unnoticed by the non-academic public – the Basel publisher Stroemfeld and Göttingen's Steidl each announced another Nietzsche edition. Karl Marx wrote that all important events in world history happen twice, "the first time as tragedy, the second as farce." In the preliminaries, sent out like signal flares in advance of the actual volumes, the editors of the new editions in fact struck a tone redolent of the postwar debates – except that this time it was not about National Socialists or Nietzsche's sister, but French philosophers and their Italian editors. "The 'French Nietzsche' who has engrossed us for decades, starting with Deleuze and Foucault, would consequently be a singular misunderstanding?," the initiator of the edition, Montinari's student Rüdiger Schmidt-Grépály, asked his interlocutor Peter Sloterdijk. "Nothing could be more alien to Nietzsche," his reply went, "than the discourse-theory version of historicism peddled today in humanities faculties all over the world by learned Last Men." For Nietzsche had ultimately not only wrestled with his publishers over every comma and line break, but had also explicitly presented himself in his autobiographical testament *Ecce homo* as an author and creator. Behind the idea of liquidating these entities, however, Sloterdijk detected an "ideology of mediocrity," which ended up flattening out the difference between literature and secondary literature. Articulated in the deconstruction of the subject and of history, Schmidt-Grépály added, was the "apologia of global capitalist reality."

Instead of lingering with Parisian postmodernism, though, the two revisionists quickly came to the actual point: namely, the philologists who, in their eyes, had enabled the philosophers' misreading in the first place. In their effort to undo Nietzsche's sister's distortions and reconstruct his authentic *Urtext*, Schmidt-Grépály explained, Colli and Montinari had made their author "almost even more unrecognizable" and, with their decision to edit the entire *Nachlass*, had facilitated a form of Nietzsche reception "that is potentially just as misleading as the appropriation of the nonexistent magnum opus by an imperialist party philosophy." Thus it was time, finally, to "ensure justice is done" to Nietzsche by returning his oeuvre to him, rather than to continue reducing it "to the footnote of an overvalued *Nachlass*." Both the twenty planned volumes of the *Ausgabe letzter Hand* by Stroemfeld and the similarly comprehensive *Werke letzter Hand* by Steidl aimed to recover the circumstances of 1889; only the works authorized by Nietzsche himself were to be included, and in a typeface and on paper that most closely approximated those of the original editions at that. On the other hand, the *Nachlass* which haunted Nietzsche philology like a ghost for more than a century would be left out. As Sloterdijk saw it, the situation, in essence, was quite simple: "If with the new edition we now attempt to call to mind Nietzsche as an author and creator, then in that very attempt lies the correction to now-despotic Deconstruction. Nietzsche only needs to be edited correctly; his image will adjust itself on its own."[36] Montinari, who had been no stranger to either the hubris or the humility of philology, would probably have acknowledged this assertion with a shrug.

NOTES

The Spoilsports: Introduction

1 In order to reduce the number of endnotes, several citations will be combined into each note. First come the direct citations and verbatim quotations – in the order in which they appear in the body text – then secondary literature. The "youth of today" in Edgar Salin, "Der Fall Nietzsche," *Merkur* 112 (1957): 573. Jürgen Habermas, "Nachwort," in *Erkenntnistheoretische Schriften*, by Friedrich Nietzsche (Frankfurt am Main: Suhrkamp, 1968), 237. The participants in the similarly ground-breaking 1966 conference "The Language of Criticism and the Sciences of Man" in Baltimore were also unaware of the significance of their meeting. Cf. Jacques Derrida, "Some Statements and Truisms about Neologisms, Newisms, Postisms, Parasitisms, and Other Small Seismisms," in *The States of "Theory": History, Art, and Critical Discourse*, ed. David Carroll, trans. Anne Tomiche (New York: Columbia University Press, 1990), 80. On the situation in France, see François Dosse, *History of Structuralism*, trans. Deborah Glassman, vol. 1 (Minneapolis: University of Minnesota Press, 1997), 202ff.

2 Karl Löwith, *My Life in Germany before and after 1933: A Report*, trans. Elizabeth King (Urbana: University of Illinois Press, 1994), 6, 145. On Jean Wahl, cf. Jacques Le Rider, *Nietzsche en France: De la fin du XIXᵉ siècle au temps présent* (Paris: Presses universitaires de France, 1999), 183.

3 Cf. Löwith, *My Life in Germany*, 83, as well as, for greater detail, Löwith's lecture given at Royaumont, "Nietzsches Versuch zur Wiedergewinnung

der Welt," in *90 Jahre philosophische Nietzsche-Rezeption*, ed. Alfredo
Guzzoni (Königstein: Hain, 1979), 89–102. The contradictions between
Löwith's cosmological and ethical exegesis of the eternal return are
pointed out by Urs Marti, *"Der große Pöbel- und Sklavenaufstand":
Nietzsches Auseinandersetzung mit Revolution und Demokratie* (Stuttgart:
J. B. Metzler, 1993), 277.

4 Gilles Deleuze, "Conclusions on the Will to Power and the Eternal Return,"
in *Desert Islands and Other Texts: 1953–1974*, by Gilles Deleuze, ed. David
Lapoujade, trans. Michael Taormina (Los Angeles, CA: Semiotext(e),
2004), 123.

5 Michel Foucault, "Nietzsche, Freud, Marx," in *Aesthetics, Method, and
Epistemology*, ed. James D. Faubion, trans. Jon Anderson and Gary
Hentzi, *Essential Works of Foucault, 1954–1984*, vol. 2 (New York: New
Press, 1998), 269–78.

6 Friedrich Nietzsche, *Kritische Studienausgabe*, ed. Giorgio Colli and
Mazzino Montinari, vol. 1 (Munich/Berlin: De Gruyter, 1988), 100
(hereafter *KSA*). On the book's dramatic structure, see Peter Sloterdijk,
Thinker on Stage: Nietzsche's Materialism, trans. Jamie Owen Daniel
(Minneapolis: University of Minnesota Press, 1989). The unusual compo-
sition also arose because the book is comprised of two originally separate
lines of thought. Cf. Mazzino Montinari, "Nietzsche lesen," in *Nietzsche
lesen*, by Mazzino Montinari (Berlin: De Gruyter, 1982), 5.

7 Mazzino Montinari in a letter to Giorgio Colli dated August 17, 1963,
quoted in Giuliano Campioni, *Leggere Nietzsche: Alle origini dell'edizione
Colli-Montinari* (Pisa: Edizioni ETS, 1992), 280. *KSA*, 1988, 1: 81. The
experience on the bus in Mazzino Montinari, "Presenza della filosofia: Il
significato dell'opera di Giorgio Colli," *Rinascità*, February 16, 1979, 42.

8 Cf. Karl Schlechta, "Philologischer Nachbericht," in *Werke in drei Bänden*,
by Friedrich Nietzsche, ed. Karl Schlechta, vol. 3 (Munich: Hanser, 1956),
1383–432. Richard Roos, "Les derniers écrits de Nietzsche et leur publication," *Revue Philosophique* 146 (1956): 262–87.

9 Erich Podach, *Friedrich Nietzsches Werke des Zusammenbruchs*
(Heidelberg: W. Rothe, 1961), 430. Karl Löwith offers criticism in his review
of this book, reprinted as "Rezension von Erich Podach, Nietzsches Werke
des Zusammenbruchs und Ein Blick in die Notizbücher Nietzsches," in
Sämtliche Schriften, by Karl Löwith, vol. 6: *Nietzsche* (Stuttgart: J. B.
Metzler, 1987), 510–17.

10 Rudolf Pannwitz, "Nietzsche-Philologie?," *Merkur* 117 (1957): 1076. Essential for the history of his sister and that of the Weimar Nietzsche Archive: David M. Hoffmann, *Zur Geschichte des Nietzsche-Archivs: Chronik, Studien und Dokumente* (Berlin: De Gruyter, 1991). A more recent biography worth reading: Ulrich Sieg, *Die Macht des Willens: Elisabeth Förster-Nietzsche und ihre Welt* (Munich: Carl Hanser Verlag, 2019).

11 Cf. Schlechta, " Philologischer Nachbericht," 1403; Richard Roos, "Règles pour une lecture philologique de Nietzsche," in *Nietzsche aujourd'hui?*, ed. Centre culturel international de Cerisy-la-Salle, vol. 2: *Passion* (Paris: Union générale d'éditions, 1973), 287. In general, Stefan Willer, *Erbfälle: Theorie und Praxis kultureller Übertragung in der Moderne* (Paderborn: Wilhelm Fink, 2014), 161–92. The teaser in Salin, "Der Fall Nietzsche," 574f.

12 Cf. Martin Heidegger, *Nietzsche*, trans. David Farrell Krell, vol. 1 (San Francisco: Harper & Row, 1979), 9. Schlechta, "Philologischer Nachbericht," 1403. Pannwitz, "Nietzsche-Philologie?," 1084.

13 Montinari in a letter to Colli dated April 8, 1961, quoted in Giuliano Campioni, "Mazzino Montinari in den Jahren von 1943 bis 1963," *Nietzsche-Studien* 17 (1988): XVf.

14 *KSA*, 1988, 3: 17. Frank Schirrmacher, "Nietzsches Wiederkehr," *Frankfurter Allgemeine Zeitung*, September 19, 1986. For the figure of the "absolute reader," cf. Hans Blumenberg, "Das finale Dilemma des Lesers," in *Lebensthemen: Aus dem Nachlaß*, by Hans Blumenberg (Stuttgart: Reclam, 1998), 29–33.

15 Antonio Gnoli, "Gli angeli di Nietzsche," *La Repubblica*, April 28, 1992. Montinari contrasted his "sanguine" temperament with Colli's "melancholic" one in a letter to the latter dated November 17, 1967, fondo Montinari, cartella 13, Archivio Scuola Normale Superiore.

16 *Mündlicher Bericht des GI "Gießhübler" vom 16.1.1970*, 1970, BArch, MfS Erfurt, 542/78, A, Bundesarchiv, Stasi-Unterlagen-Archiv Berlin Mitte. Giorgio Colli in a letter to Anna Maria Musso-Colli, September 14, 1962, fondo Giorgio Colli, b. 04, fasc. 024, Archivio Mondadori. Mazzino Montinari, "L'onorevole arte di leggere Nietzsche," *Belfagor* 41 (1986): 338; Montinari in a letter to Giorgio Colli, May 9, 1962, fondo Colli, b. 32, fasc. 185.003, Archivio Mondadori. Montinari to Colli in a letter dated August 22, 1963, quoted in Campioni, *Leggere Nietzsche*, 281.

On Montinari's interpretation, see Wolfram Groddeck, "Nietzsche lesen," *Nietzscheforschung* 25 (2018): 31–9.

17 Giorgio Colli, *Distanz und Pathos: Einleitungen zu Nietzsches Werken*, trans. Ragni Maria Gschwend and Reimar Klein (Hamburg: Europäische Verlagsanstalt, 1993), 12f. Cf. Giorgio Colli, *Dopo Nietzsche*, Milan: Adelphi, 1974, 26. Michel Foucault, "Prison Talk," in *Power/Knowledge: Selected Interviews and Other Writings, 1972–1977*, ed. and trans. Colin Gordon (New York: Pantheon Books, 1980), 53f. On a similar note, see Roland Barthes, *S/Z*, trans. Richard Howard (New York: Hill & Wang, 1974), 15: "The work of the commentary [...] consists precisely in *manhandling* the text." Montinari's suggestion in Giorgio Colli and Mazzino Montinari, "État des textes de Nietzsche," in *Nietzsche*, Cahiers de Royaumont 6 (Paris: Éditions de Minuit, 1967), 128. Walter Kaufmann, *Nietzsche: Philosopher, Psychologist, Antichrist*, 3rd ed. (Princeton: Princeton University Press, 1968). Even by the third edition of Kaufmann's influential study one may read: "The International Nietzsche Bibliography does not list any contributions by any of the two editors" (483).

18 Gilles Deleuze, "Nomadic Thought," in *Desert Islands and Other Texts: 1953–1974*, by Gilles Deleuze, ed. David Lapoujade, trans. Michael Taormina (Los Angeles, CA: Semiotext(e), 2004), 254. Heidegger's derogatory comment, according to John Rajchman, "Deleuze's Nietzsche," Nietzsche 13/13, October 25, 2016: http://blogs.law.columbia.edu /nietzsche1313/john-rajchman-deleuzes-nietzsche/. Heidegger in a letter to Richard Leutheußer dated January 12, 1938, quoted in Alfred Denker et al., eds., *Heidegger und Nietzsche* (Freiburg: Verlag Karl Alber, 2005), 26. Cf. Heidegger, *Nietzsche*, 1: 10.

19 *KSA*, 1988, 8: 23. Nietzsche in a letter to Paul Deussen, dated from the second half of October 1868, in *Sämtliche Briefe: Kritische Studienausgabe*, ed. Giorgio Colli and Mazzino Montinari, vol. 2 (Munich/Berlin: De Gruyter, 2003), 329 (hereafter *KSB*). *KSA*, 1988, 8: 32. Friedrich Nietzsche, *The Joyful Science: Idylls from Messina, Unpublished Fragments from the Period of The Joyful Science (Spring 1881–Summer 1882)*, trans. Adrian Del Caro, *The Complete Works of Friedrich Nietzsche*, vol. 6 (Stanford, CA: Stanford University Press, 2023), 250 (hereafter *CW*); *KSA*, 1988, 3: 624. Nietzsche, *CW*, 2021, 9: 269; *KSA*, 1988, 6: 325. On Nietzsche's relationship to his field, see Christian Benne, *Nietzsche und die historisch-kritische Philologie* (Berlin: De Gruyter, 2005). On the consequences of

his falling-out for the humanities, see Wolf Lepenies, "Gottfried Benn – Der Artist im Posthistoire," in *Literarische Profile: Deutsche Dichter von Grimmelshausen bis Brecht*, ed. Walter Hinderer (Königstein: Athenäum, 1982), 330.

20 Cf. James Turner, *Philology: The Forgotten Origins of the Modern Humanities* (Princeton: Princeton University Press, 2014), ix. On philology's poor reputation in France, see Bernard Cerquiglini, *In Praise of the Variant: A Critical History of Philology*, trans. Betsy Wing (Baltimore: Johns Hopkins University Press, 1999), chap. 4. More recent attempts at rehabilitating philology include Hans Ulrich Gumbrecht, *The Powers of Philology: Dynamics of Textual Scholarship* (Urbana: University of Illinois Press, 2003); Thomas Steinfeld, *Der leidenschaftliche Buchhalter: Philologie als Lebensform* (Munich: C. Hanser, 2004); and Turner, *Philology*.

21 *KSA*, 1988, 1: 268. Schirrmacher, "Nietzsches Wiederkehr." On the significance of this edition in the history of philosophical text editions, cf. Michel Espagne, *De l'archive au texte: Recherches d'histoire génétique* (Paris: Presses universitaires de France, 1998), 153.

22 On irony, see Ludger Lütkehaus, "'Ich schreibe wie ein Schwein': Die neue Nietzsche-Gesamtausgabe lässt den großen Stilisten aussehen wie einen Kritzler," *Die Zeit*, January 5, 2006. On Nietzsche as a battleground for antagonistic tendencies, see Ernst Nolte, *Nietzsche und der Nietzscheanismus* (Frankfurt am Main: Propyläen, 1990), 10f. The projection surface in Habermas, "Nachwort," 238.

23 On the philological reservation, cf. Steven E. Aschheim, *The Nietzsche Legacy in Germany, 1890–1990* (Berkeley: University of California Press, 1992), 15. Incidentally, the perpetuated "return to the origin" is what, according to Foucault, distinguishes a "founder of discursivity." Cf. "What Is an Author?," in *Aesthetics, Method, and Epistemology*, ed. James D. Faubion, trans. Robert Hurley, *Essential Works of Foucault, 1954–1984*, vol. 2 (New York: New Press, 1998), 219. On the importance of the editions, in general, for the history of Nietzsche's reception, see Eckhard Heftrich, "Zu den Ausgaben der Werke und Briefe von Friedrich Nietzsche," in *Buchstabe und Geist: Zur Überlieferung und Edition philosophischer Texte*, ed. Walter Jaeschke et al. (Hamburg: F. Meiner, 1987), 117. Among the German-language editions are: the *Klein-* and *Großoktav-Ausgabe*; the *Musarion-*, the *Beck-*, and the *Schlechta-Ausgabe*;

the apocryphal legacy editions, like Baeumler's *Unschuld des Werdens* [*Innocence of Becoming*], Würzbach's *Vermächtnis Friedrich Nietzsches* [*Legacy of Friedrich Nietzsche*], or Podach's *Nietzsches Schriften des Zusammenbruchs* [*Nietzsche's Writings of Breakdown*]; the countless anthologies still multiplying today, the mass-market, popular, and study editions, as well as the definitive editions launched in recent years by the publishers Stroemfeld and Steidl; and finally, having now grown to over forty volumes and available in German, Italian, French, Japanese, and English versions, the *Kritische Gesamtausgabe* by Colli and Montinari, which represents the gold standard of international Nietzsche research to this day. "Each kind of edition engenders a new author" (Henning Ritter, "Es gibt ihn nicht mehr, den gefährlichen Nietzsche," *Frankfurter Allgemeine Zeitung*, March 19, 2002).

24 Habermas, "Nachwort," 237f.

25 Theodor W. Adorno, "Bibliographical Musings," in *Notes to Literature*, by Theodor W. Adorno, ed. Rolf Tiedemann, trans. Shierry Weber Nicholsen (New York: Columbia University Press, 2019), 304. Mazzino Montinari, "Erinnerung an Giorgio Colli," in *Distanz und Pathos: Einleitungen zu Nietzsches Werken*, by Giorgio Colli, trans. Ragni Maria Gschwend and Reimar Klein (Hamburg: Europäische Verlagsanstalt, 1993), 170.

26 Referring to the correspondence, Michel Espagne speaks of the "roman d'une édition" ("novel of an edition"), *De l'archive au texte*, 154. Cf. Adriano Sofri, "Federico il pendolare," *Panorama*, February 22, 1987, 139. A similarly motivated investigation of "political philology" is undertaken by Robert Pursche, "Philologie als Barrikadenkampf: Rolf Tiedemann und die Arbeit für Walter Benjamins Nachleben," *Mittelweg 36: Zeitschrift des Hamburger Instituts für Sozialforschung* 30, no. 3 (2021): 12–40.

Chapter 1 Beyond the Gothic Line: Lucca, 1943–4

1 Cf. also Albert Kesselring, *The Memoirs of Field-Marshal Kesselring*, trans. Lynton Hudson (Novato, CA: Presidio, 1989), 167ff.; Enno Rintelen, *Mussolini als Bundesgenosse: Erinnerungen des deutschen Militärattachés in Rom, 1936–1943* (Tübingen: R. Wunderlich, 1951), 228f.

2 On what he was reading, see Benito Mussolini, *Storia di un anno* (Milan: Mondadori, 1944), 89f. With skepticism, Renzo De Felice, *Mussolini l'alleato: La guerra civile* (Turin: Einaudi, 1997), 17. On the young Mussolini and Nietzsche, cf. Domenico M. Fazio, "Nietzsche und der Faschismus:

Eine Politik des Nietzsche-Archivs in Italien," in *Widersprüche: Zur frühen Nietzsche-Rezeption*, ed. Andreas Schirmer and Rüdiger Schmidt (Weimar: Verlag Hermann Böhlaus Nachfolger, 2000), 221ff.

3 For Colli's reading recommendations, see Campioni, "Mazzino Montinari," xvii.

4 Mussolini's intellectual interests in Ernst Nolte, *Three Faces of Fascism: Action Française, Italian Fascism, National Socialism*, trans. Leila Vennewitz (London: Weidenfeld & Nicolson, 1965), 151. On Gentile's education reform, see Mario Mirri, "Postfazione," in *L'impegno di una generazione: Il gruppo di Lucca dal Liceo Machiavelli alla Normale nel clima del Dopoguerra*, ed. Mario Mirri, Renzo Sabbatini, and Luigi Imbasciati (Milan: FrancoAngeli, 2014), 170ff.; M.E. Moss, *Mussolini's Fascist Philosopher: Giovanni Gentile Reconsidered* (New York: Peter Lang, 2004).

5 Cf. Eugenio Garin, "Storicismo," Enciclopedia del Novecento, Alfabeto Treccani, 1984, https://www.treccani.it/enciclopedia/storicismo _%28Enciclopedia-del-Novecento%29/. On Croce's and Gentile's roles, cf. Karl Eugen Gass, *Pisaner Tagebuch* (Heidelberg: L. Schneider, 1961), 44. Colli's distance from Croce in Mazzino Montinari, "Lavò la faccia al Superuomo," *L'Espresso*, January 21, 1979, 71. For the Schmitt episode, cf. Wolfgang Schieder, *Mythos Mussolini: Deutsche in Audienz beim Duce* (Munich: Oldenbourg, 2013), 315f.; from another perspective, see Löwith, *My Life in Germany*, 91. On the lack of a fascist Nietzsche cult, cf. Domenico Fazio, "Nietzsche in Italien: Ein historischer Abriß der Nietzsche-Rezeption in Italien anhand der Übersetzungen seiner Schriften (1872–1940)," *Nietzsche-Studien* 22 (1993): 316ff. On the German legend of such a cult, see Fazio, "Nietzsche und der Faschismus," 223. Not least because of the valorization of philosophy instruction, there seem to have been numerous cases of philosophy teachers critical of the regime in fascist Italy. Cf. Mirri, "Postfazione," 168f.

6 Benedetto Croce, "Antihistoricismo." *La Critica: Rivista di Letteratura, Storia e Filosifia* 28 (1930): 409. Gass, *Pisaner Tagebuch*, 45. Cesare Cases writes of Italy as "a belated colony of German Idealism" in "Der Mythos der deutschen Kultur in Italien," in *Wissenschaftskolleg zu Berlin: Jahrbuch 1987/88* (Berlin: Siedler, 1989), 182.

7 Giorgio Colli, *Apollineo e dionisiaco* (Milan: Adelphi, 2010), 28. Cf. Giorgio Colli, *La Ragione errabonda: Quaderni postumi* (Milan: Adelphi, 1982),

184: "Philosophy can exist only as philosophical life." Luigi Imbasciati, "Il ricordo di uno studente," in *L'impegno di una generazione: Il gruppo di Lucca dal Liceo Machiavelli alla Normale nel clima del Dopoguerra*, ed. Mario Mirri, Renzo Sabbatini, and Luigi Imbasciati (Milan: FrancoAngeli, 2014), 27. Colli's criticism of modern philosophy, for instance, in *Apollineo e dionisiaco*, 38; *Dopo Nietzsche*, 177f. On the loss of philosophy's "practical purpose," see also Michael Hampe, *Erkenntnis und Praxis: Zur Philosophie des Pragmatismus* (Frankfurt am Main: Suhrkamp, 2006), 11ff.

8 Colli, *La Ragione errabonda*, 84. Colli, *Dopo Nietzsche*, 81, 141. On the "Chosen Few," cf. Montinari, "Erinnerung an Giorgio Colli," 167; Linda Bimbi, "Parlerò di Mazzino," in *L'impegno di una generazione: Il gruppo di Lucca dal Liceo Machiavelli alla Normale nel clima del Dopoguerra*, ed. Mario Mirri, Renzo Sabbatini, and Luigi Imbasciati (Milan: FrancoAngeli, 2014), 55. For the "Dionysian" secret, see, for example, the letter from Angelo Pasquinelli to Giorgio Colli, February 17, 1943, fondo Colli, b. 32, fasc. 134, Archivio Mondadori. Whether Plato is indeed the author of the Seventh Letter is disputed.

9 Nietzsche in a letter to Franz Overbeck dated November 6, 1884, in *KSB*, 2003, 6: 554. Colli, *Dopo Nietzsche*, 32, cf. 141. On Nietzsche's self-contradictory existence as a man of letters, cf. *KSB*, 2003, 6: 109, 128f., 132; *Selected Letters of Friedrich Nietzsche*, ed. and trans. Christopher Middleton (Chicago: University of Chicago Press, 1969), 179.

10 Colli, *La Ragione errabonda*, 109, 83. On Colli's dynamism, cf. Federica Montevecchi, *Giorgio Colli: Biografia intellettuale* (Turin: Bollati Boringhieri, 2004). Characteristic examples of Nietzscheanism in the first half of the century in Aschheim, *The Nietzsche Legacy in Germany, 1890–1990*.

11 Nietzsche, *KSA*, 1988, 8: 65. Nietzsche to Reinhart von Seydlitz on September 24, 1876, in *KSB*, 2003, 5: 188. Nietzsche to Erwin Rohde on December 15, 1870, in *KSB*, 2003, 3: 165f. Cf. Hubert Cancik and Hildegard Cancik-Lindemaier, "'Das Gymnasium in der Knechtschaft des Staates': Zu Entstehung, Situation und Thema von Friedrich Nietzsches 'Wir Philologen,'" in *Disciplining Classics*, ed. Glenn Most (Göttingen: Vandenhoeck & Ruprecht, 2002), 97–113.

12 George quoted in Steven E. Aschheim, *Nietzsche und die Deutschen: Karriere eines Kultus* (Stuttgart: J.B. Metzler, 1996), 76; cf. Aschheim,

The Nietzsche Legacy in Germany, 1890–1990, 75. "Only George *is* what Nietzsche convulsively coveted to be," wrote Georgean Kurt Hildebrandt. Quoted in Kaufmann, *Nietzsche*, 12. On Colli's interest in Ernst Bertram, cf. Alberto Banfi, "Giorgio Colli: Il coraggio del pensiero (profilo biografico)," *Kleos: Estemporaneo di studi e testi sulla fortuna dell'antico* 9 (2004): 255. Schwabing's "Cosmic Circle," in Max L. Baeumer, *Dionysos und das Dionysische in der antiken und deutschen Literatur* (Darmstadt: Wissenschaftliche Buchgesellschaft, 2006), 353.

13 Bataille quoted in Gerd Bergfleth, "Nietzsche redivivus," in *Wiedergutmachung an Nietzsche: Das Nietzsche-Memorandum und andere Texte*, by Georges Bataille, trans. Gerd Bergfleth (Munich: Matthes & Seitz, 1999), 341f. On Acéphale, cf. Stephan Moebius, *Die Zauberlehrlinge: Soziologiegeschichte des Collège de Sociologie (1937–39)* (Konstanz: UVK Verlagsgesellschaft, 2006), 253ff.

14 On Colli's "intense and searching" gaze, cf. Anna Maria Musso-Colli, "Ricordo di Giorgio Colli," in *Saggi su Nietzsche*, ed. Giorgio Penzo (Brescia: Morcelliana, 1980), 12. Colli, *Apollineo e dionisiaco*, 36. Cf. Clara Valenziano, "La Lucca della guerra e di Giorgio Colli," in *L'impegno di una generazione: Il gruppo di Lucca dal Liceo Machiavelli alla Normale nel clima del Dopoguerra*, ed. Mario Mirri, Renzo Sabbatini, and Luigi Imbasciati (Milan: FrancoAngeli, 2014), 97.

15 Colli's credo in Colli, *Apollineo e dionisiaco*, 199. On his abilities as a magnetic figure, see Claire Isoz and Giuliana Lanata, "Ricordo di Pietro Giorgetti," in *L'impegno di una generazione: Il gruppo di Lucca dal Liceo Machiavelli alla Normale nel clima del Dopoguerra*, ed. Mario Mirri, Renzo Sabbatini, and Luigi Imbasciati (Milan: FrancoAngeli, 2014), 80. Banfi, "Giorgio Colli," is extremely readable as an intellectual biography. On the antifascist milieu of Turin, cf. Maike Albath, *Der Geist von Turin: Pavese, Ginzburg, Einaudi und die Wiedergeburt Italiens nach 1943* (Berlin: Berenberg, 2010).

16 Cf. Musso-Colli, "Ricordo di Giorgio Colli."

17 Pavese quoted in Albath, *Der Geist von Turin*, 76.

18 Nietzsche, *KSA*, 1988, 1: 247. Nietzsche, *CW*, 2020, 16: 230; *KSA*, 1988, 11: 679. Lou Andreas-Salomé, *Nietzsche*, ed. and trans. Siegfried Mandel (Urbana: University of Illinois Press, 2001), 7. Nietzsche, *KSA*, 1988, 8: 45. "Student panic" figures in Henning Ritter, *Notizhefte* (Berlin: Berlin Verlag, 2010), 333. On Nietzsche's transformation of the educational program of

ancient philology, cf. Nikolaus Wegmann, "Was heißt einen 'klassischen' Text lesen? Philologische Selbstreflexion zwischen Wissenschaft und Bildung," in *Wissenschaftsgeschichte der Germanistik im 19. Jahrhundert*, ed. Jürgen Fohrmann and Wilhelm Voßkamp (Stuttgart: J.B. Metzler, 1994), 419ff.

19 Colli, *Apollineo e dionisiaco*, 50. Colli, *Dopo Nietzsche*, 122ff. Montinari preferred the *Eroica*: cf. his letter to Sigrid Oloff-Montinari, July 1, 1971, fondo Montinari, cartella 20, Archivio Scuola Normale Superiore. Reminiscences of former *paides* in Bimbi, "Parlerò di Mazzino," 56, and Valenziano, "La Lucca della guerra e di Giorgio Colli," 97ff. On German music as an expression of the ineffable, cf. Helmut Plessner, *Die verspätete Nation* (Frankfurt am Main: Suhrkamp, 1974), 103.

20 Bimbi, "Parlerò di Mazzino," 56.

21 Bimbi, "Parlerò di Mazzino," 56.

22 Cf. Giorgio Colli, *Filosofi sovrumani* (Milan: Adelphi, 2009), 133ff. On the *Symposium*, see also Florian Rötzer, "Jacob Taubes," in *Denken, das an der Zeit ist*, ed. Florian Rötzer (Frankfurt am Main: Suhrkamp, 1987), 309f.

23 Plato, *Plato's Symposium*, trans. Seth Benardete (Chicago: University of Chicago Press, 2001), sec. 209b (40), cf. 206c–e (37), 209a–e (39–40). Colli's thoughts of pedagogical eros in *Apollineo e dionisiaco*, 34f., and *Dopo Nietzsche*, 73f.

24 Mazzino Montinari to Giorgio Colli, February 3, 1944, fondo Colli, b. 34, fasc. 185.001, Archivio Mondadori.

25 Mazzino Montinari to Giorgio Colli, April 6, 1968, fondo Montinari, cartella 13, Archivio Scuola Normale Superiore.

26 Mazzino Montinari to Giorgio Colli, November 3, 1943, fondo Colli, b. 34, fasc. 185.001, Archivio Mondadori. Mazzino Montinari to Giorgio Colli, December 29, 1943, fondo Colli, b. 34, fasc. 185.001, Archivio Mondadori. Mazzino Montinari to Giorgio Colli, n.d., fondo Colli, b. 34, fasc. 185.001, Archivio Mondadori. Giorgio Colli to Anna Maria Musso-Colli, December 13, 1943, fondo Giorgio Colli, b. 03, fasc. 006, Archivio Mondadori.

27 One who writes of Montinari's "radicality" is, for example, Cesare Cases, "Der Großherzog von Weimar: Erinnerung an Mazzino Montinari," *Nietzsche-Studien* 18 (1989): 20. On his worldviews, see Valenziano, "La Lucca della guerra e di Giorgio Colli," 98. Cf. Imbasciati, "Il ricordo di uno studente," 27.

28 Montinari to Colli, December 29, 1943. Giorgio Colli to Anna Maria Musso-Colli, November 29, 1943, fondo Giorgio Colli, b. 03, fasc. 006, Archivio Mondadori. The crucifix in Cases, "Der Großherzog von Weimar," 21.

29 Bimbi's recollection in "Parlerò di Mazzino," 56. Colli, *Distanz und Pathos*, 27. On school discipline running wild, cf. Lea Stefanelli, "Il ricordo di una 'principiante,'" in *L'impegno di una generazione: Il gruppo di Lucca dal Liceo Machiavelli alla Normale nel clima del Dopoguerra*, ed. Mario Mirri, Renzo Sabbatini, and Luigi Imbasciati (Milan: FrancoAngeli, 2014), 21. On (pedagogical) eros in the George circle, cf. Thomas Karlauf, *Stefan George: Die Entdeckung des Charisma* (Munich: Blessing, 2007), 365–95.

30 Angelo Pasquinelli to Giorgio Colli, March 1, 1943, fondo Colli, b. 32, fasc. 134, Archivio Mondadori.

31 Leonardo Sciascia, *The Moro Affair; And, The Mystery of Majorana*, trans. Sacha Rabinovitch (Manchester: Carcanet, 1987), 82. On Italian familialism, see also Gass, *Pisaner Tagebuch*, 77f. Valenziano, "La Lucca della guerra e di Giorgio Colli," 96. Similarly, Bimbi, "Parlerò di Mazzino," 55.

32 Mazzino Montinari to Anna Maria Musso-Colli, March 11, 1981, fondo Montinari, cartella 18, Archivio Scuola Normale Superiore.

33 The quotation attributed to George in Jan Andres, "'Hellas ewig unsre liebe': Erlesenes und erlebtes Griechenland bei Rudolf Fahrner," in *Hellas verstehen: Deutsch–griechischer Kulturtransfer im 20. Jahrhundert*, ed. Chryssoula Kambas and Marilisa Mitsou (Vienna: Böhlau, 2010), 73. On Colli's learned bearing, see Gino Moretti, "Ricordo di Giorgio Colli," in *Giorgio Colli e l'enigma greco*, ed. Giuseppe Auteri (Catania: CUECM, 2000), 44–7.

34 Ulrich von Wilamowitz-Moellendorff, "Future Philology! A Reply to Friedrich Nietzsche's 'Birth of Tragedy,'" trans. Gertrude Postl, Babette Babich, and Holger Schmid, *New Nietzsche Studies* 4, no. 1/2 (Summer/ Fall 2000): 24. On Nietzsche's philhellenism, see Cancik and Cancik-Lindemaier, "Das Gymnasium in der Knechtschaft des Staates."

35 Mazzino Montinari, "Die neue kritische Gesamtausgabe von Nietzsches Werken," *Literaturmagazin* 12: *Nietzsche* (1980): 317. Colli, *Apollineo e dionisiaco*, 56: "The footnote is the typical instrument of modern laziness and spiritual hypocrisy."

36 Giorgio Colli, *Filosofia dell'espressione* (Milan: Adelphi, 1969), 236. Colli, *Apollineo e dionisiaco*, 53, cf. 32. Cf. Luigi Anzalone and Giuliano

Minichiello, *Lo specchio di Dionisio: Saggi su Giorgio Colli* (Bari: Dedalo, 1984), 149ff.

37 Colli, *Apollineo e dionisiaco*, 17. On the rituals of secrecy, cf. Jürgen Frese, "Intellektuellen-Assoziationen," in *Kreise, Gruppen, Bünde: Zur Soziologie moderner Intellektuellenassoziationen*, ed. Richard Faber and Christine Holste (Würzburg: Königshausen & Neumann, 2000), 441–62. On the German traditions of inspirited reading, see Stephan Wackwitz, "Text als Mythos: Zur Frankfurter Hölderlin-Ausgabe und ihrer Rezeption," *Merkur*, no. 492 (1990): 134–43.

38 Colli, *Dopo Nietzsche*, 140, cf. 69, 143. In addition, see Chiara Colli Staude, *Friedrich Nietzsche, Giorgio Colli und die Griechen: Philologie und Philosophie zwischen Unzeitgemäßheit und Leben* (Würzburg: Königshausen & Neumann, 2019), 113.

39 Adriano Sofri, "Dal morbillo a Nietzsche," *Panorama*, July 31, 1988, 121. Colli, *Dopo Nietzsche*, 141, 30. Cf. also Alessandro Fersen, "La memoria in Giorgio Colli," in *Giorgio Colli: Incontro di studio*, ed. Giuseppe Menichetti, Sandro Barbera, and Giuliano Campioni (Milan: Angeli, 1983), 30.

40 Cf. Manfred Landfester, "Griechen und Deutsche: Der Mythos einer 'Wahlverwandtschaft,'" in *Mythos und Nation: Studien zur Entwicklung des kollektiven Bewußtseins in der Neuzeit*, ed. Helmut Berding, vol. 3 (Frankfurt am Main: Suhrkamp, 1996), 198–219. On the German culture complex, see Wolf Lepenies, *The Seduction of Culture in German History* (Princeton: Princeton University Press, 2006).

41 *KSA*, 1988, 14: 472. See also Nietzsche's letter to Georg Brandes from early December 1888 in *KSB*, 2002, 8: 500. Nietzsche, *CW*, 2021, 9: 306; *KSA*, 1988, 6: 366. On the nature of Nietzsche's political prophesies, see Eric Voegelin, "Nietzsche, the Crisis and the War," *The Journal of Politics* 6, no. 2 (May 1944): 177–212.

42 Colli, *Dopo Nietzsche*, 193. Montinari, "Erinnerung an Giorgio Colli," 173.

43 Colli, *Apollineo e dionisiaco*, 48. Colli, *Dopo Nietzsche*, 82. Giorgio Colli, "Diario 1944–1945," Archivio Giorgio Colli, http://www.giorgiocolli.it/it/content/diario-1944-1945, entry from August 27, 1944. On Colli's aversion to Romans, see Stefanelli, "Il ricordo di una 'principiante,'" 23. On his liberalism, see Banfi, "Coraggio del pensiero," 222. His reaction to Stalingrad in Bimbi, "Parlerò di Mazzino," 56.

44 On the politicization of Colli's students, see Imbasciati, "Il ricordo di uno

studente," 25; Mirri, "Postfazione," 177ff. The course of the war from 1943 according to Lutz Klinkhammer, *Zwischen Bündnis und Besatzung: Das nationalsozialistische Deutschland und die Republik von Salò 1943–1945* (Tübingen: M. Niemeyer, 1993).

45 Angelo Pasquinelli to Giorgio Colli, January 4, 1943, fondo Colli, b. 32, fasc. 134, Archivio Mondadori; Angelo Pasquinelli to Giorgio Colli, July 16, 1943, fondo Colli, b. 32, fasc. 134, Archivio Mondadori; Angelo Pasquinelli to Giorgio Colli, August 12, 1943, fondo Colli, b. 32, fasc. 134, Archivio Mondadori. On Pasquinelli, cf. also Montinari, "Die neue kritische Gesamtausgabe von Nietzsches Werken," 317: "The best of us became freedom fighters." On the connection of another classmate, Giorgio Giorgetti, to the *Resistenza* in Viareggio, cf. "Breve note biografiche: Giorgio Giorgetti," n.d., fondo Montinari, cartella 18, Archivio Scuola Normale Superiore.

46 Montinari to Colli, November 3, 1943; Mazzino Montinari to Giorgio Colli, November 7, 1943, fondo Colli, b. 34, fasc. 185.001, Archivio Mondadori.

47 Cf. Imbasciati, "Il ricordo di uno studente," 28f. See also Campioni, "Mazzino Montinari," xviii, and Montinari to Colli, February 3, 1944.

48 Montinari to Colli, December 29, 1943.

49 Bimbi, "Parlerò di Mazzino," 56. Colli, *La Ragione errabonda*, 103. Montinari, "Die neue kritische Gesamtausgabe von Nietzsches Werken," 317. The politically lethal consequences of German Graecophilia have been emphasized particularly by Eliza M. Butler, *The Tyranny of Greece over Germany* (Cambridge: Cambridge University Press, 1935). On indirect politicization, see Reinhart Koselleck, *Critique and Crisis: Enlightenment and the Pathogenesis of Modern Society* (Cambridge, MA: MIT Press, 1988).

50 On civil resistance, cf. Mirri, "Postfazione," 182. Montinari speaks of "pranks to the annoyance of the fascists" ("Die neue kritische Gesamtausgabe von Nietzsches Werken," 317); Schirrmacher, "Nietzsches Wiederkehr."

51 On Gentile's murder, cf. Schirrmacher, "Nietzsches Wiederkehr"; and Montinari, "Lavò la faccia al Superuomo," 71. The memorable birthday celebration in Campioni, "Mazzino Montinari," xviii. Colli's entries in Colli, "Diario 1944–1945." On the events in the Valtellina, see Giorgio Colli to Anna Maria Musso-Colli, April 20, 1944, fondo Giorgio Colli, b. 03, fasc. 006, Archivio Mondadori.

52 Colli, "Diario 1944–1945", entries of June 4 and August 27, 1944. Giorgio Colli to Anna Maria Musso-Colli, June 27, 1944, fondo Giorgio Colli, b. 03, fasc. 006, Archivio Mondadori. On his time in Switzerland, see also Fersen, "La memoria in Giorgio Colli." Valenziano, "La Lucca della guerra e di Giorgio Colli," 96.

53 Giorgio Colli to Anna Maria Musso-Colli, July 24, 1944, fondo Giorgio Colli, b. 03, fasc. 006, Archivio Mondadori. On the pupils' experiences, cf. Mirri, "Postfazione," 175f., 211ff. On the atmosphere of the final months of the war in Lucchesia, see also Rudolf Borchardt, *Anabasis: Aufzeichnungen, Dokumente, Erinnerungen 1943–1945* (Munich: Edition Tenschert bei Hanser, 2003).

Chapter 2 Painstaking Care and Class Warfare: Pisa, 1948

1 Gass, *Pisaner Tagebuch*, 19.

2 Pisa after war in Antonio La Penna, "Incontri pisani degli anni quaranta," *Critica Marxista* 24 (1986): 155ff. On the social and political climate, see Albath, *Der Geist von Turin*, 161. On the supply situation in Italy, cf. Tony Judt, *Postwar: A History of Europe since 1945* (London: Vintage, 2010), 86.

3 Jean-Paul Sartre, "Palmiro Togliatti," in *Situations, IX: Mélanges*, by Jean-Paul Sartre (Paris: Gallimard, 1972), 150–1. Palmiro Togliatti, "Utopisti e riformatori sociali," in *La politica nel pensiero e nell'azione: Scritti e discorsi 1917–1964*, by Palmiro Togliatti, ed. Michele Ciliberto and Giuseppe Vacca (Milan: Bompiani, 2014), 1272. On the expectations of the Left, cf. Judt, *Postwar*, 79ff.

4 Michael Hardt and Antonio Negri, *Empire* (Cambridge, MA: Harvard University Press, 2000), 413. On Montinari's conversion, cf. Giuseppe Garritano, "Il clima politico," in *L'impegno di una generazione: Il gruppo di Lucca dal Liceo Machiavelli alla Normale nel clima del Dopoguerra*, ed. Mario Mirri, Renzo Sabbatini, and Luigi Imbasciati (Milan: FrancoAngeli, 2014), 48.

5 Cf. Togliatti, "Utopisti e riformatori sociali," 1272, 1274. The quotation according to Sartre, "Palmiro Togliatti," 144. On Stalin's nimbus, cf. Garritano, "Il clima politico," 48.

6 Sartre, "Palmiro Togliatti," 150–1. Togliatti, "Utopisti e riformatori sociali," 1274f. On Togliatti's cultural politics more generally, see Stephen Gundle, *Between Hollywood and Moscow: The Italian Communists and the*

Challenge of Mass Culture, 1943–1991 (Durham, NC: Duke University Press, 2000).

7 Very much worth reading: Joseph A. Buttigieg, "Introduction," in *Prison Notebooks*, by Antonio Gramsci, vol. 1: Notebooks 1–2, ed. and trans. Joseph A. Buttigieg (New York: Columbia University Press, 1992), 1–64.

8 Luigi Russo, "Antonio Gramsci e l'educazione democratica in Italia," *Belfagor* 2, no. 4 (1947): 395–411.

9 On the "message in a bottle," cf. Karl Markus Michel, "Versuch, die 'Ästhetische Theorie' zu verstehen," in *Materialien zur ästhetischen Theorie: Theodor W. Adornos Konstruktion der Moderne*, ed. Burkhardt Lindner and Martin Lüdke (Frankfurt am Main: Suhrkamp, 1979), 71. "Philosophy of praxis" was the name Gramsci himself chose for his theoretical undertaking. Cf. Russo, "Antonio Gramsci," 403. On the contrast between Gramsci and Adorno, see also Domenico Losurdo, *Der Marxismus Antonio Gramscis: Von der Utopie zum "kritischen Kommunismus,"* trans. Erdmute Brielmayer (Hamburg: VSA-Verlag, 2000), 164.

10 Russo, "Antonio Gramsci," 10. A good depiction of Gramsci's theory is in Eric J. Hobsbawm, *How to Change the World: Marx and Marxism, 1840–2011* (London: Little, Brown, 2011), 314ff. In his belief in the importance of intellectuals, Gramsci was strongly shaped by Croce's idealism. Cf. Cases, "Der Mythos der deutschen Kultur in Italien," 184. On Togliatti's appropriation, cf. Gundle, *Between Hollywood and Moscow*, 22f.

11 On "molecular" power and patience as a revolutionary virtue, see Adriano Sofri, "Genosse Hiob: Über Antonio Gramsci," in *Nahaufnahmen*, by Adriano Sofri (Berlin: Transit, 1999), 14–17. *KSA*, 1988, 1: 1. Mussolini's state prosecutor quoted in Russo, "Antonio Gramsci," 402. On Gramsci's mantra, see Mazzino Montinari, "Equivoci marxisti," in *Su Nietzsche*, by Mazzino Montinari (Rome: Editori riuniti, 1981), 103. On Nietzsche's origins, see Henning Ritter, "Tanz ohne Ketten: Zu Mazzino Montinaris unvollendetem Nietzsche-Kommentar," *Frankfurter Allgemeine Zeitung*, December 3, 1986. About the personal verification of philosophical truths, cf. Hannah Arendt, "Truth and Politics," *The New Yorker*, February 25, 1967, 62, 67.

12 For the self-understanding of the younger generation, a comment by Italo Calvino from 1959 is revealing: "We the younger ones – who had become partisans in the nick of time – felt not crushed, conquered, or 'burned,' but like winners, like the exclusive bearers of something." Quoted in

Albath, *Der Geist von Turin*, 177. On the political goings-on, see Judt, *Postwar*, 86ff., 127. In general – for the following as well – see Rudolf Lill, *Geschichte Italiens in der Neuzeit* (Darmstadt: Wissenschaftliche Buchgesellschaft, 1988), 372ff.

13 The fellow student: Garritano, "Il clima politico," 48. Angelo Pasquinelli to Giorgio Colli, August 30, 1946, fondo Colli, b. 32, fasc. 134, Archivio Mondadori. Delio Cantimori to Mazzino Montinari, October 31, 1962, fondo Montinari, cartella 13, Archivio Scuola Normale Superiore.

14 On Montinari's alienation, see Giuliano Campioni, "Da Lucca a Weimar: Mazzino Montinari e Nietzsche," in *L'impegno di una generazione: Il gruppo di Lucca dal Liceo Machiavelli alla Normale nel clima del Dopoguerra*, ed. Mario Mirri, Renzo Sabbatini, and Luigi Imbasciati (Milan: FrancoAngeli, 2014), 154. Montinari's accusation in a letter to Colli, November 17, 1967.

15 The comparison originally in Campioni, "Da Lucca a Weimar," 159.

16 On Cantimori as the "god" of learnedness, cf. Valentino Parlato, "Angelo, Mazzino e Fausto," in *L'impegno di una generazione: Il gruppo di Lucca dal Liceo Machiavelli alla Normale nel clima del Dopoguerra*, ed. Mario Mirri, Renzo Sabbatini, and Luigi Imbasciati (Milan: FrancoAngeli, 2014), 92f. On his style as a university instructor, see Licia Giusti, "Mazzino, Giorgio e Fausto," in *L'impegno di una generazione: Il gruppo di Lucca dal Liceo Machiavelli alla Normale nel clima del Dopoguerra*, ed. Mario Mirri, Renzo Sabbatini, and Luigi Imbasciati (Milano: FrancoAngeli, 2014), 75f; La Penna, "Incontri pisani degli anni quaranta," 153, 159; Silvana Seidel Menchi, "'Ein Neues Leben': Contributo allo studio di Delio Cantimori," *Studi Storici* 34 (1993): 778. For an apologia of archival work, see Delio Cantimori, *Conversando di storia* (Bari: Laterza, 1967), 155ff. For a concise take on his perspective, which emphasizes the continuities between Reformation and humanism and the social-revolutionary aspects of heresies, see Anne Jacobson Schutte, "Periodization of Sixteenth-Century Italian Religious History: The Post-Cantimori Paradigm Shift," *The Journal of Modern History* 61 (1989): 270f.

17 Paul Veyne, "Histoire et historiens," *Annales* 27 (1972): 668. On Cantimori's spectrum of interests, see Eric Cochrane and John Tedeschi, "Delio Cantimori: Historian," *The Journal of Modern History* 39 (1967): 438–45.

18 On Togliatti's reference, see Claudio Cesa, "Il clima culturale," in *L'impegno di una generazione: Il gruppo di Lucca dal Liceo Machiavelli alla Normale*

nel clima del Dopoguerra, ed. Mario Mirri, Renzo Sabbatini, and Luigi Imbasciati (Milan: FrancoAngeli, 2014), 37. On Cantimori's role, cf. Eugenio Di Rienzo, *Delio Cantimori e la cultura politica del Novecento* (Florence: Le lettere, 2009), 82.

19 On the subversive aura of Cantimori's research, cf. Ernesto Sestan, "Cantimori e i Giacobini," *Annali della Scuola Normale Superiore di Pisa: Lettere, Storia e Filosofia, Serie II* 37 (1968): 233; Cochrane and Tedeschi, "Delio Cantimori: Historian," 441ff.

20 Mazzino Montinari to Delio Cantimori, February 11, 1948, fondo Delio Cantimori, serie carteggio, fasc. Mazzino Montinari, Archivio Scuola Normale Superiore. Cf. Campioni, "Da Lucca a Weimar," 156.

21 Calvino's allusion to Cantimori in "Nota 1960," in *I nostri antenati*, by Italo Calvino (Milan: Garzanti, 1996), 418. Carlo Ginzburg, *The Cheese and the Worms: The Cosmos of a Sixteenth-Century Miller*, trans. John Tedeschi and Anne C. Tedeschi (Baltimore: Johns Hopkins University Press, 2013), xxxii. On the relationship between Ginzburg and Cantimori, see Anne Jacobson Schutte, "Carlo Ginzburg," *The Journal of Modern History* 48 (1976): 296–315.

22 Delio Cantimori, *Italienische Haeretiker der Spätrenaissance*, trans. Werner Kaegi (Basel: B. Schwabe, 1949), v. On the perception of Cantimori after the war, see La Penna, "Incontri pisani degli anni quaranta," 158. See also Nicola D'Elia, *Delio Cantimori e la cultura politica tedesca (1927–1940)* (Rome: Viella, 2007), 22, 118.

23 Cantimori, *Conversando di storia*, 138. Criticism in Di Rienzo, *Delio Cantimori e la cultura politica del Novecento*, 79ff. The counterargument in Adriano Prosperi, "Delio Cantimori, maestro di tolleranza," *il manifesto*, March 30, 2005.

24 Cantimori quoted in D'Elia, *Delio Cantimori*, 33, 70, cf. 118.

25 Carl Schmitt to Delio Cantimori, April 21, 1935, fondo Delio Cantimori, serie carteggio, fasc. Vari, Archivio Scuola Normale Superiore; Carl Schmitt to Delio Cantimori, June 6, 1935, fondo Delio Cantimori, serie carteggio, fasc. Vari, Archivio Scuola Normale Superiore. Löwith, *My Life in Germany*, 86, cf. 91. See also Schieder, *Mythos Mussolini*, 123. On Cantimori and Schmitt, cf. Pierangelo Schiera, "Carl Schmitt und Delio Cantimori," in *Complexio Oppositorum: Über Carl Schmitt*, ed. Helmut Quaritsch (Berlin: Duncker & Humblot, 1988), 529–35.

26 Delio Cantimori, "Interpretazioni tedesche di Marx nel periodo

1929–1945," in *Studi di storia*, by Delio Cantimori (Turin: Einaudi, 1959), 237. The "beautiful souls" quoted in D'Elia, *Delio Cantimori*, 21, cf. 72. On Cantimori's conception of the political, cf. D'Elia, *Delio Cantimori*, 33; Michele Ciliberto, *Intellettuali e fascismo: Saggio su Delio Cantimori* (Bari: De Donato, 1977), 69.

27 The "demon of the political" is addressed in Antonio Gnoli, "Il libro segreto di Cantimori," *La Repubblica*, May 27, 2004. Cf. D'Elia, *Delio Cantimori*, 57f., 118; Di Rienzo, *Delio Cantimori e la cultura politica del Novecento*, 81ff.

28 Nietzsche, *CW*, 2020, 16: 398f.; *KSA*, 1988, 12: 165. *Querfront* intellectuals, for instance, in Cantimori, "Interpretazioni tedesche," 179. Cf. Mazzino Montinari, "Delio Cantimori e Nietzsche," in *Su Nietzsche*, by Mazzino Montinari (Rome: Editori riuniti, 1981), 104–22. On Nietzsche's modernity, for example, Karl Löwith, *From Hegel to Nietzsche: The Revolution in Nineteenth-Century Thought*, trans. David E. Green (New York: Columbia University Press, 1991), 218.

29 Nietzsche, *CW*, 2023, 6: 254, cf. 64; *KSA*, 1988, 3: 629, cf. 401. Nietzsche, *CW*, 2021, 9: 116; *KSA*, 1988, 6: 144. Delio Cantimori, "Recensione di Hugo Fischer, Nietzsche Apostata," in *Politica e storia contemporanea: Scritti (1927–1942)*, by Delio Cantimori, ed. Luisa Mangoni (Turin: Einaudi, 1991), 158. Hugo Fischer, *Nietzsche Apostata; oder, die Philosophie des Ärgernisses* (Erfurt: K. Stenger, 1931), 9f. Nietzsche, *CW*, 2023, 6: 145; *KSA*, 1988, 3: 500. The "believing doubter" in Ernst Bertram, *Nietzsche: Attempt at a Mythology*, trans. Robert Edward Norton (Urbana: University of Illinois Press, 2009), 8.

30 On the trauma, see Rossana Rossanda, *Vergebliche Reise oder Politik als Education sentimentale*, trans. Barbara Kleiner (Frankfurt am Main: Suhrkamp, 1985), 14. On the events in Pisa and the vicinity, see Carla Forti, *Dopoguerra in provincia: Microstorie pisane e lucchesi (1944–1948)* (Milan: FrancoAngeli, 2007), 290ff. The discussions among the students in Garritano, "Il clima politico," 49.

31 The prefect is quoted in Forti, *Dopoguerra in provincia*, 237. Cf. Albertina Vittoria, "La commissione culturale del Pci dal 1948 al 1956," *Studi Storici* 31 (1990): 135–70. On the "Russo case," see the documentation, of which Cantimori and Montinari were signatories, "Il 'libro bianco' di una vendetta nera," *Belfagor* 3, no. 6 (1948): 722–7, "Il 'libro bianco' di una vendetta nera," *Belfagor* 4, no. 1 (1949): 94–112.

32 Rossanda, *Vergebliche Reise oder Politik als Education sentimentale*, 14. Direzione des PCI, Sezione Propaganda, to Delio Cantimori, August 4, 1945, fondo Delio Cantimori, serie carteggio, fasc. Partito Comunista Italiano, Archivio Scuola Normale Superiore. Mario Alicata to Delio Cantimori, October 28, 1955, fondo Delio Cantimori, serie carteggio, fasc. Partito Comunista Italiano, Archivio Scuola Normale Superiore. Palmiro Togliatti to Delio Cantimori, February 18, 1949, fondo Delio Cantimori, serie carteggio, fasc. vari, Archivio Scuola Normale Superiore. Cantimori quoted in Daniele Menozzi and Francesco Torchiani, eds., *Delio Cantimori (1904–1966): Libri, documenti e immagini dai fondi della Scuola Normale Superiore* (Pisa: Edizioni della Normale, 2016), 106.

33 For his "total politicization" see Montinari, "Erinnerung an Giorgio Colli," 168. Cf. Paolo Chiarini, "Il comunista che amava Nietzsche," *Rinascità*, December 13, 1986. The restaurants in Rome are found in Giusti, "Mazzino, Giorgio e Fausto," 76; Cases, "Der Großherzog von Weimar," 21; Parlato, "Angelo, Mazzino e Fausto," 92. Ernst Bloch, "Italy and Porosity," in *Literary Essays*, by Ernst Bloch, trans. Andrew Joron (Stanford, CA: Stanford University Press, 1998), 450–7. Montinari's two sides in Cases, "Der Großherzog von Weimar," 20, 24.

34 Valentino Gerratana, "Le inquietudine di Mazzino," in *L'impegno di una generazione: Il gruppo di Lucca dal Liceo Machiavelli alla Normale nel clima del Dopoguerra*, ed. Mario Mirri, Renzo Sabbatini, and Luigi Imbasciati (Milan: FrancoAngeli, 2014), 71. Montinari's work for the party in Campioni, "Mazzino Montinari," xxiif. On the strategies of the culture wars, see Gundle, *Between Hollywood and Moscow*, 39, cf. 43, 56ff. On media competition, see Régis Debray, "Socialism: A Life-Cycle," *New Left Review* 46 (2007): 5–28.

35 Mazzino Montinari to Delio Cantimori, March 1950, fondo Cantimori, fasc. Montinari, Archivio Scuola Normale Superiore.

36 Mazzino Montinari to Delio Cantimori, June 2, 1950, fondo Cantimori, fasc. Montinari, Archivio Scuola Normale Superiore.

37 The *FAZ* correspondent is quoted in Klaus Heitmann, "Das Deutschland der Adenauer-Zeit, von italienischen Autoren gesehen," in *Italien in Deutschland, Deutschland in Italien: Die deutsch–italienischen Wechselbeziehungen in der Belletristik des 20. Jahrhunderts*, ed. Anna Comi and Alexandra Pontzen (Berlin: E. Schmidt, 1999), 89, cf. 87. Mazzino Montinari, "Lettere dalla Germania," *Nuovo Corriere*, May 6/7, 1950.

38 Angelo Pasquinelli to Giorgio Colli, October 17, 1951, fondo Colli, b. 32, fasc. 134, Archivio Mondadori.

39 Quoted in Michele Sisto, "Gli intellettuali italiani e la Germania socialista: Un percorso attraverso gli scritti di Cesare Cases," in *Riflessioni sulla DDR: Prospettive internazionali e interdisciplinari vent'anni dopo*, ed. Magda Martini and Thomas Schaarschmidt (Bologna: Il mulino, 2011), 104f. On the genre, cf. Philipp Felsch and Frank Witzel, *BRD Noir* (Berlin: Matthes & Seitz, 2016).

40 Cesare Cases to Delio Cantimori, January 16, 1957, fondo Cantimori, serie carteggio, fasc. vari, Archivio Scuola Normale Superiore.

41 For the *Doctor Zhivago* episode, see Sergio d'Angelo, "Der Roman des Romans," *Osteuropa* 18 (1968): 489–501.

42 Georg Lukács, *The Destruction of Reason*, trans. Peter Palmer (London: Verso, 2021), 315ff., 328. Lukács's book is a reckoning with his own early Nietzsche fascination, according to Henning Ottmann, "Anti-Lukács: Eine Kritik der Nietzsche-Kritik von Georg Lukács," *Nietzsche-Studien* 13 (1984): 570–86. Cf. also Mazzino Montinari, "Nietzsche zwischen Alfred Baeumler und Georg Lukács," in *Nietzsche lesen*, by Mazzino Montinari (Berlin: De Gruyter, 1982), 169–206.

43 Mazzino Montinari, "Nel partito non mi piace fare l'intellettuale," *il manifesto*, February 11, 1983. On his readings, cf. Montinari, "L'onorevole arte di leggere Nietzsche," 336. The events according to Judt, *Postwar*, 176f., 309f.

44 Mazzino Montinari to "Helga," July 24, 1955, fondo Montinari, cartella 2, Archivio Scuola Normale Superiore. Montinari's self-understanding in Campioni, "Mazzino Montinari," xxiv.

45 Mann quoted in Hans Wysling and Yvonne Schmidlin, eds., *Thomas Mann: Ein Leben in Bildern* (Zurich: Artemis, 1994), 425. On Mann's significance for the Italian Left, see Charis Pöthig, *Italien und die DDR: Die politischen, ökonomischen und kulturellen Beziehungen von 1949 bis 1980* (Frankfurt am Main: Peter Lang, 2000), 147f. On the evolution of his political ideas, see Lepenies, *The Seduction of Culture in German History*, 27ff. Cf. Heinz Riedt to Mazzino Montinari, June 2, 1956, fondo Montinari, cartella 2, Archivio Scuola Normale Superiore. Mazzino Montinari, "Otto lettere inedite di Thomas Mann," *Il Contemporaneo*, December 31, 1955.

46 The memo is cited in Pöthig, *Italien und die DDR*, 152. "Wiedervereinigung in Rom," *Der Spiegel*, April 17, 1956, 23.

47 Montinari and the brochure are quoted from "Wiedervereinigung in Rom," 23. Azio de Franciscis, "Pankows Kulturoffensive in Rom," *Die Zeit*, April 11, 1957. On the activities of the Centro, see Pöthig, *Italien und die DDR*, 147ff.

48 Judt, *Postwar*, 321. On the PCI, see Nikolas Dörr, *Die Rote Gefahr: Der italienische Eurokommunismus als sicherheitspolitische Herausforderung für die USA und Westdeutschland 1969–1979* (Cologne: Böhlau, 2017), 81.

49 Montinari, quoted in Campioni, "Mazzino Montinari," xxiii. See also Mazzino Montinari to Paolo Chiarini, May 28, 1967, fondo Montinari, cartella 6, Archivio Scuola Normale Superiore.

Chapter 3 Operation Nietzsche: Florence, 1958

1 Colli, "Diario 1944–1945", entry from July 25, 1944. Colli to Musso-Colli, July 24, 1944.

2 Colli, "Diario 1944–1945", entry from June 4, 1944. Giorgio Colli to Anna Maria Musso-Colli, December 1, 1944, fondo Giorgio Colli, b. 03, fasc. 006, Archivio Mondadori.

3 Giuseppe Colli to Giorgio Colli, October 14, 1948, fondo Giorgio Colli, b. 05, fasc. 006, Archivio Mondadori.

4 On Colli's book and his first translation proposals, cf. Sofri, "Dal morbillo a Nietzsche," 121; Banfi, "Giorgio Colli," 229f., 234, 252. His anticommunism is very explicit in his entry from June 20, 1944, and his undated entry in "Diario 1944–1945." On the importance of Einaudi, cf. Albath, *Der Geist von Turin*.

5 Albath, *Der Geist von Turin*, 161.

6 "Bollettino editoriale Einaudi" (Turin, 1955), Archivio Giorgio Colli.

7 See, for instance, Colli, *La Ragione errabonda*, 27ff.

8 Giorgio Colli to Gino Moretti, June 8, 1957, fondo Giorgio Colli, b. 31, fasc. 124, Archivio Mondadori.

9 Cf. Banfi, "Giorgio Colli," 245; Campioni, "Da Lucca a Weimar," 157. Director Regina Schilling referred to the generation of those born in the mid-1920s living through the West German Economic Miracle as "Generation Heart Attack" (*Kulenkampffs Schuhe*, documentary film, 2018). Does that also pertain to Italy? After Angelo Pasquinelli, Colli and Montinari also die of cardiovascular diseases at sixty-one and fifty-eight, respectively.

10 Mazzino Montinari to Giorgio Colli, March 25, 1957, fondo Colli, b. 34, fasc. 185.001, Archivio Mondadori.

11 Sergio d'Angelo to Mazzino Montinari, February 9, 1958, fondo Montinari, cartella 2, Archivio Scuola Normale Superiore. Cantimori is quoted from Campioni, "Da Lucca a Weimar," 158.

12 Montinari to Colli, April 6, 1968.

13 Colli, *La Ragione errabonda*, 598f. See also Colli's more extensive reflections on a philosophy of expression – three years later in the same place: "As the waterfall which strikes rock imparts energy to it, so does the world of expression arise," *La Ragione errabonda*, 57. For more, see Colli Staude, *Friedrich Nietzsche, Giorgio Colli und die Griechen*, 99.

14 Colli, *Dopo Nietzsche*, 193. Colli, *La Ragione errabonda*, 103, 565, cf. as a whole 83–112. The "dirty business" from the entry dated August 27, 1944, in Colli, "Diario 1944–1945."

15 Colli, *La Ragione errabonda*, 565, cf. 89, 105.

16 Colli to Moretti, June 8, 1957. Cf. Banfi, "Giorgio Colli," 231, 248.

17 Giuliana Lanata, "L'Enciclopedia' di Giorgio Colli," in *Giorgio Colli: Incontro di studio*, ed. Giuseppe Menichetti, Sandro Barbera, and Giuliano Campioni (Milan: Angeli, 1983), 36. A selection of Colli's forewords in Giorgio Colli, *Per una enciclopedia di autori classici* (Milan: Adelphi, 1983).

18 Colli, *Dopo Nietzsche*, 32. Bobbio quoted in Banfi, "Giorgio Colli," 241f.

19 Colli, *La Ragione errabonda*, 102, 108. Cf. Philipp Felsch, *The Summer of Theory: History of a Rebellion, 1960–1990*, trans. Tony Crawford (Cambridge: Polity, 2022).

20 Quoted in Campioni, "Mazzino Montinari," xxxix, xlii.

21 Cf. Montinari, "L'onorevole arte di leggere Nietzsche," 336.

22 Voegelin, "Nietzsche, the Crisis and the War," 177. François Menthon quoted in "Thirty-Sixth Day: Thursday, 17 January 1946," in *Trial of the Major War Criminals before the International Military Tribunal, Nuremberg, 14 November 1945–1 October 1946*, vol. 5 (Nuremberg: International Military Tribunal, 1947), 377. Giorgio Colli, "Recensione di K.A. Goetz, Nietzsche als Ausnahme," *Rivista di filosofia* 16 (1950): 230f. On the Nietzsche journalism after the war, cf. Herbert W. Reichert, "The Present Status of Nietzsche: Nietzsche Literature in the Post-War Era," *Monatshefte* 51 (1959): 103–20.

23 Thomas Mann, *Nietzsche's Philosophy in the Light of Contemporary Events*

(Washington, DC: US Government Printing Office, 1947), 36. Cf. Karl Schlechta, *Der Fall Nietzsche: Aufsätze und Vorträge* (Munich: C. Hanser, 1959), 97.

24 Mazzino Montinari to Giorgio Colli, October 31, 1967, fondo Montinari, cartella 13, Archivio Scuola Normale Superiore. On Schlechta, see Jens Thiel, "Monumentalisch – antiquarisch – kritisch? Archiv und Edition als Institutionen der Distanzierung: Der Fall des Nietzsche-Herausgebers Karl Schlechta," in *"Einige werden posthum geboren": Friedrich Nietzsches Wirkungen*, ed. Renate Reschke and Marco Brusotti (Berlin: De Gruyter, 2012), 475–88.

25 Schlechta, *Der Fall Nietzsche*, 12. Schlechta, "Philologischer Nachbericht," 1383, 1403. Horneffer quoted in Schlechta, "Philologischer Nachbericht," 1399.

26 Schlechta, "Philologischer Nachbericht," 1393, 1398, 1403. Schlechta, *Der Fall Nietzsche*, 41.

27 Walter Jens, "Zarter Zeichner des großen Mittags," *Texte und Zeichen* 3 (1957): 309. "Also sprach Lisbeth Förster," *Der Spiegel*, January 29, 1958, 32–41. *Time* magazine quoted in Reichert, "The Present Status of Nietzsche," 118. Karl Löwith, "Rezension von Karl Schlechta, Der Fall Nietzsche," in *Sämtliche Schriften*, by Karl Löwith, vol. 6: *Nietzsche* (Stuttgart: J.B. Metzler, 1987), 521. Karl Löwith, "Rezension von Friedrich Nietzsche, Werke in drei Bänden," in *Sämtliche Schriften*, by Karl Löwith, vol. 6: *Nietzsche* (Stuttgart: J.B. Metzler, 1987), 513.

28 All quotations come from Pannwitz, "Nietzsche-Philologie?," 1074, 1080, 1076, 1084. On Pannwitz's "postmodern man," cf. Marc-Oliver Schuster, "Rudolf Pannwitz' kulturphilosophische Verwendung des Begriffs 'postmodern,'" *Archiv für Begriffsgeschichte* 47 (2005): 191–213. On hermeneutic and philological propriety, see Erika Thomalla, *Anwälte des Autors: Zur Geschichte der Herausgeberschaft im 18. und 19. Jahrhundert* (Göttingen: Wallstein, 2020), 327ff.

29 Walter Kaufmann, "German Thought Today," *The Kenyon Review* 19 (1957): 21f. Heidegger, *Nietzsche*, 1: 9. On Kaufmann's assessment of Nietzsche's literary remains, see "A Book for Thinking," *The Times Literary Supplement*, May 15, 1969.

30 Justus W. Hedemann to Nietzsche-Archiv, March 2, 1945, Nietzsche-Archiv (72), 1801, Goethe- und Schiller-Archiv. Here, too, the pledge from Reemtsma Cigarettenfabriken GmbH. Karl Schlechta to Max Oehler,

March 6, 1945, Nietzsche-Archiv (72), 1801, Goethe- und Schiller-Archiv. On Schlechta's war experience, see Thiel, "Monumentalisch – antiquarisch – kritisch?," 483. Steinway & Sons, Hamburg, to Nietzsche-Archiv, October 25, 1945, Nietzsche-Archiv (72), 1801, Goethe- und Schiller-Archiv.

31 Schlechta, "Philologischer Nachbericht," 1405, 1431f. By way of correction, see Podach, *Friedrich Nietzsches Werke des Zusammenbruchs*, 393ff. The historical facts in Manfred Riedel, *Nietzsche in Weimar: Ein deutsches Drama* (Leipzig: Reclam, 1997), 153ff.; Wolfgang Stephan, "Der Zugriff der sowjetischen Militäradministration auf Nietzsches Nachlass 1946 und seine Retter," *Nietzsche-Studien* 27 (1998): 527–34. On the methods of the Soviet Trophy Brigades, see Renatur Deckert, "Eisenregale, vom Feuer verformt," *Süddeutsche Zeitung*, February 11, 2020.

32 Pannwitz, "Nietzsche-Philologie?," 1084, cf. 1074. Reichert quoted in Podach, *Friedrich Nietzsches Werke des Zusammenbruchs*, 396, who of course highlights his own interpretation.

33 Giorgio Colli to Luciano Foà, July 3, 1958, Archivio Giorgio Colli.

34 The "undeciphered manuscripts" in Pannwitz, "Nietzsche-Philologie?," 1075. Colli, *Distanz und Pathos*, 125f. Nietzsche, *CW*, 2014, 8: 192; *KSA*, 1988, 5: 234. On esoteric Nietzsche, see also Colli, *Dopo Nietzsche*, 69; Pannwitz, "Nietzsche-Philologie?," 1079. Roos's parallel initiative: "Les derniers écrits de Nietzsche et leur publication."

35 Colli to Foà, July 3, 1958. On the locational advantage of the Italians, see Werner Brede, "Rezension der Kritischen Studienausgabe für den SFB" (typescript, 1980), Nachlass Mazzino Montinari (177), Kasten 30.4, Goethe- und Schiller-Archiv. The Montinari *Nachlass* in Weimar has not yet been indexed by the archive, thus the call numbers are preliminary.

36 Nietzsche, *KSA*, 1988, 8: 44, cf. 68. "Freemasonry" in Michel Foucault, *Society Must Be Defended: Lectures at the Collège de France, 1975–76*, ed. Mauro Bertani and Alessandro Fontana, trans. David Macey (New York: Picador, 2003), 5. Colli, "Diario 1944–1945", entry from August 27, 1944. Explicit echoes of Renaissance philology in Colli, *Apollineo e dionisiaco*, 31ff. On Gramsci, see Buttigieg, "Introduction," 58ff. On Sofri, see Gustav Seibt, "Freigängerbriefe," in *Nahaufnahmen*, by Adriano Sofri, trans. Martina Bartel (Berlin: Transit, 1999), 8f. For the tip about Pasolini, I am grateful to Margaret Scarborough. In general, see Cerquiglini, *In Praise of the Variant*, 87f.

37 Colli to Foà, July 3, 1958.
38 Mazzino Montinari to "Laura," February 9, 1960, fondo Montinari, cartella 5, Archivio Scuola Normale Superiore. Cf. Campioni, "Mazzino Montinari," xxxvii.
39 Cases, "Der Großherzog von Weimar," 21, and Cesare Cases to Mazzino Montinari, March 27, 1978, Nachlass Mazzino Montinari (177), Kasten 33.1, Goethe- und Schiller-Archiv. Cf. Banfi, "Giorgio Colli," 257.

Chapter 4 Over the Wall and into the Desert: Weimar, 1961

1 Montinari to Colli, April 8, 1961, quoted from Campioni, *Leggere Nietzsche*, 255f.
2 Regarding the preparations, cf. Cesare Cases to Mazzino Montinari, December 2, 1960, fondo Montinari, cartella 5, Archivio Scuola Normale. On January 31, 1961, the Akademie der Künste issues the permit: fondo Montinari, cartella 3, Archivio Scuola Normale.
3 Walter Benjamin, "The Work of Art in the Age of Its Technological Reproducibility: Second Version," in *The Work of Art in the Age of Its Technological Reproducibility, and Other Writings on Media*, by Walter Benjamin, ed. Michael William Jennings, Brigid Doherty, and Thomas Y. Levin, trans. Edmund Jephcott, Rodney Livingstone, and Howard Eiland (Cambridge, MA: The Belknap Press of Harvard University Press, 2008), 21, 23f.
4 Cf. Almuth Grésillon, *Literarische Handschriften: Einführung in die "critique génétique"* (Bern: Peter Lang, 1999), 222.
5 Hellingrath quoted in Ute Oelmann, "Norbert von Hellingrath," in *Hölderlin-Handbuch: Leben – Werk – Wirkung*, ed. Johann Kreuzer (Stuttgart: J.B. Metzler, 2011), 424. Cf. Birgit Wägenbaur, "Norbert von Hellingrath und Karl Wolfskehl: Eine biographische Skizze," in *Norbert von Hellingrath und die Ästhetik der europäischen Moderne*, ed. Jürgen Brokoff, Joachim Jacob, and Marcel Lepper (Göttingen: Wallstein, 2013), 161–89. On the *Nachlass* fascination at the turn of the century, cf. Willer, *Erbfälle*, 173f. More generally, Kai Sina and Carlos Spoerhase, "Nachlassbewusstsein: Zur literaturwissenschaftlichen Erforschung seiner Entstehung und Entwicklung," *Zeitschrift für Germanistik, Neue Folge* 23 (2013): 607–23.
6 Gerhard Neumann, *Selbstversuch* (Freiburg im Breisgau: Rombach Verlag, 2018), 33. Nietzsche, *KSA*, 1988, 8: 31.

7 On the holdings, see Karl-Heinz Hahn, "Das Nietzsche-Archiv," *Nietzsche-Studien* 18 (1989): 2ff. The 111 Russian crates in Riedel, *Nietzsche in Weimar*, 157.

8 Schlechta, "Philologischer Nachbericht," 1399. Montinari to Colli, April 8, 1961, quoted in Campioni, *Leggere Nietzsche*, 255f.

9 Banfi, "Giorgio Colli," 259. The reference about the "Nietzsche Boys," for instance, may be found in Stella Cervasio, "Il fascino di Nietzsche: Gli scritti di un filosofo che diventò profeta," *La Repubblica*, July 8, 2009.

10 Montinari to Giorgio Colli, in a letter dated August 12, 1962, quoted in Campioni, *Leggere Nietzsche*, 267. Giorgio Colli to Anna Maria Musso-Colli, August 16, 1962, fondo Giorgio Colli, b. 04, fasc. 024, Archivio Mondadori.

11 Montinari in letters to Colli dated August 3, 4, and 21, 1961, quoted in Campioni, *Leggere Nietzsche*, 258, 255, 262. Wolfgang Harich, "Nietzsche und seine Brüder: Eine Streitschrift in sieben Dialogen," in *Friedrich Nietzsche: Der Wegbereiter des Faschismus*, by Wolfgang Harich, ed. Andreas Heyer (Baden-Baden: Tectum, 2019), 208.

12 Montinari to Colli in a letter dated August 21, 1961, quoted in Campioni, *Leggere Nietzsche*, 261. Cf. Helmut Holtzhauer, *Weimarer Tagesnotizen 1958–1973*, ed. Martin Holtzhauer, Konrad Kratzsch, and Rainer Krauß (Hamburg: Tredition, 2017). On the distinctiveness of this milieu, cf. Uwe Tellkamp, *The Tower: Tales from a Lost Country*, trans. Mike Mitchell (London: Penguin Books, 2016).

13 Colli to Musso-Colli, September 14, 1962. Holtzhauer "is the best one of all," writes Mazzino Montinari to Delio Cantimori, July 9, 1966, fondo Cantimori, serie carteggio, fasc. Montinari, Archivio Scuola Normale Superiore. On his close relationship with Holtzhauer, see also *Bericht des GI "Gießhübler" (Tonbandaufnahme) v. 19. 1. 1966*, cassette recording, 1966, BArch, MfS Erfurt, 542/78, A, Bundesarchiv, Stasi-Unterlagen-Archiv Berlin Mitte. For Holtzhauer's support and his own Italy plans, cf., for instance, Helmut Holtzhauer to Mazzino Montinari, January 9, 1962, fondo Montinari, cartella 9, Archivio Scuola Normale Superiore.

14 Amos Elon, *Journey through a Haunted Land: The New Germany*, trans. Michael Roloff (New York: Holt, Rinehart and Winston, 1967), 100; Amos Elon, *In einem heimgesuchten Land: Reise eines israelischen Journalisten in beide deutsche Staaten* (Munich: Kindler, 1966), 196.

15 Montinari to Colli, August 3, 1961, quoted in Campioni, *Leggere Nietzsche*, 258. Nietzsche, *CW*, 2021, 9: 234; *KSA*, 1988, 6: 283.

16 Montinari to Colli on March 14, 1964, and August 21, 1961, quoted in Campioni, *Leggere Nietzsche*, 296, 264. Cf. Colli to Musso-Colli, September 14, 1962. *Mündlicher Bericht des GI "Gießhübler" vom 16.1.1970.*

17 Nietzsche, *CW*, 2023, 6: 202; Nietzsche, *CW*, 2011, 5: 6; *KSA*, 1988, 3: 568, 17. Montinari's newspaper reading in letter to Cantimori, July 9, 1966. Conversations with Montinari are recorded in Holtzhauer, *Weimarer Tagesnotizen 1958–1973*, passim. Regarding Montinari's remove from the present, see also Matthias Steinbach, "'Der Donnerer hinter der Mauer': Nietzsche-Lesarten und -Orte in der DDR," in *"Ins Nichts mit ihm!" Ins Nichts mit ihm? Zur Rezeption Friedrich Nietzsches in der DDR* (Berlin: "Helle Panke" e.V. – Rosa-Luxemburg-Stiftung Berlin, 2016), 15.

18 Giorgio Colli to Anna Maria Musso-Colli, September 13, 1962, fondo Giorgio Colli, b. 04, fasc. 024, Archivio Mondadori; Colli to Musso-Colli, September 14, 1962; Giorgio Colli to Anna Maria Musso-Colli, September 18, 1962, fondo Giorgio Colli, b. 04, fasc. 024, Archivio Mondadori; Giorgio Colli to Anna Maria Musso-Colli, September 19, 1963, fondo Giorgio Colli, b. 04, fasc. 025, Archivio Mondadori; Giorgio Colli to Anna Maria Musso-Colli, August 24, 1964, fondo Giorgio Colli, b. 04, fasc. 026, Archivio Mondadori; Giorgio Colli to Anna Maria Musso-Colli, September 6, 1966, fondo Giorgio Colli, b. 04, fasc. 028, Archivio Mondadori. Colli, *La Ragione errabonda*, 195.

19 Giorgio Colli to Anna Maria Musso-Colli, April 16, 1963, fondo Giorgio Colli, b. 04, fasc. 025, Archivio Mondadori; Giorgio Colli to Anna Maria Musso-Colli, September 23, 1963, fondo Giorgio Colli, b. 04, fasc. 025, Archivio Mondadori. Elon, *Journey through a Haunted Land*, 142.

20 Montinari's uncertainty in his letter to Colli dated April 8, 1961, quoted in Campioni, *Leggere Nietzsche*, 255f. Regarding criticism of Schlechta, cf. Mazzino Montinari, "Vorwort," in *Sämtliche Werke: Kritische Studienausgabe*, by Friedrich Nietzsche, ed. Giorgio Colli and Mazzino Montinari, vol. 14 (Munich/Berlin: Deutscher Taschenbuch-Verlag, 1988), 13.

21 Delio Cantimori to Montinari, August 26, 1961, quoted in Giuliano Campioni, "'Der Karren unserer Arbeit . . .': Sechzehn Briefe von Mazzino Montinari an Delio Cantimori," *Nietzsche-Studien* 36 (2007): 61. Traces of Montinari's engagement with editorial philology are scattered across his entire *Nachlass*.

22 Nietzsche, *KSA*, 1988, 8: 14. Karl Lachmann, *Ausgaben classischer Werke*

darf jeder nachdrucken: Eine Warnung für Herausgeber (Berlin: W. Besser, 1841), 14. On Lachmann's philology, see Sebastiano Timpanaro, *The Genesis of Lachmann's Method*, ed. and trans. Glenn W. Most (Chicago: University of Chicago Press, 2005); Wegmann, "Was heißt einen 'klassischen' Text lesen?," 399–419; Hans-Gert Roloff, "Karl Lachmann, seine Methode und die Folgen," in *Geschichte der Editionsverfahren vom Altertum bis zur Gegenwart im Überblick*, ed. Hans-Gert Roloff (Berlin: Weidler, 2003), 63–81.

23 Montinari, "Vorwort," 11. The bottom line in Mazzino Montinari, "Nietzsches Nachlaß von 1885 bis 1888 oder Textkritik und Wille zur Macht," in *Nietzsche lesen*, by Mazzino Montinari (Berlin: De Gruyter, 1982), 118.

24 Montinari to Colli, August 21, 1961, quoted in Campioni, *Leggere Nietzsche*, 263f.

25 On these two different conceptions, cf. Montinari, "Nietzsches Nachlaß von 1885 bis 1888 oder Textkritik und Wille zur Macht," 92. Karl Lachmann, *Kleinere Schriften zur deutschen Philologie*, ed. Karl Müllenhoff (Berlin: Reimer, 1876), 566. Wilhelm Dilthey, "Archive für Literatur," in *Zur Geistesgeschichte des 19. Jahrhunderts*, by Wilhelm Dilthey, ed. Ulrich Herrmann, *Gesammelte Schriften* (Göttingen: Vandenhoeck & Ruprecht, 1991), 6. Kaufmann quoted in "A Book for Thinking," 501. For the complementary notion of modern literature as "craft," cf. Roland Barthes, *Writing Degree Zero*, trans. Annette Lavers and Colin Smith (New York: Hill & Wang, 1968), 62–6.

26 Beißner quoted in Grésillon, *Literarische Handschriften*, 226.

27 Montinari, "L'onorevole arte di leggere Nietzsche," 338. Montinari also deals with the *critica delle varianti* of the Italian philologist Gianfranco Contini – see the corresponding excerpts in fondo Montinari, cartella 39, Archivio Scuola Normale.

28 Mazzino Montinari to Helmut Holtzhauer, October 10, 1962, fondo Colli, b. 34, fasc. 185.003, Archivio Mondadori. Mazzino Montinari, manuscript page (n.d.), fondo Montinari, cartella 8, Archivio Scuola Normale Superiore. See also Mazzino Montinari to Giorgio Colli, August 3, 1969, fondo Montinari, cartella 13, Archivio Scuola Normale Superiore: "There is something unsettling about Nietzsche's extreme clarity unto the end regarding what he wanted to say, even down to the typographical details."

29 Mazzino Montinari to Giorgio Colli, August 17 and October 14, 1963, August 21, 1961, and August 22, 1963, quoted in Campioni, *Leggere Nietzsche*, 279, 285, 264, 281. Montinari to Colli, November 17, 1967. Mazzino Montinari to Giorgio Colli, October 7, 1963, fondo Colli, b. 34, fasc. 185.003, Archivio Mondadori.

30 Cf. Cesare Cases, "Gli incontri romani con Mazzino e Codino," in *L'impegno di una generazione: Il gruppo di Lucca dal Liceo Machiavelli alla Normale nel clima del Dopoguerra*, ed. Mario Mirri, Renzo Sabbatini, and Luigi Imbasciati (Milan: FrancoAngeli, 2014), 68. On nineteenth-century historical erudition as a "religion of the text," see Cerquiglini, *In Praise of the Variant*, 1.

31 Mazzino Montinari to Giorgio Colli, October 14, 1963, quoted in Campioni, *Leggere Nietzsche*, 285. Cf. also Montinari to Colli, November 11, 1963, quoted in Campioni, *Leggere Nietzsche*, 291f.; The "finicky aesthete" in a private note dated May 29, 1967, quoted in Campioni, "Mazzino Montinari," liii. On the dramatic structure of pietistic confessional literature, cf. Michael Multhammer, "Benjamin von Stuckrad-Barres Bekenntnisse," *Merkur* 811 (2016): 67–71.

32 Gött quoted in Andreas Urs Sommer, *Nietzsche und die Folgen* (Stuttgart: J.B. Metzler, 2017), 113. Mann, *Nietzsche's Philosophy in the Light of Contemporary Events*, 33. Jean-François Lyotard, "Notes on the Return and Capital," trans. Roger McKeon, *Semiotext(e)* 3, no. 1 (1978): 44–53. Montinari quoted in Campioni, "Der Karren unserer Arbeit ...," 70.

33 Mazzino Montinari to Giorgio Colli, August 26, October 16, and October 23, 1962, quoted in Campioni, *Leggere Nietzsche*, 269, 272, 274. Incidentally, the existence of Thermos canisters in the GDR is a sign that the standard of living improved considerably here, too, in the 1960s. Cf. Ulrich Herbert, *A History of Twentieth-Century Germany*, trans. Ben Fowkes (New York: Oxford University Press, 2019), 669ff. Montinari to Colli, November 15, August 22, and November 11, 1963, quoted in Campioni, *Leggere Nietzsche*, 281, 292f.

34 Quoted from Campioni, "Mazzino Montinari," xxiv. Montinari to Colli, May 9, 1962. Montinari to Colli, August 22, 1963, quoted in Campioni, *Leggere Nietzsche*, 281. On philology's "pathos of correctness," cf. Ritter, *Notizhefte*, 75. On "trust in the factual nature of texts" as "one of the moral principles of our modernity," see Cerquiglini, *In Praise of the Variant*, 1f.

35 Nietzsche, *CW*, 2014, 8: 338, 5; *KSA*, 1988, 5: 399, 15. On Mussolini,

see Rosarita Russo, "Die Anfänge der Nietzsche-Rezeption in Italien," in *Widersprüche: Zur frühen Nietzsche-Rezeption*, ed. Andreas Schirmer and Rüdiger Schmidt (Weimar: Hermann Böhlaus Nachfolger, 2000), 241f.

36 Nietzsche, *CW*, 2011, 5: 224; *KSA*, 1988, 3: 265. Nietzsche, *CW*, 2014, 8: 347; *KSA*, 1988, 5: 409f. Nietzsche, *CW*, 2021, 9: 218; *KSA*, 1988, 6: 264. On "How the Will to Truth Overcomes Itself," cf. Karl Jaspers, *Nietzsche: An Introduction to the Understanding of His Philosophical Activity*, trans. Charles F. Wallraff and Frederick J. Schmitz (Baltimore: Johns Hopkins University Press, 1997), 209ff.

37 Montinari to Colli, May 9, 1962. On Podach, see Dieter Haller, "Short Portrait: Erich Podach," 2011, Interviews with German Anthropologists: http://www.germananthropology.com/short-portrait/erich-podach/256. A critique of Podach's psychologizing Nietzsche interpretation in Eckhard Heftrich, "Die Grenzen der psychologischen Nietzsche-Erklärung," *Revue Internationale de Philosophie* 18 (1964): 74–90.

38 Mazzino Montinari to Giorgio Colli, April 26, 1962, fondo Colli, b. 32, fasc. 185.003, Archivio Mondadori.

39 Erich Podach to Giorgio Colli, April 22, 1962, fondo Colli, b. 34, fasc. 185.002, Archivio Mondadori. Mazzino Montinari to Giorgio Colli, August 17, 1963, quoted in Campioni, *Leggere Nietzsche*, 280. Montinari to Colli, April 26, 1962. Regarding Podach's book, see Heftrich, "Die Grenzen der psychologischen Nietzsche-Erklärung," 79.

40 On the founding of Adelphi, see Banfi, "Giorgio Colli," 261. He was "stunned" and unable to perceive the new state of affairs, Colli wrote when the definitive acceptance from Gallimard finally arrived in August 1962, whereby the financing for their edition was assured for the first time. Giorgio Colli to Mazzino Montinari, August 20, 1962, fondo Colli, b. 34, fasc. 185.002, Archivio Mondadori.

41 Erich Podach to Mazzino Montinari, August 29, 1962, fondo Montinari, cartella 6, Archivio Scuola Normale. Montinari to Colli, April 26, 1962. Mazzino Montinari to Erich Podach, October 27, 1963, fondo Colli, b. 35, fasc. 190, Archivio Mondadori. For Montinari's "literal" reading, see also Groddeck, "Nietzsche lesen."

42 Campano quoted in Anthony Grafton, "Humanist Philologies: Texts, Antiquities, and Their Scholarly Transformations in the Early Modern West," in *World Philology*, ed. Sheldon Pollock, Benjamin A. Elman, and Ku-ming Kevin Chang (Cambridge, MA: Harvard University Press, 2015),

164, cf. 168. On the long tradition of collating in textual criticism, see also Timpanaro, *The Genesis of Lachmann's Method*, 45ff.

43 Nietzsche, *KSA*, 1988, 8: 68, 44. On Valla, see Grafton, "Humanist Philologies," 171. On du Tillet, see Jacob Soll, "Empirical History and the Transformation of Political Criticism in France from Bodin to Bayle," *Journal of the History of Ideas* 64 (2003): 298ff. On the relationship between philological and historical criticism, see Hans Gerhard Senger, "Die historisch-kritische Edition historisch-kritisch betrachtet," in *Buchstabe und Geist: Zur Überlieferung und Edition philosophischer Texte*, ed. Walter Jaeschke et al. (Hamburg: F. Meiner, 1987), 1–20.

44 Nietzsche, *CW*, 2023, 6: 138; *KSA*, 1988, 3: 491. On the role of Protestantism, cf. Grafton, "Humanist Philologies," 161; Timpanaro, *The Genesis of Lachmann's Method*, 58ff. On biblical philology, see Koselleck, *Critique and Crisis*, 105ff.; Anthony Grafton, "Prolegomena to Friedrich August Wolf," *Journal of the Warburg and Courtauld Institutes* 44 (1981): 120. On the Protestant scriptural fixation as a "trap," see Eckhard Nordhofen, "Die Tragik des Protestantismus," *Merkur* 834 (2019): 71–9.

45 Ernst Cassirer, *The Philosophy of the Enlightenment*, trans. Fritz C.A. Koelln and James P. Pettegrove (Princeton: Princeton University Press, 2009), 207, 205. See also Anthony Grafton, "The Footnote from De Thou to Ranke," *History and Theory* 33 (1994): 53–76.

46 Pierre Bayle, "Project for a Critical Dictionary," in *Political Writings*, by Pierre Bayle, ed. and trans. Sally L. Jenkinson (Cambridge: Cambridge University Press, 2000), 10ff., 14.

47 Nietzsche, *CW*, 2020, 16: 376; *KSA*, 1988, 12: 315, 140. Nietzsche, *CW*, 2021, 9: 190; *KSA*, 1988, 6: 233. Cf. Colli, *Dopo Nietzsche*, 196: "Nietzsche said everything, and the opposite of everything."

48 Nietzsche, *CW*, 1997, 3: 17, 184; *KSA*, 1988, 2: 25, 223. Cf. Nietzsche, *CW*, 2023, 6: 241ff.; *KSA*, 1988, 3: 614ff., on the opposition between academic and literary intelligence. Hendrik Birus, "'Wir Philologen' … Überlegungen zu Nietzsches Begriff der Interpretation," *Revue Internationale de Philosophie* 38 (1984): 373–95. On the translation of the philological method into philosophy, see also Benne, *Nietzsche und die historisch-kritische Philologie*, especially 101.

49 Mazzino Montinari to Giorgio Colli, August 22, 1963, quoted in Campioni, *Leggere Nietzsche*, 281. Nietzsche, *CW*, 1997, 3: 17, 264; *KSA*, 1988, 2: 25, 317. Cf. Wolfgang Müller-Lauter, "Ständige Herausforderung:

Über Mazzino Montinaris Verhältnis zu Nietzsche," *Nietzsche-Studien* 18 (1989): 37.

50 Montinari, "Nel partito non mi piace fare l'intellettuale."

51 Quoted in Luisa Mangoni, "Europa sotterranea," in *Politica e storia contemporanea: Scritti (1927–1942)*, by Delio Cantimori, ed. Luisa Mangoni (Turin: Einaudi, 1991), xli. Echoes of the historical-critical virtuosity of countless Protestant heretics in Delio Cantimori, *Eretici italiani del Cinquecento* (Florence: Sansoni, 1939), *passim*. On his predilection for Bayle, see Cesa, "Il clima culturale," 38.

52 Quoted in Mangoni, "Europa sotterranea," xlif. On Cantimori's alcohol consumption, cf. Adriano Prosperi, "'Io ci provo, ma quello degli storici sta diventando un mestiere inutile,'" *La Repubblica*, June 29, 2015.

53 On Cantimori's diagnoses, cf. Ciliberto, *Intellettuali e fascismo*, 20. Cases to Cantimori, January 16, 1957. "In the library, the usual grind continues, and we are all a bit tired," Cantimori writes Mazzino Montinari, August 26, 1962, fondo Montinari, cartella 5, Archivio Scuola Normale Superiore. On *posthistoire* see Lutz Niethammer, *Posthistoire: Has History Come to an End?*, trans. Patrick Camiller (London; New York: Verso, 1992).

54 Delio Cantimori to Mazzino Montinari, September 25, 1963, fondo Montinari, cartella 5, Archivio Scuola Normale Superiore; Delio Cantimori to Mazzino Montinari, September 14/15, 1963, fondo Montinari, cartella 5, Archivio Scuola Normale Superiore. Cantimori's identity as a craftsman quoted in Mangoni, "Europa sotterranea," xlii.

55 Mazzino Montinari to Giorgio Colli, September 29, 1967, quoted in Campioni, *Leggere Nietzsche*, 436. Montinari, "Nel partito non mi piace fare l'intellettuale."

56 Gilles Deleuze to Mazzino Montinari, November 8, 1963, fondo Montinari, cartella 8, Archivio Scuola Normale Superiore.

Chapter 5 Waiting for Foucault: Cerisy-la-Salle, 1972

1 Nietzsche, *CW*, 2021, 9: 250; *KSA*, 1988, 6: 301. On the preestablished harmony between Nietzsche and his French readers, cf. Mazzino Montinari, "Nietzsche in Cosmopolis: Französisch–deutsche Wechselbeziehungen in der Décadence," *Frankfurter Allgemeine Zeitung*, July 19, 1986; Mazzino Montinari, "Aufgaben der Nietzsche-Forschung heute: Nietzsches Auseinandersetzung mit der französischen Literatur des 19. Jahrhunderts," in *Nietzsche heute: Die Rezeption seines Werks*

nach 1968, ed. Sigrid Bauschinger, Susan L. Cocalis, and Sara Lennox (Bern: Francke, 1988), 137–48. See also Werner Hamacher, "Echolos," in *Nietzsche aus Frankreich*, ed. Werner Hamacher (Hamburg: Europäische Verlagsanstalt, 2007), 7ff.

2 Cf. Le Rider, *Nietzsche en France*, 153ff. On Deleuze, see François Dosse, *Gilles Deleuze & Félix Guattari: Intersecting Lives*, trans. Deborah Glassman (New York: Columbia University Press, 2010), 129.

3 Giorgio Colli to Mazzino Montinari, May 20, 1964, fondo Colli, b. 34, fasc. 185.002, Archivio Mondadori. Löwith, "Rezension von Erich Podach," 534. Giorgio Colli to Mazzino Montinari, May 1, 1964, fondo Colli, b. 34, fasc. 185.002, Archivio Mondadori. Colli's theory of a concerted campaign in Mazzino Montinari to Giorgio Colli, May 10, 1964, fondo Colli, b. 34, fasc. 185.004, Archivio Mondadori. On Boehm's plans for an edition, see Mazzino Montinari to Giorgio Colli, April 26, 1964, quoted in Campioni, *Leggere Nietzsche*, 309f.; Rudolf Boehm, "Le problème du 'Wille zur Macht', oeuvre posthume de Nietzsche: À propos d'une nouvelle édition," *Revue Philosophique de Louvain, Troisième série* 61 (1963): 402–34. On the Royaumont trip in general, see Giuliano Campioni, "'Die Kunst, gut zu lesen': Mazzino Montinari und das Handwerk des Philologen," *Nietzsche-Studien* 18 (1989): xliiff.

4 Montinari to Colli, May 10, 1964. Colli to Montinari, May 20, 1964.

5 Colli and Montinari, "État des textes de Nietzsche," 127, 136. Nietzsche's advice in Nietzsche, *CW*, 2021, 9: 189f.; *KSA*, 1988, 6: 233.

6 Mann, *Nietzsche's Philosophy in the Light of Contemporary Events*, 33. Kaufmann, *Nietzsche: Philosopher, Psychologist, Antichrist*, 72. At the center of Nietzsche's practical philosophy, according to Kaufmann, is "self-overcoming," the "sublimation" of desires (cf. Kaufmann, *Nietzsche*, chaps 6–8). Even his own interpretation of Nietzsche can be described as sublimating. On the metaphysical–metaphoric shift, cf. Kurt Flasch, "Und er war doch ein Zerstörer der Vernunft," *Frankfurter Allgemeine Zeitung*, February 21, 2003.

7 Gilles Deleuze, "Nietzsche," in *Pure Immanence: Essays on a Life*, by Gilles Deleuze, trans. Anne Boyman (New York: Zone Books, 2001), 92. Cf. Deleuze, "Conclusions on the Will to Power and the Eternal Return," 123f. Pierre Klossowski, "Forgetting and Anamnesis in the Experience of the Eternal Return of the Same," trans. Susan Hanson, *Semiotext(e)* 3, no. 1 (1978): 138–49. Foucault, "Nietzsche, Freud, Marx," 1998, 275.

8 Deleuze, "Conclusions on the Will to Power and the Eternal Return," 124. Giorgio Colli to Mazzino Montinari, March 17, 1968, fondo Montinari, cartella 13, Archivio Scuola Normale Superiore. Giorgio Colli to Mazzino Montinari, December 1, 1965, fondo Colli, b. 34, fasc. 186.001, Archivio Mondadori. Mazzino Montinari to Giorgio Colli, March 3, 1967, quoted in Campioni, *Leggere Nietzsche*, 403.

9 Deleuze, "Nomadic Thought," 256. Henning Ritter, "Stille Penelopearbeit: Nietzsche ist ein anderer geworden," *Frankfurter Allgemeine Zeitung*, April 21, 1993.

10 The question of interpretation is cited in Foucault, "Nietzsche, Freud, Marx," 1998, 277f. Cf. Wilhelm Dilthey, "The Essence of Philosophy," in *Selected Works*, by Wilhelm Dilthey, ed. Rudolf A. Makkreel and Frithjof Rodi, trans. John Krois and Rudolf A. Makkreel, *Ethical and World-View Philosophy*, vol. IV (Princeton: Princeton University Press, 2019), 171–247. On hermeneutics, see Hans Ulrich Gumbrecht, "Das Nicht-Hermeneutische: Skizze einer Genealogie," in *Präsenz*, by Hans Ulrich Gumbrecht, ed. Jürgen Klein (Frankfurt am Main: Suhrkamp, 2019), 190–209; Nibras Chehayed, "Nietzsche and Gadamer on Truth and Interpretation," *The New Centennial Review* 19 (2019): 251–72. On Jacob Taubes's expectations for hermeneutics, see Jacob Taubes, "Einleitende Wort zum Hermeneutische Colloquium mit Herrn Professor Hans Georg Gadamer am 28. 11. 1966" (typescript, November 28, 1966), Nachlass Jacob Taubes, Zentrum für Literatur- und Kulturforschung Berlin.

11 Wahl quoted in Michel Foucault, "Nietzsche, Freud, Marx," in *Dits et écrits: 1954–1988*, ed. Daniel Defert and François Ewald, vol. 1: *1954–1969* (Paris: Gallimard, 1994), 576. Herbert Schnädelbach, "Morbus hermeneuticus: Thesen über eine philosophische Krankheit," in *Vernunft und Geschichte: Vorträge und Abhandlungen*, by Herbert Schnädelbach (Frankfurt am Main: Suhrkamp, 1987), 279–84. The "systems of discursive multiplication" in Friedrich Kittler, "Ein Verwaiser," in *Anschlüsse: Versuche nach Michel Foucault*, ed. Gesa Dane (Tübingen: Edition Diskord, 1985), 142. Cf. Michel Foucault, *The Order of Things: An Archaeology of the Human Sciences*, trans. Alan Sheridan (New York: Vintage Books, 1994), 297f.; Birus, "'Wir Philologen,'" 374ff. Jacob Taubes to Jürgen Habermas, February 17, 1967, Nachlass Jabob Taubes, Zentrum für Literatur- und Kulturforschung Berlin. Susan Sontag, "Against Interpretation," in *Essays of the 1960s & 70s*, ed. David Rieff (New York: The Library of America, 2013), 18.

12 Colli, *Distanz und Pathos*, 12. Sontag, "Against Interpretation," 13, 14f. In Sontag's image of "mass ravishment," incidentally, one can also recognize an echo of her reading of Nietzsche. In one of *his* tirades against the intemperance of interpreters, Nietzsche writes in *Human, All Too Human*: "The worst readers are those who behave like plundering soldiers: they take the few things they can use, leave the rest dirty and disordered, and slander the whole" (Nietzsche, *CW*, 2013, 4: 60; *KSA*, 1988, 2: 436).

13 Colli writes in hindsight to Claude Gallimard, August 19, 1975, fondo Colli, b. 29, fasc. 069, Archivio Mondadori.

14 Mazzino Montinari to Giorgio Colli, March 14, 1964, quoted in Campioni, *Leggere Nietzsche*, 296. Colli to Musso-Colli, September 14, 1962; Giorgio Colli to Anna Maria Musso-Colli, September 1, 1964, fondo Giorgio Colli, b. 04, fasc. 026, Archivio Mondadori.

15 Giorgio Colli to Anna Maria Musso-Colli, September 9, 1964, fondo Giorgio Colli, b. 04, fasc. 026, Archivio Mondadori. Mazzino Montinari to Giorgio Colli, September 27, 1964, fondo Colli, b. 34, fasc. 185.004, Archivio Mondadori; Mazzino Montinari to Giorgio Colli, October 26, 1964, fondo Colli, b. 34, fasc. 185.004, Archivio Mondadori. Giorgio Colli to Mazzino Montinari, October 27, 1964, fondo Colli, b. 34, fasc. 185.002, Archivio Mondadori; Giorgio Colli to Mazzino Montinari, November 7, 1964, fondo Colli, b. 34, fasc. 185.002, Archivio Mondadori.

16 Montinari, manuscript page; Montinari to Colli, October 26, 1964; Mazzino Montinari to Giorgio Colli, December 23, 1964, fondo Colli, b. 34, fasc. 185.004, Archivio Mondadori; Mazzino Montinari to Giorgio Colli, May 11, 1965, fondo Colli, b. 34, fasc. 186.002, Archivio Mondadori. Giorgio Colli to Mazzino Montinari, May 17, 1965, fondo Colli, b. 34, fasc. 186.001, Archivio Mondadori; cf. Giorgio Colli to Mazzino Montinari, May 18, 1965, fondo Colli, b. 34, fasc. 186.001, Archivio Mondadori.

17 Mazzino Montinari to Giorgio Colli, October 23, 1962, fondo Colli, b. 32, fasc. 185.003, Archivio Mondadori. Mazzino Montinari to Giorgio Colli, April 13, 1964, quoted in Campioni, *Leggere Nietzsche*, 304. Walter Boehlich to Karl Löwith, January 19, 1965, fondo Colli, b. 31, fasc. 104, Archivio Mondadori. Siegfried Unseld to Luciano Foà, January 20, 1965, fondo Colli, b. 30, fasc. 086, Archivio Mondadori. On the atmosphere of the negotiations, cf. Siegfried Unseld to Giorgio Colli, August 27, 1964, fondo Colli, b. 30, fasc. 086, Archivio Mondadori. Giorgio Colli to Karl Löwith, February 6, 1965, fondo Colli, b. 31, fasc. 104, Archivio Mondadori.

18 Mazzino Montinari to Giorgio Colli, January 28, 1965, fondo Colli, b. 34, fasc. 186.002, Archivio Mondadori. Löwith quoted in Mazzino Montinari to Giorgio Colli, October 14, 1965, quoted in Campioni, *Leggere Nietzsche*, 376. Cf. Mazzino Montinari to Giorgio Colli, January 5, 1966, fondo Colli, b. 34, fasc. 185.003, Archivio Mondadori; Mazzino Montinari to Giorgio Colli, January 14, 1966, fondo Colli, b. 34, fasc. 185.003, Archivio Mondadori.

19 Mazzino Montinari to Giorgio Colli, June 13, 1965, fondo Colli, b. 34, fasc. 186.002, Archivio Mondadori. Mazzino Montinari to Giorgio Colli, August 2, 1965, quoted in Campioni, *Leggere Nietzsche*, 373. On the negotiations, cf. Montinari to Colli, May 11, 1965; Montinari to Colli, June 13, 1965. See also Cases, "Der Großherzog von Weimar," 24.

20 Cf. Cases, "Der Großherzog von Weimar," 23f; Karl-Heinz Hahn, "Nachruf auf Professor Dr. Mazzino Montinari," *Goethe-Jahrbuch* 104 (1987): 389.

21 Mazzino Montinari to "Dino," November 28, 1969, fondo Montinari, cartella 36, Archivio Scuola Normale Superiore. Cf. Mazzino Montinari to Giorgio Colli, January 15, 1968, fondo Montinari, cartella 13, Archivio Scuola Normale Superiore. Wolfgang Harich, "Rezension von Lukács, Die Zerstörung der Vernunft," *Deutsche Zeitschrift für Philosophie* 3 (1955): 135. On his reception history in the GDR, cf. Riedel, *Nietzsche in Weimar*, 208ff. See also Jürgen Staszak, "Beobachtungen an der Wirkungsweise des Lukácsschen Literaturkonzepts," *Weimarer Beiträge* 31 (1985): 573–9.

22 Cf. Matthias Steinbach, *"Also sprach Sarah Tustra": Nietzsches sozialistische Irrfahrten* (Halle: Mitteldeutscher Verlag, 2020), 227f.

23 Cf. Steinbach, "Der Donnerer hinter der Mauer."

24 *Bericht des GI "Gießhübler" (Tonbandaufnahme) v. 19. 1. 1966.*

25 *Bericht des GI "Gießhübler" (Tonbandaufnahme) v. 19. 1. 1966*, 50. Cf. Steinbach, *"Also sprach Sarah Tustra,"* 162.

26 "Vorschlag zur Anwerbung" (December 16, 1963), 4, 6, BArch, MfS Erfurt, 542/78, A, Bundesarchiv, Stasi-Unterlagen-Archiv Berlin Mitte. Cf. GI "Schaller," "Bericht" (March 12, 1963), 22, BArch, MfS Erfurt, 542/78, I, Bundesarchiv, Stasi-Unterlagen-Archiv Berlin Mitte; "Bericht über durchgeführte Werbung" (April 10, 1964), 58–60, BArch, MfS Erfurt, 542/78, I, Bundesarchiv, Stasi-Unterlagen-Archiv Berlin Mitte.

27 "Treffbericht" (November 12, 1970), 10, BArch, MfS Erfurt, 542/78, II, Bundesarchiv, Stasi-Unterlagen-Archiv Berlin Mitte.

28 Montinari to Cantimori, July 9, 1966. On the inadequacy of the older

apparatuses, cf. Mazzino Montinari, "Glanz und Elend der philologischen Arbeit," *Deutsche Akademie für Sprache und Dichtung: Jahrbuch* 1985 (1986): 57.

29 Nietzsche, *CW*, 2021, 9: 270; *KSA*, 1988, 6: 326. Nietzsche, *CW*, 2023, 6: 241; *KSA*, 1988, 3: 614. Mazzino Montinari to Giorgio Colli, June 25, 1966, quoted in Campioni, "'Die Kunst, gut zu lesen,'" xlii. Wagner quoted in Mazzino Montinari, "Nietzsche und Wagner vor hundert Jahren," in *Nietzsche lesen*, by Mazzino Montinari (Berlin: De Gruyter, 1982), 45, cf. 52. On Montinari's study of source material, cf. Campioni, "Die Kunst, gut zu lesen," xlii–xlix.

30 Quoted in Campioni, "'Die Kunst, gut zu lesen,'" xlvii. Mazzino Montinari to Giorgio Colli, December 14, 1964, fondo Colli, b. 34, fasc. 185.004, Archivio Mondadori. Mazzino Montinari to Giorgio Colli, September 10, 1967, quoted in Campioni, *Leggere Nietzsche*, 434. Mazzino Montinari to Delio Cantimori, November 4, 1963, quoted in Campioni, "Der Karren unserer Arbeit . . .," 75.

31 Quoted in Campioni, "Die Kunst, gut zu lesen," xlix, xlvii. Montinari, "Aufgaben der Nietzsche-Forschung heute," 137f. On the broadening of the concept of the preliminary stage, cf. Ritter, "Tanz ohne Ketten."

32 Giorgio Colli to Mazzino Montinari, February 7, 1968, fondo Montinari, cartella 18, Archivio Scuola Normale Superiore; Giorgio Colli to Mazzino Montinari, November 16, 1965, fondo Montinari, cartella 13, Archivio Scuola Normale Superiore; Giorgio Colli to Mazzino Montinari, September 24, 1967, fondo Montinari, cartella 18, Archivio Scuola Normale Superiore; Giorgio Colli to Mazzino Montinari, October 5, 1967, fondo Montinari, cartella 18, Archivio Scuola Normale Superiore; Giorgio Colli to Mazzino Montinari, November 13, 1967, fondo Montinari, cartella 18, Archivio Scuola Normale Superiore. Wolfgang Müller-Lauter, a professor of philosophy at the Kirchliche Hochschule Berlin (Ecclesiastical University Berlin), was intimately involved in the *Kritische Gesamtausgabe* as an advisor to De Gruyter. Initial academic plans were already mentioned by Montinari in a letter to Giorgio Colli, September 23, 1962, fondo Colli, b. 32, fasc. 185.003, Archivio Mondadori.

33 Giorgio Colli to Mazzino Montinari, June 25, 1967, fondo Montinari, cartella 18, Archivio Scuola Normale Superiore. Before publication: "Michel Foucault et Gilles Deleuze veulent rendre à Nietzsche son vrai visage," *Le Figaro*, September 15, 1966. On the publication date: "L'éclat de

rire de Nietzsche (Entretien avec Gilles Deleuze)," *Le Nouvel Observateur*, April 5, 1967; "La publication des Oeuvres complètes de Nietzsche (Entretien avec Michel Foucault)," *Le Monde*, May 24, 1967. In the first volume: Michel Foucault and Gilles Deleuze, "Introduction générale," in *Dits et écrits: 1954–1988*, ed. Daniel Defert and François Ewald, vol. 1: *1954–1969* (Paris: Gallimard, 1994), 561–4.

34 Foucault, *The Order of Things*, 263, 305, 298. "Michel Foucault et Gilles Deleuze veulent rendre à Nietzsche son vrai visage." Gallimard's disinterest in Colli to Montinari, December 1, 1965.

35 "La publication des Oeuvres complètes de Nietzsche (Entretien avec Michel Foucault)." Jacques Derrida, *Of Grammatology*, trans. Gayatri Chakravorty Spivak (Baltimore: Johns Hopkins University Press, 1998), 18. Cf. Jacques Derrida, "Ellipsis," in *Writing and Difference*, trans. Alan Bass (Chicago: University of Chicago Press, 1978), 294f. Maurice Blanchot, *The Infinite Conversation*, trans. Susan Hanson (Minneapolis: University of Minnesota Press, 1993), 166. Gilles Deleuze, "On Nietzsche and the Image of Thought," in *Desert Islands and Other Texts: 1953–1974*, by Gilles Deleuze, ed. David Lapoujade, trans. Michael Taormina (Los Angeles: Semiotext(e), 2004), 141. Philippe Lacoue-Labarthe, "The Detour," in *The Subject of Philosophy*, ed. Thomas Trezise, trans. Thomas Trezise et al. (Minneapolis: University of Minnesota Press, 1993), 17f. Rüdiger Schmidt, "Die verratenen Gedanken: Wie Nietzsche erst gefälscht und dann rekonstruiert wurde," *Süddeutsche Zeitung*, November 24/5, 2001. On Nietzsche's "philologization" in France, cf. Wegmann, "Was heißt einen 'klassischen' Text lesen?," 420. On the inability to end books as a symptom of twentieth-century thought, see Rötzer, "Jacob Taubes," 311.

36 Giorgio Colli to Mazzino Montinari, March 12, 1967, fondo Montinari, cartella 18, Archivio Scuola Normale Superiore. Jean Beaufret, "Les inédits de Nietzsche," *Le Monde*, June 7, 1967. Giorgio Colli and Mazzino Montinari, "Principes des éditeurs," in *Gai Savoir: Fragments posthumes 1881–1882*, by Friedrich Nietzsche, ed. Giorgio Colli and Mazzino Montinari, trans. Pierre Klossowski (Paris: Gallimard, 1967), 294. Jean-Michel Palmier, "La réédition d'"Humain, trop humain,'" *Le Monde*, July 7, 1969. On the lapse in the afterword, cf. Colli to Gallimard, August 19, 1975. On Beaufret's role, see Lutz Hachmeister, *Heideggers Testament: Der Philosoph, der Spiegel und die SS* (Berlin: Propyläen, 2015), 79.

37 On the challenging collaboration, see Giorgio Colli to Mazzino Montinari,

January 11, 1966, fondo Colli, b. 34, fasc. 186.001, Archivio Mondadori. Colli to Gallimard, August 19, 1975. Dionys Mascolo to Mazzino Montinari, October 7, 1969, fondo Montinari, cartella 19, Archivio Scuola Normale Superiore. Dionys Mascolo to Giorgio Colli, April 1, 1968, fondo Colli, b. 29, fasc. 069, Archivio Mondadori. See also Dionys Mascolo to Giorgio Colli, October 16, 1975, fondo Colli, b. 29, fasc. 069, Archivio Mondadori.

38 Montinari to Holtzhauer, October 10, 1962.

39 Foucault, "What Is an Author?," 207f.

40 Foucault, "What Is an Author?," 205f., 221.

41 Julia Kristeva, "Word, Dialogue and Novel," in *The Kristeva Reader*, ed. Toril Moi, trans. Alice Jardine, Thomas Gora, and Léon S. Roudiez (New York: Columbia University Press, 1986), 37. Roland Barthes, "The Death of the Author," in *Image, Music, Text: Essays*, trans. Stephen Heath (New York: Hill & Wang, 2007), 148, 146.

42 Friedrich Nietzsche, "On Truth and Lie in an Extra-Moral Sense," in *Writings from the Early Notebooks*, ed. Raymond Geuss and Alexander Nehamas, trans. Ladislaus Löb (Cambridge: Cambridge University Press, 2009), 257; *KSA*, 1988, 1: 880. The "scribbling" in Nietzsche's letter to Heinrich Köselitz, August 1881, quoted in Pannwitz, "Nietzsche-Philologie?," 1082. The translation mentioned is Friedrich Nietzsche, "Rhétorique et langage: Textes traduits, présentés et annotés par Philippe Lacoue-Labarthe et Jean-Luc Nancy," *Poétique* 5 (1971): 99–130. Cf. Lacoue-Labarthe, "The Detour," 16f., 25. Sarah Kofman, "Le/les 'concepts' de culture dans les 'Intempestives' ou la double dissimulation," in *Nietzsche aujourd'hui*, ed. Centre culturel international de Cerisy-la-Salle, vol. 2: *Passion* (Paris: Union générale d'éditions, 1973), 146; Ritter, "Stille Penelopearbeit."

43 Gerhard Neumann, "Werk oder Schrift? Vorüberlegungen zur Edition von Kafkas 'Bericht für eine Akademie,'" in *Edition und Interpretation*, ed. Louis Hay and Winfried Woesler (Bern: Peter Lang, 1982), 163. Mazzino Montinari to Giorgio Colli, May 18, 1967, quoted in Campioni, *Leggere Nietzsche*, 420. Montinari to Oloff-Montinari, July 1, 1971. Montinari to Colli, May 7, 1967, quoted in Campioni, *Leggere Nietzsche*, 417. Mazzino Montinari to Giorgio Colli, October 28, 1968, fondo Montinari, cartella 13, Archivio Scuola Normale Superiore. For examples of his decipherings of *Zarathustra*, see Mazzino Montinari, "Zum Verhältnis

Lektüre – Nachlaß – Werk bei Nietzsche," *Editio* 1 (1987): 245–9. Reports from Berlin in, for example, Mazzino Montinari to Giorgio Colli, August 15, 1967, fondo Montinari, cartella 13, Archivio Scuola Normale Superiore; Mazzino Montinari to Sigrid Oloff-Montinari, June 26, 1971, fondo Montinari, cartella 20, Archivio Scuola Normale Superiore.

44 Nietzsche, *CW*, 2021, 9: 221; *KSA*, 1988, 6: 268. Mazzino Montinari to Giorgio Colli, June 4, 1969, fondo Montinari, cartella 13, Archivio Scuola Normale Superiore; Mazzino Montinari to Giorgio Colli, July 25, 1969, fondo Montinari, cartella 13, Archivio Scuola Normale Superiore. The reconstruction of Nietzsche's library, including annotations and dog-eared corners, in fact later became a multi-year research project; cf. Giuliani Campioni, ed., *Nietzsches persönliche Bibliothek* (Berlin: De Gruyter, 2003). On this project, see Ulrich Raulff, "Das Labyrinth des Lesens und das Eselsohr der Philologie," *Süddeutsche Zeitung*, October 4, 2003.

45 Mazzino Montinari to Giorgio Colli, September 10, 1967, quoted in Campioni, *Leggere Nietzsche*, 434. Giorgio Colli to Mazzino Montinari, August 7, 1969, fondo Montinari, cartella 18, Archivio Scuola Normale Superiore. Mazzino Montinari to Giorgio Colli, August 28, 1969, fondo Montinari, cartella 13, Archivio Scuola Normale Superiore; Mazzino Montinari to Giorgio Colli, June 4, 1970, fondo Montinari, cartella 13, Archivio Scuola Normale Superiore. On Colli's dropping out, cf. Montinari to Colli, December 13, 1967, quoted in Campioni, *Leggere Nietzsche*, 446, and Giorgio Colli to Mazzino Montinari, March 31, 1969, fondo Montinari, cartella 18, Archivio Scuola Normale Superiore. See also Montinari, "Erinnerung an Giorgio Colli," 171.

46 Montinari to Colli, August 28, 1969. *Mündlicher Bericht des GI "Gießhübler" vom 16.1.1970*, 95. *Mündlicher Bericht des IMS "Gießhübler" vom 11.11.1970*, 1970, 11, BArch, MfS Erfurt, 542/78, II, Bundesarchiv, Stasi-Unterlagen-Archiv Berlin Mitte. Regarding their preparations for return, see, for example, the correspondence in fondo Montinari, cartella 36, Archivio Scuola Normale.

47 Colli to Gallimard, August 19, 1975. Montinari to Colli, September 29, 1967, quoted in Campioni, *Leggere Nietzsche*, 437.

48 Lyotard, "Notes on the Return and Capital," 52f. Deleuze, "Nomadic Thought," 259, 252, 254, 256, 260. Barthes, "The Death of the Author," 145, 144. Deleuze, "On Nietzsche and the Image of Thought," 138, cf. 140f.

49 Jacques Derrida, *Spurs: Nietzsche's Styles/Éperons: Les Styles de Nietzsche*,
    trans. Barbara Harlow (Chicago: University of Chicago Press, 1979), 131,
    123, 127, 125, 105. Cf. Ulrich J. Beil, "'Anführungszeichen': Anmerkungen
    zur Literaturtheorie von Jacques Derrida und Paul de Man," *Pandaemonium
    Germanicum* 6 (2002): 17–46. As Andreas Urs Sommer discovered, the
    "*Regenschirm*" sentence is a quotation from Grandville's satiric novel *Un
    autre monde* (1844). Cf. Andreas Urs Sommer, *Band 5.1 Kommentar zu
    Nietzsches "Jenseits von Gut und Böse"* (Berlin: De Gruyter, 2016), 796. I
    thank Bettina Wahrig-Schmidt for the reference.
50 Roos, "Règles pour une lecture philologique de Nietzsche," 291, 289, 294,
    285. The assessment of Maurice Gandillac, "Le colloque de Cerisy-la-
    Salle," *Nietzsche-Studien* 4 (1975): 328.
51 All quotations from Roos, "Règles pour une lecture philologique de
    Nietzsche," 321ff. On philology as a disciplining science, cf. Neumann,
    "Werk oder Schrift?," 166; Cerquiglini, *In Praise of the Variant*, 50.
52 Foucault, "Prison Talk," 53f. On the reader as poacher, cf. Philipp Felsch,
    "Der Leser als Partisan," *Zeitschrift für Ideengeschichte* 6 (2012): 35–49.

Chapter 6 Burn after Reading: Berlin, 1985

1 Sigrid Oloff-Montinari, "Begründung meines Antrages zur Übersiedlung
   nach Italien," January 27, 1970, fondo Montinari, cartella 36, Archivio
   Scuola Normale Superiore.
2 Cf. Judt, *Postwar*, 473. For a comparison between the Italian and the West
   German Left, cf. Seibt, "Freigängerbriefe," 7.
3 Mazzino Montinari, "Intervento al dibattito sulla Germania" (typescript,
   November 1970), fondo Montinari, cartella 39, Archivio Scuola Normale
   Superiore. On his academic career in Italy, see Campioni, "'Die Kunst, gut
   zu lesen,'" xixff. On his conception of politics, see Montinari, "Nel partito
   non mi piace fare l'intellettuale." On the Historical Compromise, see Judt,
   Postwar, 495f.
4 Montinari, "Delio Cantimori e Nietzsche," 105. Claudio Magris, "'Ich bin
   die Einsamkeit als Mensch': Nietzsche und die neue Linke," *Süddeutsche
   Zeitung*, January 3/4, 1981. On Esposti, cf. Alberto Moravia to Mazzino
   Montinari, n.d., fondo Montinari, cartella 19, Archivio Scuola Normale.
   On the Nietzsche reception among leftwing and rightwing terrorists, see
   Alessandro Orsini, *Anatomy of the Red Brigades: The Religious Mind-Set
   of Modern Terrorists* (Ithaca, NY: Cornell University Press, 2011), 268f.

The "Nietzscheanization of the Left" features in Alan Bloom, *The Closing of the American Mind* (New York: Simon & Schuster, 1987), 217ff.

5 Nietzsche, *CW*, 2021, 9: 17f.; *KSA*, 1988, 6: 27.

6 Montinari, "Delio Cantimori e Nietzsche," 105. In a personal note, Montinari writes in 1978: "Nietzsche's current success is, all things considered, a phenomenon to be judged negatively. He fits into a general disorientation that has reached a critical stage. The disoriented believe Nietzsche has answers for them, but that is not true." Quoted in Campioni, "'Die Kunst, gut zu lesen,'" XX.7 Colli as "rediscoverer" in "Colloquio con l'italiano che riscopre Federico," *Corriere della Sera*, July 23, 1974. Giorgio Colli to Mazzino Montinari, September 17, 1968, fondo Montinari, cartella 18, Archivio Scuola Normale Superiore. On Colli's joy, see Sofri, "Dal morbillo a Nietzsche," 120. Marco Colli's documentary *Modi di vivere – Giorgio Colli: una conoscenza per cambiare la vita*, documentary film, 1980. On the writing of *Dopo Nietzsche*, cf. Colli, *La Ragione errabonda*, 601.

8 Colli, *La Ragione errabonda*, 601. Shortly after the Nietzsche book – and in a similarly popular vein – he publishes *The Birth of Philosophy*: *La nascita della filosofia* (Milan: Adelphi, 1975). On the end of Colli's life, see Antonio Gnoli, "Giorgio Colli, il profeta di Nietzsche," *La Repubblica*, October 23, 1991. "French arrogance: Bataille – Foucault – Klossowski. Confusion and sickness of intellect and character," Colli notes in 1972. *La Ragione errabonda*, 503.

9 His unsettledness in Anneliese Clauss to Mazzino Montinari, February 8, 1979, Nachlass Mazzino Montinari (177), Kasten 30.1, Goethe- und Schiller-Archiv. For the editors' claims, see "Ein neuer Hölderlin? Verlag Roter Stern stellt den ersten Band seiner Hölderlin-Ausgabe vor," *Frankfurter Rundschau*, August 8, 1975.

10 All quotations from Michel Leiner, D.E. Sattler, and K.D. Wolff, "Vorwort," in *Sämtliche Werke*, by Friedrich Hölderlin, Frankfurter Ausgabe, vol.: *Einleitung* (Frankfurt am Main: Roter Stern, 1975), 9–19, and from D.E. Sattler, "Friedrich Hölderlin, 'Frankfurter Ausgabe': Editionsprinzipien und Editionsmodell," *Hölderlin-Jahrbuch* 19/20 (1975): 112–30. Cerquiglini quoted in Grésillon, *Literarische Handschriften*, 222, cf. 226. The diagnosis of self-affirmation relayed orally by Wolfgang Groddeck.

11 Rolf Michaelis, "Roter Stern über Hölderlin," *Die Zeit*, August 8, 1975. Sattler, "Friedrich Hölderlin, 'Frankfurter Ausgabe,'" 112, 123, 125. On

the capacities of Hölderlin, see Volker Hage, "Ein neuer Hölderlin oder: Abschied von der Endgültigkeit," *Frankfurter Allgemeine Zeitung*, August 8, 1975. The success among the public is mentioned by Wackwitz, "Text als Mythos," 140. See also Wolfram Groddeck, "Fünf Jahrzehnte Editionsphilologie: Erinnerungen aus Forschung und Lehre," *Text: Kritische Beiträge* 16 (2020): 2–8.

12 Sattler, "Friedrich Hölderlin, 'Frankfurter Ausgabe,'" 116f., 124. On the return of the author, cf. Michel Contat, "La question d'auteur au regard des manuscrits," in *L'auteur et le manuscrit*, ed. Michel Contat (Paris: Presses universitaires de France, 1991), 7–34; Neumann, "Werk oder Schrift?"

13 Nietzsche, *CW*, 2023, 6: 243; *KSA*, 1988, 3: 616. Nietzsche to Erwin Rohde, mid-July 1882, in Nietzsche, *Selected Letters of Friedrich Nietzsche*, 187; *KSB*, 2003, 6: 226. *KSA*, 1988, 12: 450. Hans Blumenberg, "Für wen einer schreibt," *Süddeutsche Zeitung*, February 23, 1997.

14 D.E. Sattler to René Stockmar, April 18, 2002, friedrich hoelderlin, historisch-kritische ausgabe, arbeitsstelle bremen, http://www.hoelderlin .de/kritik/stockmar.html. Luciano Zagari, "Ricordo berlinese di Mazzino Montinari," in *L'impegno di una generazione: Il gruppo di Lucca dal Liceo Machiavelli alla Normale nel clima del Dopoguerra*, ed. Mario Mirri, Renzo Sabbatini, and Luigi Imbasciati (Milan: FrancoAngeli, 2014), 111. Michaelis, "Roter Stern über Hölderlin." On Montinari's skepticism about the text-genetic method, see also Ritter, "Tanz ohne Ketten," 3f.

15 On the paperback edition, see the correspondence in the Goethe- und Schiller-Archiv, Nachlass Montinari (177), Kasten 30.8. Ivo Frenzel, "Die gescheiterte Hoffnung: Die Kritische Gesamtausgabe der Werke Friedrich Nietzsches und das Ende eines Mythos," *Süddeutsche Zeitung*, February 14/15, 1976. Friedrich Kabermann, "Unter Glocke und Sturzglas," *Merkur* 354 (1977): 1112–18. Sepp Schelz, "Fragen und Denken am Abgrund: Literarische Symptome einer Wiederkunft," *Deutsches Allgemeines Sonntagsblatt*, March 1, 1981. Magris, "'Ich bin die Einsamkeit als Mensch.'" "Ein Nietzsche für Grüne und Alternative? Jakob Augstein zur Philosophie vom Übermenschen," *Der Spiegel*, June 7, 1981, 157, 160, 165f.

16 Willy Hochkeppel, "Nietzsche, unzeitgemäßer denn je: Über seine mögliche Wiederkehr," *Die Zeit*, September 11, 1981. "In Weimar entziffert," *Der Spiegel*, August 13, 1967, 98. Frenzel, "Die gescheiterte Hoffnung."

17 Ulrich Raulff, "Klickeradoms: Nietzsche liegt in Stücken," *Süddeutsche Zeitung*, November 24, 2001. On Suhrkamp's edition of Hegel, cf. Jürgen Kaube, *Hegels Welt* (Berlin: Rowohlt, 2020), 591. Ben Mercer, "The Paperback Revolution: Mass-Circulation Books and the Cultural Origins of 1968 in Western Europe," *Journal of the History of Ideas* 72 (2011): 613–36.

18 The "intellectual diary" in Mazzino Montinari, *Friedrich Nietzsche: Eine Einführung*, trans. Renate Müller-Beck (Berlin: De Gruyter, 1991), 100. Kaufmann is quoted in "A Book for Thinking," 501. Ritter, "Tanz ohne Ketten." The "dust cloud" is mentioned by Michel Foucault in "La publication des Oeuvres complètes de Nietzsche (Entretien avec Michel Foucault)." On the opposition between work and text, cf. also Reinhard Mehring, *Heideggers "große Politik": Die semantische Revolution der Gesamtausgabe* (Tübingen: Mohr Siebeck, 2016), 244.

19 Henning Ritter, "Nietzsche für Philologen? Zu einer Tagung über seine philosophischen Anfänge," *Frankfurter Allgemeine Zeitung*, March 25, 1992. Ritter, "Stille Penelopearbeit." Glenn Most, "Friedrich Nietzsche zwischen Philosophie und Philologie," *Ruperto-Carola* 2 (1994): 17.

20 Montinari to Musso-Colli, March 11, 1981. Montinari, "Erinnerung an Giorgio Colli," 170. On the expansion of the notion of work, cf. Montinari, "Aufgaben der Nietzsche-Forschung heute," 137f. Montinari's response to the French Nietzsche also consists in demonstrating how greatly Nietzsche had in turn been influenced by French authors. See chapter 5, note 1.

21 Heinz Malorny, "Tendenzen der Nietzsche-Rezeption in der BRD," *Deutsche Zeitschrift für Philosophie* 27 (1979): 1493, 1500. The Stasi is quoted in Riedel, *Nietzsche in Weimar*, 251, 254. On Hager's change in tack, see Jürgen Große, *Ernstfall Nietzsche: Debatten vor und nach 1989* (Bielefeld: Aisthesis, 2010), 23f. On the Stasi's role, see also Steinbach, *"Also sprach Sarah Tustra,"* 220. On the beginnings of the Nietzsche renaissance in the GDR more generally, see Renate Reschke and Rüdiger Schmidt-Grépály, "Über Zugänge zu Nietzsche: Renate Reschke im Gespräch mit Rüdiger Schmidt-Grépály," in *Zur Rückkehr des Autors: Gespräche über das Werk Friedrich Nietzsches*, ed. Rüdiger Schmidt-Grépály (Göttingen: LSD, 2013), 63–93.

22 Friedrich Nietzsche, *Ecce homo: Faksimileausgabe der Transkription* (Leipzig: Edition Leipzig, 1985). Cases, "Der Großherzog von Weimar," 26. According to information related orally by Bettina Wahrig-Schmidt,

Montinari behaved loyally toward the GDR until the last. Cf. Campioni, "Die Kunst, gut zu lesen."

23 Wolfgang Harich to Willi Stoph, December 22, 1985, in Wolfgang Harich, *Friedrich Nietzsche: Der Wegbereiter des Faschismus*, ed. Andreas Heyer (Baden-Baden: Tectum, 2019), 496f. The episode according to Steinbach, *"Also sprach Sarah Tustra"*, 186ff. Cf. also Reschke and Schmidt-Grépály, "Über Zugänge zu Nietzsche," 70f.

24 Wolfgang Harich to Klaus Höpke, January 25, 1986, and to Kurt Hager, January 30, 1986. Harich, "Nietzsche und seine Brüder." Wolfgang Harich to the cultural association, October 16, 1987. All documents in Harich, *Friedrich Nietzsche*, 503, 508–15, 201, 541.

25 Heinz Pepperle, "Revision des marxistischen Nietzsche-Bildes?," *Sinn und Form* 38 (1986): 935, 938. The essay mentioned is Montinari, "Nietzsche zwischen Alfred Baeumler und Georg Lukács," 191. On the assessment of the Nietzsche debate, see Große, *Ernstfall Nietzsche*, 12ff., 24, 73.

26 Wolfgang Harich, "Revision des marxistischen Nietzschebildes?," in *Friedrich Nietzsche: Der Wegbereiter des Faschismus*, by Wolfgang Harich, ed. Andreas Heyer (Baden-Baden: Tectum, 2019), 556, 560, 563. Harich says that Nietzsche had been "worse" than Hitler in "'Hager war mein Hauptfeind': Wolfgang Harich antwortet seinem Kritiker," *taz*, February 22, 1990. Cf. Große, *Ernstfall Nietzsche*, 36, 55.

27 Harich, "Nietzsche und seine Brüder," 207f. Harich's view of the events may be found here at 218f., 253, 256. On Hager's responsibility, cf. 255, as well as Wolfgang Harich to Christoph Links, July 2, 1990, and to Wilfried Träder, July 5, 1990, in Harich, *Friedrich Nietzsche*, 708, 711. Manfred Buhr, "Meinungen zu einem Streit: Es geht um das Phänomen Nietzsche!," *Sinn und Form* 40 (1988): 200–9. Cf. Steinbach, *"Also sprach Sarah Tustra,"* 208f.

28 Cf. Harich, "Nietzsche und seine Brüder," 201, 251, 257. See also Riedel, *Nietzsche in Weimar*, 295.

29 Chiarini, "Il comunista che amava Nietzsche." Marino Freschi, "Montinari: Nietzsche e martello," *Il Mattino*, December 9, 1986. Marianello Marianelli, "L'ultimo patriarca della grande filologia," *La Nazione*, January 6, 1987. Frank Schirrmacher, "Lust auf Leben: Zum Tode von Mazzino Montinari," *Frankfurter Allgemeine Zeitung*, November 26, 1986. "Mazzino Montinari," *Der Spiegel*, December 1, 1986. Montinari's death according to Cases, "Der Großherzog von Weimar," 20.

30 Schirrmacher, "Lust auf Leben." For a retrospective account of the

project's status upon Montinari's death, see Barbara von Reibnitz, "Die Handschrift lesen: Der Nachlass des späten Nietzsche in neuer Edition," *Neue Zürcher Zeitung*, October 30, 2002.

31 Wolfram Groddeck, "Einleitung," in *"Dionysos-Dithyramben": Textgenetische Edition der Vorstufen und Reinschriften*, by Friedrich Nietzsche, ed. Wolfram Groddeck, vol. 1 (Berlin: De Gruyter, 1991), ix. Wolfram Groddeck, "Die Überwindung der Editions-Metaphysik: Zur geplanten Neuedition von Nietzsches spätem Nachlass," *Neue Zürcher Zeitung*, October 15/16, 1994. Cf. Wolfram Groddeck, "'Vorstufe' und 'Fragment': Zur Problematik einer traditionellen textkritischen Unterscheidung in der Nietzsche-Philologie," in *Textkonstitution bei mündlicher und schriftlicher Überlieferung*, ed. Martin Stern (Berlin: De Gruyter, 1991), 165–75. On the editors' change in course, see also Reibnitz, "Die Handschrift lesen"; Raulff, "Klickeradoms."

32 Raulff, "Klickeradoms." Hubert Thüring, "Tertium datum: Der 'Nachlass' zwischen Leben und Werk: Zur Neuausgabe der handschriftlichen Dokumente des 'späten Nietzsche,'" *IASL online*, May 25, 2003. See also Gustav Seibt, "Wie in neuen Werkausgaben mit Nietzsche, Marx und Burckhardt umgegangen wird," *Die Zeit*, October 19, 2000. On the paradoxes of literality, see Heinz Sieburg, "Die Buchstäblichkeit der Buchstaben," in *Buchstäblichkeit: Theorie, Geschichte, Übersetzung*, ed. Achim Geisenhanslüke (Bielefeld: Transcript, 2020), 11–28.

33 Beat Röllin and René Stockmar, "Nietzsche lesen mit KGW IX: Zum Beispiel Arbeitsheft W II 1, Seite 1," in *Text/Kritik: Nietzsche und Adorno*, ed. Martin Endres (Berlin: de Gruyter, 2017), 3. Groddeck speaks of a "pallid grandchild" of older Nietzsche philology in "'Vorstufe' und 'Fragment,'" 169. "Ein Buch für alle und keinen: Nietzsche wird nicht mehr sein, der er war: Ein Gespräch mit Rüdiger Schmidt," *Süddeutsche Zeitung*, November 24/5, 2001. Lütkehaus, "Ich schreibe wie ein Schwein."

34 Jörg Lau, "Der Jargon der Uneigentlichkeit," *Merkur* 594/5 (1998): 944. On the close reading more recently, and with numerous references in the literature, see Anna-Lisa Dieter, "Close Reading," in *Enzyklopädie der Genauigkeit*, ed. Markus Krajewski, Antonia von Schöning, and Mario Wimmer (Konstanz: Konstanz University Press, 2021), 50–61. Franco Moretti, "The Slaughterhouse of Literature," *Modern Language Quarterly* 61 (2000): 208. Cf. Hans Ulrich Gumbrecht, "Was ist aus der Dekonstruktion geworden?," *Neue Zürcher Zeitung*, December 6, 2015.

35 Domenico Losurdo, *Nietzsche, the Aristocratic Rebel: Intellectual Biography and Critical Balance-Sheet*, trans. Gregor Benton (Leiden; Boston: Brill, 2020), 821, 1001, 1008, 1009f. The approach of the *Kritische Gesamtausgabe* as an "excellent way of hiding essential things behind inessential things" also in Hans-Georg Gadamer, "Das Drama Zarathustras," *Nietzsche-Studien* 15 (1986): 4.

36 Karl Marx, "The Eighteenth Brumaire of Louis Bonaparte," in *Collected Works*, by Friedrich Engels and Karl Heinrich Marx, trans. Clemens Dutt, Rodney Livingstone, and Christopher Upward, vol. 11: *Marx and Engels: 1851–53* (New York: International Publishers, 1979), 103. All quotations from Peter Sloterdijk and Rüdiger Schmidt-Grépály, "Nietzsche, Autor, Reformator: Peter Sloterdijk im Gespräch mit Rüdiger Schmidt-Grépály," in *Zur Rückkehr des Autors: Gespräche über das Werk Friedrich Nietzsches*, ed. Rüdiger Schmidt-Grépály (Göttingen: LSD, 2013), 27–62. On the return to 1889, cf. Schmidt-Grépály, "Über Zugänge zu Nietzsche," 88f. Montinari's sense of futility in Montinari, "Glanz und Elend der philologischen Arbeit," 57.

BIBLIOGRAPHY

Archives
Bundesarchiv
Stasi-Unterlagen-Archiv Berlin-Mitte
Karl-Liebknecht-Straße 31/33
10178 Berlin
Germany

Centro Archivistico della Scuola Normale Superiore
Piazza dei Cavalieri 7
56126 Pisa
Italy

Fondazione Arnoldo e Alberto Mondadori
Via Riccione 8
20156 Milan
Italy

Goethe- und Schiller-Archiv
Jenaer Straße 1
99425 Weimar
Germany

Leibniz-Zentrum für Literatur- und Kulturforschung
Nachlass Jacob Taubes
Schützenstraße 18
10117 Berlin
Germany

Internet sources

Colli, Giorgio. "Diario 1944–1945," Archivio Giorgio Colli, http://www
.giorgiocolli.it/it/content/diario-1944-1945.
Garin, Eugenio. "Storicismo," Enciclopedia del Novecento, Alfabeto Treccani,
1984. https://www.treccani.it/enciclopedia/storicismo_%28Enciclopedia
-del-Novecento%29/.
Haller, Dieter. "Short Portrait: Erich Podach," 2011. Interviews with German
Anthropologists.   http://www.germananthropology.com/short-portrait
/erich-podach/256.
Rajchman, John. "Deleuze's Nietzsche," Nietzsche 13/13, October 25, 2016.
http://blogs.law.columbia.edu/nietzsche1313/john-rajchman-deleuzes
-nietzsche/.
Sattler, D.E. to René Stockmar, April 18, 2002, friedrich hoelderlin, historisch-
kritische ausgabe, arbeitsstelle bremen. http://www.hoelderlin.de/kritik
/stockmar.html.

Films

Colli, Marco, dir. *Modi di vivere – Giorgio Colli: una conoscenza per cambiare
la vita*. Documentary film, 1980.
Schilling, Regina, dir. *Kulenkampffs Schuhe*. Documentary film, 2018.

Literature

"A Book for Thinking." *The Times Literary Supplement*, May 15, 1969.
Adorno, Theodor W. "Bibliographical Musings." In *Notes to Literature*, by
Theodor W. Adorno, 298–308, ed. Rolf Tiedemann, trans. Shierry Weber
Nicholsen. New York: Columbia University Press, 2019.
Albath, Maike. *Der Geist von Turin: Pavese, Ginzburg, Einaudi und die
Wiedergeburt Italiens nach 1943*. Berlin: Berenberg, 2010.
"Also sprach Lisbeth Förster." *Der Spiegel*, January 29, 1958, 32–41.
Andreas-Salomé, Lou. *Nietzsche*, ed. and trans. Siegfried Mandel. Urbana:
University of Illinois Press, 2001.

Andres, Jan. "'Hellas ewig unsre liebe': Erlesenes und erlebtes Griechenland bei Rudolf Fahrner." In *Hellas verstehen: Deutsch–griechischer Kulturtransfer im 20. Jahrhundert*, ed. Chryssoula Kambas and Marilisa Mitsou, 73–94. Vienna: Böhlau, 2010.

Anzalone, Luigi, and Giuliano Minichiello. *Lo specchio di Dionisio: Saggi su Giorgio Colli*. Bari: Dedalo, 1984.

Arendt, Hannah. "Truth and Politics." *The New Yorker*, February 25, 1967.

Aschheim, Steven E. *Nietzsche und die Deutschen: Karriere eines Kultus*. Stuttgart: J.B. Metzler, 1996.

Aschheim, Steven E. *The Nietzsche Legacy in Germany, 1890–1990*. Berkeley: University of California Press, 1992.

Baeumer, Max L. *Dionysos und das Dionysische in der antiken und deutschen Literatur*. Darmstadt: Wissenschaftliche Buchgesellschaft, 2006.

Banfi, Alberto. "Giorgio Colli: Il coraggio del pensiero (profilo biografico)." *Kleos: Estemporaneo di studi e testi sulla fortuna dell'antico* 9 (2004): 221–71.

Barthes, Roland. *S/Z*, trans. Richard Howard. New York: Hill & Wang, 1974.

Barthes, Roland. "The Death of the Author." In *Image, Music, Text: Essays*, trans. Stephen Heath, 142–8. New York: Hill & Wang, 2007.

Barthes, Roland. *Writing Degree Zero*, trans. Annette Lavers and Colin Smith. New York: Hill & Wang, 1968.

Bayle, Pierre. "Project for a Critical Dictionary." In *Political Writings*, by Pierre Bayle, 1–16, ed. and trans. Sally L. Jenkinson. Cambridge: Cambridge University Press, 2000.

Beaufret, Jean. "Les inédits de Nietzsche." *Le Monde*, June 7, 1967.

Beil, Ulrich J. "'Anführungszeichen': Anmerkungen zur Literaturtheorie von Jacques Derrida und Paul de Man." *Pandaemonium Germanicum* 6 (2002): 17–46.

Benjamin, Walter. "The Work of Art in the Age of Its Technological Reproducibility: Second Version." In *The Work of Art in the Age of Its Technological Reproducibility, and Other Writings on Media*, by Walter Benjamin, 19–55, ed. Michael William Jennings, Brigid Doherty, and Thomas Y. Levin, trans. Edmund Jephcott, Rodney Livingstone, and Howard Eiland. Cambridge, MA: The Belknap Press of Harvard University Press, 2008.

Benne, Christian. *Nietzsche und die historisch-kritische Philologie*. Berlin: De Gruyter, 2005.

Bergfleth, Gerd. "Nietzsche redivivus." In *Wiedergutmachung an Nietzsche: Das Nietzsche-Memorandum und andere Texte*, by Georges Bataille, 299–396, trans. Gerd Bergfleth. Munich: Matthes & Seitz, 1999.

Bertram, Ernst. *Nietzsche: Attempt at a Mythology*, trans. Robert Edward Norton. Urbana: University of Illinois Press, 2009.

Bimbi, Linda. "Parlerò di Mazzino." In *L'impegno di una generazione: Il gruppo di Lucca dal Liceo Machiavelli alla Normale nel clima del Dopoguerra*, ed. Mario Mirri, Renzo Sabbatini, and Luigi Imbasciati, 55–8. Milan: FrancoAngeli, 2014.

Birus, Hendrik. "'Wir Philologen' . . . Überlegungen zu Nietzsches Begriff der Interpretation." *Revue Internationale de Philosophie* 38 (1984): 373–95.

Blanchot, Maurice. *The Infinite Conversation*, trans. Susan Hanson. Minneapolis: University of Minnesota Press, 1993.

Bloch, Ernst. "Italy and Porosity." In *Literary Essays*, by Ernst Bloch, 450–7, trans. Andrew Joron. Stanford, CA: Stanford University Press, 1998.

Bloom, Alan. *The Closing of the American Mind*. New York: Simon & Schuster, 1987.

Blumenberg, Hans. "Das finale Dilemma des Lesers." In *Lebensthemen: Aus dem Nachlaß*, by Hans Blumenberg, 29–33. Stuttgart: Reclam, 1998.

Blumenberg, Hans. "Für wen einer schreibt." *Süddeutsche Zeitung*, February 23, 1997.

Boehm, Rudolf. "Le problème du 'Wille zur Macht', oeuvre posthume de Nietzsche: À propos d'une nouvelle édition." *Revue Philosophique de Louvain, Troisième série* 61 (1963): 402–34.

Borchardt, Rudolf. *Anabasis: Aufzeichnungen, Dokumente, Erinnerungen 1943–1945*. Munich: Edition Tenschert bei Hanser, 2003.

Buhr, Manfred. "Meinungen zu einem Streit: Es geht um das Phänomen Nietzsche!" *Sinn und Form* 40 (1988): 200–9.

Butler, Eliza M. *The Tyranny of Greece over Germany*. Cambridge: Cambridge University Press, 1935.

Buttigieg, Joseph A. "Introduction." In *Prison Notebooks*, by Antonio Gramsci, vol. 1: Notebooks 1–2, 1–64, ed. and trans. Joseph A. Buttigieg. New York: Columbia University Press, 1992.

Calvino, Italo. "Nota 1960." In *I nostri antenati*, by Italo Calvino, 411–22. Milan: Garzanti, 1996.

Campioni, Giuliano. "Da Lucca a Weimar: Mazzino Montinari e Nietzsche." In *L'impegno di una generazione: Il gruppo di Lucca dal Liceo Machiavelli alla Normale nel clima del Dopoguerra*, ed. Mario Mirri, Renzo Sabbatini, and Luigi Imbasciati, 151–65. Milan: FrancoAngeli, 2014.

Campioni, Giuliano. "'Der Karren unserer Arbeit . . .': Sechzehn Briefe von Mazzino Montinari an Delio Cantimori." *Nietzsche-Studien* 36 (2007): 48–79.

Campioni, Giuliano. "'Die Kunst, gut zu lesen': Mazzino Montinari und das Handwerk des Philologen." *Nietzsche-Studien* 18 (1989): xv–lxxiv.

Campioni, Giuliano. *Leggere Nietzsche: Alle origini dell'edizione Colli-Montinari*. Pisa: Edizioni ETS, 1992.

Campioni, Giuliano. "Mazzino Montinari in den Jahren von 1943 bis 1963." *Nietzsche-Studien* 17 (1988): xv–lx.

Campioni, Giuliani, ed. *Nietzsches persönliche Bibliothek*. Berlin: De Gruyter, 2003.

Cancik, Hubert, and Hildegard Cancik-Lindemaier. "'Das Gymnasium in der Knechtschaft des Staates': Zu Entstehung, Situation und Thema von Friedrich Nietzsches 'Wir Philologen.'" In *Disciplining Classics*, ed. Glenn Most, 97–113. Göttingen: Vandenhoeck & Ruprecht, 2002.

Cantimori, Delio. *Conversando di storia*. Bari: Laterza, 1967.

Cantimori, Delio. *Eretici italiani del Cinquecento*. Florence: Sansoni, 1939.

Cantimori, Delio. "Interpretazioni tedesche di Marx nel periodo 1929–1945." In *Studi di storia*, by Delio Cantimori, 139–237. Turin: Einaudi, 1959.

Cantimori, Delio. *Italienische Haeretiker der Spätrenaissance*, trans. Werner Kaegi. Basel: B. Schwabe, 1949.

Cantimori, Delio. "Recensione di Hugo Fischer, Nietzsche Apostata." In *Politica e storia contemporanea: Scritti (1927–1942)*, by Delio Cantimori, 154–9, ed. Luisa Mangoni. Turin: Einaudi, 1991.

Cases, Cesare. "Der Großherzog von Weimar: Erinnerung an Mazzino Montinari." *Nietzsche-Studien* 18 (1989): 20–6.

Cases, Cesare. "Der Mythos der deutschen Kultur in Italien." In *Wissenschaftskolleg zu Berlin: Jahrbuch 1987/88*, 175–90. Berlin: Siedler, 1989.

Cases, Cesare. "Gli incontri romani con Mazzino e Codino." In *L'impegno di una generazione: Il gruppo di Lucca dal Liceo Machiavelli alla Normale nel clima del Dopoguerra*, ed. Mario Mirri, Renzo Sabbatini, and Luigi Imbasciati, 67–9. Milan: FrancoAngeli, 2014.

Cassirer, Ernst. *The Philosophy of the Enlightenment*, trans. Fritz C.A. Koelln and James P. Pettegrove. Princeton: Princeton University Press, 2009.

Cerquiglini, Bernard. *In Praise of the Variant: A Critical History of Philology*, trans. Betsy Wing. Baltimore: Johns Hopkins University Press, 1999.

Cervasio, Stella. "Il fascino di Nietzsche: Gli scritti di un filosofo che diventò profeta." *La Repubblica*, July 8, 2009.

Cesa, Claudio. "Il clima culturale." In *L'impegno di una generazione: Il gruppo di Lucca dal Liceo Machiavelli alla Normale nel clima del Dopoguerra*, ed. Mario Mirri, Renzo Sabbatini, and Luigi Imbasciati, 33–43. Milan: FrancoAngeli, 2014.

Chehayed, Nibras. "Nietzsche and Gadamer on Truth and Interpretation." *The New Centennial Review* 19 (2019): 251–72.

Chiarini, Paolo. "Il comunista che amava Nietzsche." *Rinascità*, December 13, 1986.

Ciliberto, Michele. *Intellettuali e fascismo: Saggio su Delio Cantimori*. Bari: De Donato, 1977.

Cochrane, Eric, and John Tedeschi. "Delio Cantimori: Historian." *The Journal of Modern History* 39 (1967): 438–45.

Colli, Giorgio. *Apollineo e dionisiaco*. Milan: Adelphi, 2010.

Colli, Giorgio. *Distanz und Pathos: Einleitungen zu Nietzsches Werken*, trans. Ragni Maria Gschwend and Reimar Klein. Hamburg: Europäische Verlagsanstalt, 1993.

Colli, Giorgio. *Dopo Nietzsche*. Milan: Adelphi, 1974.

Colli, Giorgio. *Filosofi sovrumani*. Milan: Adelphi, 2009.

Colli, Giorgio. *Filosofia dell'espressione*. Milan: Adelphi, 1969.

Colli, Giorgio. *La nascita della filosofia*. Milan: Adelphi, 1975.

Colli, Giorgio. *La Ragione errabonda: Quaderni postumi*. Milan: Adelphi, 1982.

Colli, Giorgio. *Per una enciclopedia di autori classici*. Milan: Adelphi, 1983.

Colli, Giorgio. "Recensione di K.A. Goetz, Nietzsche als Ausnahme." *Rivista di filosofia* 16 (1950): 227–31.

Colli, Giorgio, and Mazzino Montinari. "État des textes de Nietzsche." In *Nietzsche*, 127–40. Cahiers de Royaumont 6. Paris: Éditions de Minuit, 1967.

Colli, Giorgio, and Mazzino Montinari. "Principes des éditeurs." In *Gai Savoir: Fragments posthumes 1881–1882*, by Friedrich Nietzsche, 294, ed. Giorgio Colli and Mazzino Montinari, trans. Pierre Klossowski. Paris: Gallimard, 1967.

Colli Staude, Chiara. *Friedrich Nietzsche, Giorgio Colli und die Griechen:*

Philologie und Philosophie zwischen Unzeitgemäßheit und Leben. Würzburg: Königshausen & Neumann, 2019.

"Colloquio con l'italiano che riscopre Federico." *Corriere della Sera,* July 23, 1974.

Contat, Michel. "La question d'auteur au regard des manuscrits." In *L'auteur et le manuscrit,* ed. Michel Contat, 7–34. Paris: Presses universitaires de France, 1991.

Croce, Benedetto. "Antihistoricismo." *La Critica: Rivista di Letteratura, Storia e Filosifia* 28 (1930): 400–9.

d'Angelo, Sergio. "Der Roman des Romans." *Osteuropa* 18 (1968): 489–501.

De Felice, Renzo. *Mussolini l'alleato: La guerra civile.* Turin: Einaudi, 1997.

de Franciscis, Azio. "Pankows Kulturoffensive in Rom," *Die Zeit,* April 11, 1957.

Debray, Régis. "Socialism: A Life-Cycle." *New Left Review* 46 (2007): 5–28.

Deckert, Renatur. "Eisenregale, vom Feuer verformt." *Süddeutsche Zeitung,* February 11, 2020.

Deleuze, Gilles. "Conclusions on the Will to Power and the Eternal Return." In *Desert Islands and Other Texts: 1953–1974,* by Gilles Deleuze, 117–27, ed. David Lapoujade, trans. Michael Taormina. Los Angeles: Semiotext(e), 2004.

Deleuze, Gilles. "Nietzsche." In *Pure Immanence: Essays on a Life,* by Gilles Deleuze, 53–102, trans. Anne Boyman. New York: Zone Books, 2001.

Deleuze, Gilles. "Nomadic Thought." In *Desert Islands and Other Texts: 1953–1974,* by Gilles Deleuze, 252–61, ed. David Lapoujade, trans. Michael Taormina. Los Angeles: Semiotext(e), 2004.

Deleuze, Gilles. "On Nietzsche and the Image of Thought." In *Desert Islands and Other Texts: 1953–1974,* by Gilles Deleuze, 135–42, ed. David Lapoujade, trans. Michael Taormina. Los Angeles: Semiotext(e), 2004.

D'Elia, Nicola. *Delio Cantimori e la cultura politica tedesca (1927–1940).* Rome: Viella, 2007.

Denker, Alfred, et al., eds. *Heidegger und Nietzsche.* Freiburg: Verlag Karl Alber, 2005.

Derrida, Jacques. "Ellipsis." In *Writing and Difference,* trans. Alan Bass, 294–300. Chicago: University of Chicago Press, 1978.

Derrida, Jacques. *Of Grammatology,* trans. Gayatri Chakravorty Spivak. Baltimore: Johns Hopkins University Press, 1998.

Derrida, Jacques. "Some Statements and Truisms about Neologisms, Newisms, Postisms, Parasitisms, and Other Small Seismisms." In *The*

States of "Theory": History, Art, and Critical Discourse, ed. David Carroll, trans. Anne Tomiche, 63–94. New York: Columbia University Press, 1990.

Derrida, Jacques. *Spurs: Nietzsche's Styles/Éperons: Les Styles de Nietzsche*, trans. Barbara Harlow. Chicago: University of Chicago Press, 1979.

Di Rienzo, Eugenio. *Delio Cantimori e la cultura politica del Novecento*. Florence: Le lettere, 2009.

Dieter, Anna-Lisa. "Close Reading." In *Enzyklopädie der Genauigkeit*, ed. Markus Krajewski, Antonia von Schöning, and Mario Wimmer, 50–61. Konstanz: Konstanz University Press, 2021.

Dilthey, Wilhelm. "Archive für Literatur." In *Zur Geistesgeschichte des 19. Jahrhunderts*, by Wilhelm Dilthey, 1–16. ed. Ulrich Herrmann. *Gesammelte Schriften*. Göttingen: Vandenhoeck & Ruprecht, 1991.

Dilthey, Wilhelm. "The Essence of Philosophy." In *Selected Works*, by Wilhelm Dilthey, 171–247, ed. Rudolf A. Makkreel and Frithjof Rodi, trans. John Krois and Rudolf A. Makkreel. *Ethical and World-View Philosophy*, vol. IV. Princeton: Princeton University Press, 2019.

Dörr, Nikolas. *Die Rote Gefahr: Der italienische Eurokommunismus als sicherheitspolitische Herausforderung für die USA und Westdeutschland 1969–1979*. Cologne: Böhlau, 2017.

Dosse, François. *Gilles Deleuze & Félix Guattari: Intersecting Lives*, trans. Deborah Glassman. New York: Columbia University Press, 2010.

Dosse, François. *History of Structuralism*, trans. Deborah Glassman, vol. 1. Minneapolis: University of Minnesota Press, 1997.

"Ein Buch für alle und keinen: Nietzsche wird nicht mehr sein, der er war: Ein Gespräch mit Rüdiger Schmidt." *Süddeutsche Zeitung*, November 24/5, 2001.

"Ein neuer Hölderlin? Verlag Roter Stern stellt den ersten Band seiner Hölderlin-Ausgabe vor." *Frankfurter Rundschau*, August 8, 1975.

"Ein Nietzsche für Grüne und Alternative? Jakob Augstein zur Philosophie vom Übermenschen." *Der Spiegel*, June 7, 1981, 156–84.

Elon, Amos. *In einem heimgesuchten Land: Reise eines israelischen Journalisten in beide deutsche Staaten*. Munich: Kindler, 1966.

Elon, Amos. *Journey through a Haunted Land: The New Germany*, trans. Michael Roloff. New York: Holt, Rinehart and Winston, 1967.

Espagne, Michel. *De l'archive au texte: Recherches d'histoire génétique*. Paris: Presses universitaires de France, 1998.

Fazio, Domenico M. "Nietzsche in Italien: Ein historischer Abriß der Nietzsche-Rezeption in Italien anhand der Übersetzungen seiner Schriften (1872–1940)." *Nietzsche-Studien* 22 (1993): 304–19.

Fazio, Domenico M. "Nietzsche und der Faschismus: Eine Politik des Nietzsche-Archivs in Italien." In *Widersprüche: Zur frühen Nietzsche-Rezeption*, ed. Andreas Schirmer and Rüdiger Schmidt, 221–33. Weimar: Verlag Hermann Böhlaus Nachfolger, 2000.

Felsch, Philipp. "Der Leser als Partisan." *Zeitschrift für Ideengeschichte* 6 (2012): 35–49.

Felsch, Philipp. *The Summer of Theory: History of a Rebellion, 1960–1990*, trans. Tony Crawford. Cambridge: Polity, 2022.

Felsch, Philipp, and Frank Witzel. *BRD Noir*. Berlin: Matthes & Seitz, 2016.

Fersen, Alessandro. "La memoria in Giorgio Colli." In *Giorgio Colli: Incontro di studio*, ed. Giuseppe Menichetti, Sandro Barbera, and Giuliano Campioni, 29–33. Milan: Angeli, 1983.

Fischer, Hugo. *Nietzsche Apostata; oder, die Philosophie des Ärgernisses*. Erfurt: K. Stenger, 1931.

Flasch, Kurt. "Und er war doch ein Zerstörer der Vernunft." *Frankfurter Allgemeine Zeitung*, February 21, 2003.

Forti, Carla. *Dopoguerra in provincia: Microstorie pisane e lucchesi (1944–1948)*. Milan: FrancoAngeli, 2007.

Foucault, Michel. "Nietzsche, Freud, Marx." In *Dits et écrits: 1954–1988*, ed. Daniel Defert and François Ewald, vol. 1: *1954–1969*, 564–79. Paris: Gallimard, 1994.

Foucault, Michel. "Nietzsche, Freud, Marx." In *Aesthetics, Method, and Epistemology*, ed. James D. Faubion, trans. Jon Anderson and Gary Hentzi, 269–78. *Essential Works of Foucault, 1954–1984*, vol. 2. New York: New Press, 1998.

Foucault, Michel. "Prison Talk." In *Power/Knowledge: Selected Interviews and Other Writings, 1972–1977*, ed. and trans. Colin Gordon, 37–54. New York: Pantheon Books, 1980.

Foucault, Michel. *Society Must Be Defended: Lectures at the Collège de France, 1975–76*, ed. Mauro Bertani and Alessandro Fontana, trans. David Macey. New York: Picador, 2003.

Foucault, Michel. *The Order of Things: An Archaeology of the Human Sciences*, trans. Alan Sheridan. New York: Vintage Books, 1994.

Foucault, Michel. "What Is an Author?" In *Aesthetics, Method, and*

Epistemology, ed. James D. Faubion, trans. Robert Hurley, 205–22. *Essential Works of Foucault, 1954–1984*, vol. 2. New York: New Press, 1998.

Foucault, Michel, and Gilles Deleuze. "Introduction générale." In *Dits et écrits: 1954–1988*, ed. Daniel Defert and François Ewald, vol. 1: *1954–1969*, 561–4. Paris: Gallimard, 1994.

Frenzel, Ivo. "Die gescheiterte Hoffnung: Die Kritische Gesamtausgabe der Werke Friedrich Nietzsches und das Ende eines Mythos." *Süddeutsche Zeitung*, February 14/15, 1976.

Freschi, Marino. "Montinari: Nietzsche e martello." *Il Mattino*, December 9, 1986.

Frese, Jürgen. "Intellektuellen-Assoziationen." In *Kreise, Gruppen, Bünde: Zur Soziologie moderner Intellektuellenassoziationen*, ed. Richard Faber and Christine Holste, 441–62. Würzburg: Königshausen & Neumann, 2000.

Gadamer, Hans-Georg. "Das Drama Zarathustras." *Nietzsche-Studien* 15 (1986): 1–15.

Gandillac, Maurice. "Le colloque de Cerisy-la-Salle." *Nietzsche-Studien* 4 (1975): 324–33.

Garritano, Giuseppe. "Il clima politico." In *L'impegno di una generazione: Il gruppo di Lucca dal Liceo Machiavelli alla Normale nel clima del Dopoguerra*, ed. Mario Mirri, Renzo Sabbatini, and Luigi Imbasciati, 45–9. Milan: FrancoAngeli, 2014.

Gass, Karl Eugen. *Pisaner Tagebuch*. Heidelberg: L. Schneider, 1961.

Gerratana, Valentino. "Le inquietudine di Mazzino." In *L'impegno di una generazione: Il gruppo di Lucca dal Liceo Machiavelli alla Normale nel clima del Dopoguerra*, ed. Mario Mirri, Renzo Sabbatini, and Luigi Imbasciati, 71–3. Milan: FrancoAngeli, 2014.

Ginzburg, Carlo. *The Cheese and the Worms: The Cosmos of a Sixteenth-Century Miller*, trans. John Tedeschi and Anne C. Tedeschi. Baltimore: Johns Hopkins University Press, 2013.

Giusti, Licia. "Mazzino, Giorgio e Fausto." In *L'impegno di una generazione: Il gruppo di Lucca dal Liceo Machiavelli alla Normale nel clima del Dopoguerra*, ed. Mario Mirri, Renzo Sabbatini, and Luigi Imbasciati, 75–7. Milan: FrancoAngeli, 2014.

Gnoli, Antonio. "Giorgio Colli, il profeta di Nietzsche." *La Repubblica*, October 23, 1991.

Gnoli, Antonio. "Gli angeli di Nietzsche." *La Repubblica*, April 28, 1992.

Gnoli, Antonio. "Il libro segreto di Cantimori." *La Repubblica*, May 27, 2004.

Grafton, Anthony. "Humanist Philologies: Texts, Antiquities, and Their Scholarly Transformations in the Early Modern West." In *World Philology*, ed. Sheldon Pollock, Benjamin A. Elman, and Ku-ming Kevin Chang, 154–77. Cambridge, MA: Harvard University Press, 2015.

Grafton, Anthony. "Prolegomena to Friedrich August Wolf." *Journal of the Warburg and Courtauld Institutes* 44 (1981): 101–29.

Grafton, Anthony. "The Footnote from De Thou to Ranke." *History and Theory* 33 (1994): 53–76.

Gramsci, Antonio. *Prison Notebooks*, ed. and trans. Joseph A. Buttigieg, vol. III: Notebooks 6–8. New York: Columbia University Press, 1992.

Grésillon, Almuth. *Literarische Handschriften: Einführung in die "critique génétique."* Bern: Peter Lang, 1999.

Groddeck, Wolfram. "Die Überwindung der Editions-Metaphysik: Zur geplanten Neuedition von Nietzsches spätem Nachlass." *Neue Zürcher Zeitung*, October 15/16, 1994.

Groddeck, Wolfram. "Einleitung." In *"Dionysos-Dithyramben": Textgenetische Edition der Vorstufen und Reinschriften*, by Friedrich Nietzsche, vii–xvi. ed. Wolfram Groddeck. Berlin: De Gruyter, 1991.

Groddeck, Wolfram. "Fünf Jahrzehnte Editionsphilologie: Erinnerungen aus Forschung und Lehre." *Text: Kritische Beiträge* 16 (2020): 2–8.

Groddeck, Wolfram. "Nietzsche lesen." *Nietzscheforschung* 25 (2018): 31–9.

Groddeck, Wolfram. "'Vorstufe' und 'Fragment': Zur Problematik einer traditionellen textkritischen Unterscheidung in der Nietzsche-Philologie." In *Textkonstitution bei mündlicher und schriftlicher Überlieferung*, ed. Martin Stern, 165–75. Berlin: De Gruyter, 1991.

Große, Jürgen. *Ernstfall Nietzsche: Debatten vor und nach 1989*. Bielefeld: Aisthesis, 2010.

Gumbrecht, Hans Ulrich. "Das Nicht-Hermeneutische: Skizze einer Genealogie." In *Präsenz*, by Hans Ulrich Gumbrecht, 190–209, ed. Jürgen Klein. Frankfurt am Main: Suhrkamp, 2019.

Gumbrecht, Hans Ulrich. *The Powers of Philology: Dynamics of Textual Scholarship*. Urbana: University of Illinois Press, 2003.

Gumbrecht, Hans Ulrich. "Was ist aus der Dekonstruktion geworden?" *Neue Zürcher Zeitung*, December 6, 2015.

Gundle, Stephen. *Between Hollywood and Moscow: The Italian Communists and the Challenge of Mass Culture, 1943–1991*. Durham, NC: Duke University Press, 2000.

Habermas, Jürgen. "Nachwort." In *Erkenntnistheoretische Schriften*, by Friedrich Nietzsche, 237–61. Frankfurt am Main: Suhrkamp, 1968.

Hachmeister, Lutz. *Heideggers Testament: Der Philosoph, der Spiegel und die SS*. Berlin: Propyläen, 2015.

Hage, Volker. "Ein neuer Hölderlin oder: Abschied von der Endgültigkeit." *Frankfurter Allgemeine Zeitung*, August 8, 1975.

"'Hager war mein Hauptfeind': Wolfgang Harich antwortet seinem Kritiker." *taz*, February 22, 1990.

Hahn, Karl-Heinz. "Das Nietzsche-Archiv." *Nietzsche-Studien* 18 (1989): 1–19.

Hahn, Karl-Heinz. "Nachruf auf Professor Dr. Mazzino Montinari." *Goethe-Jahrbuch* 104 (1987): 388–90.

Hamacher, Werner. "Echolos." In *Nietzsche aus Frankreich*, ed. Werner Hamacher, 7–18. Hamburg: Europäische Verlagsanstalt, 2007.

Hampe, Michael. *Erkenntnis und Praxis: Zur Philosophie des Pragmatismus*. Frankfurt am Main: Suhrkamp, 2006.

Hardt, Michael, and Antonio Negri. *Empire*. Cambridge, MA: Harvard University Press, 2000.

Harich, Wolfgang. *Friedrich Nietzsche: Der Wegbereiter des Faschismus*, ed. Andreas Heyer. Baden-Baden: Tectum, 2019.

Harich, Wolfgang. "Nietzsche und seine Brüder: Eine Streitschrift in sieben Dialogen." In *Friedrich Nietzsche: Der Wegbereiter des Faschismus*, by Wolfgang Harich, 57–264. ed. Andreas Heyer. Baden-Baden: Tectum, 2019.

Harich, Wolfgang. "Revision des marxistischen Nietzschebildes?" In *Friedrich Nietzsche: Der Wegbereiter des Faschismus*, by Wolfgang Harich, 542–82. ed. Andreas Heyer. Baden-Baden: Tectum, 2019.

Harich, Wolfgang. "Rezension von Lukács, Die Zerstörung der Vernunft." *Deutsche Zeitschrift für Philosophie* 3 (1955): 133–45.

Heftrich, Eckhard. "Die Grenzen der psychologischen Nietzsche-Erklärung." *Revue Internationale de Philosophie* 18 (1964): 74–90.

Heftrich, Eckhard. "Zu den Ausgaben der Werke und Briefe von Friedrich Nietzsche." In *Buchstabe und Geist: Zur Überlieferung und Edition philosophischer Texte*, ed. Walter Jaeschke et al., 117–36. Hamburg: F. Meiner, 1987.

Heidegger, Martin. *Nietzsche*, trans. David Farrell Krell, vol. 1. San Francisco: Harper & Row, 1979.

Heitmann, Klaus. "Das Deutschland der Adenauer-Zeit, von italienischen Autoren gesehen." In *Italien in Deutschland, Deutschland in Italien: Die deutsch–italienischen Wechselbeziehungen in der Belletristik des 20. Jahrhunderts*, ed. Anna Comi and Alexandra Pontzen, 81–130. Berlin: E. Schmidt, 1999.

Herbert, Ulrich. *A History of Twentieth-Century Germany*, trans. Ben Fowkes. New York: Oxford University Press, 2019.

Hobsbawm, Eric J. *How to Change the World: Marx and Marxism, 1840–2011*. London: Little, Brown, 2011.

Hochkeppel, Willy. "Nietzsche, unzeitgemäßer denn je: Über seine mögliche Wiederkehr." *Die Zeit*, September 11, 1981.

Hoffmann, David M. *Zur Geschichte des Nietzsche-Archivs: Chronik, Studien und Dokumente*. Berlin: De Gruyter, 1991.

Holtzhauer, Helmut. *Weimarer Tagesnotizen 1958–1973*, ed. Martin Holtzhauer, Konrad Kratzsch, and Rainer Krauß. Hamburg: Tredition, 2017.

"Il 'libro bianco' di una vendetta nera." *Belfagor* 3, no. 6 (1948): 722–7.

"Il 'libro bianco' di una vendetta nera." *Belfagor* 4, no. 1 (1949): 94–112.

Imbasciati, Luigi. "Il ricordo di uno studente." In *L'impegno di una generazione: Il gruppo di Lucca dal Liceo Machiavelli alla Normale nel clima del Dopoguerra*, ed. Mario Mirri, Renzo Sabbatini, and Luigi Imbasciati, 25–30. Milan: FrancoAngeli, 2014.

"In Weimar entziffert." *Der Spiegel*, August 13, 1967, 96–8.

Isoz, Claire, and Giuliana Lanata. "Ricordo di Pietro Giorgetti." In *L'impegno di una generazione: Il gruppo di Lucca dal Liceo Machiavelli alla Normale nel clima del Dopoguerra*, ed. Mario Mirri, Renzo Sabbatini, and Luigi Imbasciati, 79–83. Milan: FrancoAngeli, 2014.

Jaspers, Karl. *Nietzsche: An Introduction to the Understanding of His Philosophical Activity*, trans. Charles F. Wallraff and Frederick J. Schmitz. Baltimore: Johns Hopkins University Press, 1997.

Jens, Walter. "Zarter Zeichner des großen Mittags." *Texte und Zeichen* 3 (1957): 304–9.

Judt, Tony. *Postwar: A History of Europe since 1945*. London: Vintage, 2010.

Kabermann, Friedrich. "Unter Glocke und Sturzglas." *Merkur* 354 (1977): 1112–18.

Karlauf, Thomas. *Stefan George: Die Entdeckung des Charisma*. Munich: Blessing, 2007.

Kaube, Jürgen. *Hegels Welt*. Berlin: Rowohlt, 2020.

Kaufmann, Walter. "German Thought Today." *The Kenyon Review* 19 (1957): 15–30.

Kaufmann, Walter. *Nietzsche: Philosopher, Psychologist, Antichrist*. 3rd ed. Princeton: Princeton University Press, 1968.

Kesselring, Albert. *The Memoirs of Field-Marshal Kesselring*, trans. Lynton Hudson. Novato, CA: Presidio, 1989.

Kittler, Friedrich. "Ein Verwaiser." In *Anschlüsse: Versuche nach Michel Foucault*, ed. Gesa Dane, 141–6. Tübingen: Edition Diskord, 1985.

Klinkhammer, Lutz. *Zwischen Bündnis und Besatzung: Das nationalsozial-istische Deutschland und die Republik von Salò 1943–1945*. Tübingen: M. Niemeyer, 1993.

Klossowski, Pierre. "Forgetting and Anamnesis in the Experience of the Eternal Return of the Same," trans. Susan Hanson. *Semiotext(e)* 3, no. 1 (1978): 138–49.

Kofman, Sarah. "Le/les 'concepts' de culture dans les 'Intempestives' ou la double dissimulation." In *Nietzsche aujourd'hui*, ed. Centre culturel international de Cerisy-la-Salle, 2: *Passion*: 119–52. Paris: Union générale d'éditions, 1973.

Koselleck, Reinhart. *Critique and Crisis: Enlightenment and the Pathogenesis of Modern Society*. Cambridge, MA: MIT Press, 1988.

Kristeva, Julia. "Word, Dialogue and Novel." In *The Kristeva Reader*, ed. Toril Moi, trans. Alice Jardine, Thomas Gora, and Léon S. Roudiez, 34–61. New York: Columbia University Press, 1986.

La Penna, Antonio. "Incontri pisani degli anni quaranta." *Critica Marxista* 24 (1986): 151–62.

"La publication des Oeuvres complètes de Nietzsche (Entretien avec Michel Foucault)." *Le Monde*, May 24, 1967.

Lachmann, Karl. *Ausgaben classischer Werke darf jeder nachdrucken: Eine Warnung für Herausgeber*. Berlin: W. Besser, 1841.

Lachmann, Karl. *Kleinere Schriften zur deutschen Philologie*, ed. Karl Müllenhoff. Berlin: Reimer, 1876.

Lacoue-Labarthe, Philippe. "The Detour." In *The Subject of Philosophy*, ed. Thomas Trezise, trans. Thomas Trezise et al., 14–36. Minneapolis: University of Minnesota Press, 1993.

Lanata, Giuliana. "L''Enciclopedia' di Giorgio Colli." In *Giorgio Colli: Incontro di studio*, ed. Giuseppe Menichetti, Sandro Barbera, and Giuliano Campioni, 34–40. Milan: Angeli, 1983.

Landfester, Manfred. "Griechen und Deutsche: Der Mythos einer 'Wahlverwandtschaft.'" In *Mythos und Nation: Studien zur Entwicklung des kollektiven Bewußtseins in der Neuzeit*, ed. Helmut Berding, vol. 3, 198–219. Frankfurt am Main: Suhrkamp, 1996.

Lau, Jörg. "Der Jargon der Uneigentlichkeit." *Merkur* 594/5 (1998): 944–55.

Le Rider, Jacques. *Nietzsche en France: De la fin du XIXe siècle au temps présent*. Paris: Presses universitaires de France, 1999.

"L'éclat de rire de Nietzsche (Entretien avec Gilles Deleuze)." *Le Nouvel Observateur*, April 5, 1967.

Leiner, Michel, D.E. Sattler, and K.D. Wolff. "Vorwort." In *Sämtliche Werke*, by Friedrich Hölderlin, vol.: *Einleitung*, 9–19, Frankfurter Ausgabe. Frankfurt am Main: Roter Stern, 1975.

Lepenies, Wolf. "Gottfried Benn – Der Artist im Posthistoire." In *Literarische Profile: Deutsche Dichter von Grimmelshausen bis Brecht*, ed. Walter Hinderer, 326–37. Königstein: Athenäum, 1982.

Lepenies, Wolf. *The Seduction of Culture in German History*. Princeton.: Princeton University Press, 2006.

Lill, Rudolf. *Geschichte Italiens in der Neuzeit*. Darmstadt: Wissenschaftliche Buchgesellschaft, 1988.

Losurdo, Domenico. *Der Marxismus Antonio Gramscis: Von der Utopie zum "kritischen Kommunismus,"* trans. Erdmute Brielmayer. Hamburg: VSA-Verlag, 2000.

Losurdo, Domenico. *Nietzsche, the Aristocratic Rebel: Intellectual Biography and Critical Balance-Sheet*, trans. Gregor Benton. Leiden; Boston: Brill, 2020.

Löwith, Karl. *From Hegel to Nietzsche: The Revolution in Nineteenth-Century Thought*, trans. David E. Green. New York: Columbia University Press, 1991.

Löwith, Karl. *My Life in Germany before and after 1933: A Report*, trans. Elizabeth King. Urbana: University of Illinois Press, 1994.

Löwith, Karl. "Nietzsches Versuch zur Wiedergewinnung der Welt." In *90 Jahre philosophische Nietzsche-Rezeption*, ed. Alfredo Guzzoni, 89–102. Königstein: Hain, 1979.

Löwith, Karl. "Rezension von Erich Podach, Nietzsches Werke des Zusammenbruchs und Ein Blick in die Notizbücher Nietzsches." In

Sämtliche Schriften, by Karl Löwith, vol. 6: *Nietzsche*, 510–17. Stuttgart: J.B. Metzler, 1987.

Löwith, Karl. "Rezension von Friedrich Nietzsche, Werke in drei Bänden." In *Sämtliche Schriften*, by Karl Löwith, vol. 6: *Nietzsche*, 526–34. Stuttgart: J.B. Metzler, 1987.

Löwith, Karl. "Rezension von Karl Schlechta, Der Fall Nietzsche." In *Sämtliche Schriften*, by Karl Löwith, vol. 6: *Nietzsche*, 518–23. Stuttgart: J.B. Metzler, 1987.

Lukács, Georg. *The Destruction of Reason*, trans. Peter Palmer. London: Verso, 2021.

Lütkehaus, Ludger. "'Ich schreibe wie ein Schwein': Die neue Nietzsche-Gesamtausgabe lässt den großen Stilisten aussehen wie einen Kritzler." *Die Zeit*, January 5, 2006.

Lyotard, Jean-François. "Notes on the Return and Capital," trans. Roger McKeon. *Semiotext(e)* 3, no. 1 (1978): 44–53.

Magris, Claudio. "'Ich bin die Einsamkeit als Mensch': Nietzsche und die neue Linke." *Süddeutsche Zeitung*, January 3/4, 1981.

Malorny, Heinz. "Tendenzen der Nietzsche-Rezeption in der BRD." *Deutsche Zeitschrift für Philosophie* 27 (1979): 1493–500.

Mangoni, Luisa. "Europa sotterranea." In *Politica e storia contemporanea: Scritti (1927–1942)*, by Delio Cantimori, xliii–xlii. ed. Luisa Mangoni. Turin: Einaudi, 1991.

Mann, Thomas. *Nietzsche's Philosophy in the Light of Contemporary Events*. Washington, DC: US Government Printing Office, 1947.

Marianelli, Marianello. "L'ultimo patriarca della grande filologia." *La Nazione*, January 6, 1987.

Marti, Urs. *"Der große Pöbel- und Sklavenaufstand": Nietzsches Auseinandersetzung mit Revolution und Demokratie*. Stuttgart: J.B. Metzler, 1993.

Marx, Karl. "The Eighteenth Brumaire of Louis Bonaparte." In *Collected Works*, by Friedrich Engels and Karl Marx, vol. II: *Marx and Engels: 1851–53*, 99–197, trans. Clemens Dutt, Rodney Livingstone, and Christopher Upward. New York: International Publishers, 1979.

"Mazzino Montinari." *Der Spiegel*, December 1, 1986.

Mehring, Reinhard. *Heideggers "große Politik": Die semantische Revolution der Gesamtausgabe*. Tübingen: Mohr Siebeck, 2016.

Menozzi, Daniele, and Francesco Torchiani, eds. *Delio Cantimori (1904–1966):*

Libri, documenti e immagini dai fondi della Scuola Normale Superiore. Pisa: Edizĩoni della Normale, 2016.

Mercer, Ben. "The Paperback Revolution: Mass-Circulation Books and the Cultural Origins of 1968 in Western Europe." *Journal of the History of Ideas* 72 (2011): 613–36.

Michaelis, Rolf. "Roter Stern über Hölderlin." *Die Zeit*, August 8, 1975.

Michel, Karl Markus. "Versuch, die 'Ästhetische Theorie' zu verstehen." In *Materialien zur ästhetischen Theorie: Theodor W. Adornos Konstruktion der Moderne*, ed. Burkhardt Lindner and Martin Lüdke, 41–107. Frankfurt am Main: Suhrkamp, 1979.

"Michel Foucault et Gilles Deleuze veulent rendre à Nietzsche son vrai visage." *Le Figaro*, September 15, 1966.

Mirri, Mario. "Postfazione." In *L'impegno di una generazione: Il gruppo di Lucca dal Liceo Machiavelli alla Normale nel clima del Dopoguerra*, ed. Mario Mirri, Renzo Sabbatini, and Luigi Imbasciati, 167–362. Milan: FrancoAngeli, 2014.

Moebius, Stephan. *Die Zauberlehrlinge: Soziologiegeschichte des Collège de Sociologie (1937–39)*. Konstanz: UVK Verlagsgesellschaft, 2006.

Montevecchi, Federica. *Giorgio Colli: Biografia intellettuale*. Turin: Bollati Boringhieri, 2004.

Montinari, Mazzino. "Aufgaben der Nietzsche-Forschung heute: Nietzsches Auseinandersetzung mit der französischen Literatur des 19. Jahrhunderts." In *Nietzsche heute: Die Rezeption seines Werks nach 1968*, ed. Sigrid Bauschinger, Susan L. Cocalis, and Sara Lennox, 137–48. Bern: Francke, 1988.

Montinari, Mazzino. "Delio Cantimori e Nietzsche." In *Su Nietzsche*, by Mazzino Montinari, 104–22. Rome: Editori riuniti, 1981.

Montinari, Mazzino. "Die neue kritische Gesamtausgabe von Nietzsches Werken." *Literaturmagazin* 12: *Nietzsche* (1980): 317–28.

Montinari, Mazzino. "Equivoci marxisti." In *Su Nietzsche*, by Mazzino Montinari, 90–103. Rome: Editori riuniti, 1981.

Montinari, Mazzino. "Erinnerung an Giorgio Colli." In *Distanz und Pathos: Einleitungen zu Nietzsches Werken*, by Giorgio Colli, 165–73, trans. Ragni Maria Gschwend and Reimar Klein. Hamburg: Europäische Verlagsanstalt, 1993.

Montinari, Mazzino. *Friedrich Nietzsche: Eine Einführung*, trans. Renate Müller-Beck. Berlin: De Gruyter, 1991.

Montinari, Mazzino. "Glanz und Elend der philologischen Arbeit." *Deutsche Akademie für Sprache und Dichtung: Jahrbuch* 1985 (1986): 56–7.

Montinari, Mazzino. "Lavò la faccia al Superuomo." *L'Espresso*, January 21, 1979.

Montinari, Mazzino. "Lettere dalla Germania." *Nuovo Corriere*, May 6/7, 1950.

Montinari, Mazzino. "L'onorevole arte di leggere Nietzsche." *Belfagor* 41 (1986): 335–40.

Montinari, Mazzino. "Nel partito non mi piace fare l'intellettuale." *il manifesto*, February 11, 1983.

Montinari, Mazzino. "Nietzsche in Cosmopolis: Französisch–deutsche Wechselbeziehungen in der Décadence." *Frankfurter Allgemeine Zeitung*, July 19, 1986.

Montinari, Mazzino. "Nietzsche lesen." In *Nietzsche lesen*, by Mazzino Montinari, 1–9. Berlin: De Gruyter, 1982.

Montinari, Mazzino. "Nietzsche und Wagner vor hundert Jahren." In *Nietzsche lesen*, by Mazzino Montinari, 38–55. Berlin: De Gruyter, 1982.

Montinari, Mazzino. "Nietzsche zwischen Alfred Baeumler und Georg Lukács." In *Nietzsche lesen*, by Mazzino Montinari, 169–206. Berlin: De Gruyter, 1982.

Montinari, Mazzino. "Nietzsches Nachlaß von 1885 bis 1888 oder Textkritik und Wille zur Macht." In *Nietzsche lesen*, by Mazzino Montinari, 92–119. Berlin: De Gruyter, 1982.

Montinari, Mazzino. "Otto lettere inedite di Thomas Mann." *Il Contemporaneo*, December 31, 1955.

Montinari, Mazzino. "Presenza della filosofia: Il significato dell'opera di Giorgio Colli." *Rinascità*, February 16, 1979.

Montinari, Mazzino. "Vorwort." In *Sämtliche Werke: Kritische Studienausgabe*, by Friedrich Nietzsche, 7–17, ed. Giorgio Colli and Mazzino Montinari. Munich/Berlin: Deutscher Taschenbuch-Verlag, 1988.

Montinari, Mazzino. "Zum Verhältnis Lektüre – Nachlaß – Werk bei Nietzsche." *Editio* 1 (1987): 245–9.

Moretti, Franco. "The Slaughterhouse of Literature." *Modern Language Quarterly* 61 (2000): 207–27.

Moretti, Gino. "Ricordo di Giorgio Colli." In *Giorgio Colli e l'enigma greco*, ed. Giuseppe Auteri, 44–7. Catania: CUECM, 2000.

Moss, M.E. *Mussolini's Fascist Philosopher: Giovanni Gentile Reconsidered.* New York: Peter Lang, 2004.

Most, Glenn. "Friedrich Nietzsche zwischen Philosophie und Philologie." *Ruperto-Carola* 2 (1994): 12–17.

Müller-Lauter, Wolfgang. "Ständige Herausforderung: Über Mazzino Montinaris Verhältnis zu Nietzsche." *Nietzsche-Studien* 18 (1989): 32–82.

Multhammer, Michael. "Benjamin von Stuckrad-Barres Bekenntnisse." *Merkur* 811 (2016): 67–71.

Musso-Colli, Anna Maria. "Ricordo di Giorgio Colli." In *Saggi su Nietzsche*, ed. Giorgio Penzo, 11–14. Brescia: Morcelliana, 1980.

Mussolini, Benito. *Storia di un anno*. Milan: Mondadori, 1944.

Neumann, Gerhard. *Selbstversuch*. Freiburg im Breisgau: Rombach Verlag, 2018.

Neumann, Gerhard. "Werk oder Schrift? Vorüberlegungen zur Edition von Kafkas 'Bericht für eine Akademie.'" In *Edition und Interpretation*, ed. Louis Hay and Winfried Woesler, 154–73. Bern: Peter Lang, 1982.

Niethammer, Lutz. *Posthistoire: Has History Come to an End?*, trans. Patrick Camiller. London; New York: Verso, 1992.

Nietzsche, Friedrich. *Human, All Too Human I*, trans. Gary J. Handwerk, *The Complete Works of Friedrich Nietzsche*, vol. 3. Stanford, CA: Stanford University Press, 1997.

Nietzsche, Friedrich. *Human, All Too Human II and Unpublished Fragments from the Period of Human, All Too Human II (Spring 1878–Fall 1879)*, trans. Gary J. Handwerk, *The Complete Works of Friedrich Nietzsche*, vol. 4. Stanford, CA: Stanford University Press, 2013.

Nietzsche, Friedrich. *Dawn: Thoughts on the Presumptions of Morality*, trans. Brittain Smith, *The Complete Works of Friedrich Nietzsche*, vol. 5. Stanford, CA: Stanford University Press, 2011.

Nietzsche, Friedrich. *The Joyful Science: Idylls from Messina, Unpublished Fragments from the Period of The Joyful Science (Spring 1881–Summer 1882)*, trans. Adrian Del Caro, *The Complete Works of Friedrich Nietzsche*, vol. 6. Stanford, CA: Stanford University Press, 2023.

Nietzsche, Friedrich. *Beyond Good and Evil, On the Genealogy of Morality*, trans. Adrian Del Caro, *The Complete Works of Friedrich Nietzsche*, vol. 8. Stanford, CA: Stanford University Press, 2014.

Nietzsche, Friedrich. *The Case of Wagner, Twilight of the Idols, The Antichrist, Ecce Homo, Dionysus Dithyrambs, Nietzsche Contra Wagner*, trans. Adrian Del Caro et al., *The Complete Works of Friedrich Nietzsche*, vol. 9. Stanford, CA: Stanford University Press, 2021.

Nietzsche, Friedrich. *Unpublished Fragments (Spring 1885–Spring 1886)*, trans. Adrian Del Caro, *The Complete Works of Friedrich Nietzsche*, vol. 16. Stanford, CA: Stanford University Press, 2020.

Nietzsche, Friedrich. *Ecce homo: Faksimileausgabe der Transkription*. Leipzig: Edition Leipzig, 1985.

Nietzsche, Friedrich. *Kritische Studienausgabe*, ed. Giorgio Colli and Mazzino Montinari, vol. 1. Munich/Berlin: De Gruyter, 1988.

Nietzsche, Friedrich. *Kritische Studienausgabe*, ed. Giorgio Colli and Mazzino Montinari, vol. 2. Munich/Berlin: De Gruyter, 1988.

Nietzsche, Friedrich. *Kritische Studienausgabe*, ed. Giorgio Colli and Mazzino Montinari, vol. 3. Munich/Berlin: De Gruyter, 1988.

Nietzsche, Friedrich. *Kritische Studienausgabe*, ed. Giorgio Colli and Mazzino Montinari, vol. 5. Munich/Berlin: De Gruyter, 1988.

Nietzsche, Friedrich. *Kritische Studienausgabe*, ed. Giorgio Colli and Mazzino Montinari, vol. 6. Munich/Berlin: De Gruyter, 1988.

Nietzsche, Friedrich. *Kritische Studienausgabe*, ed. Giorgio Colli and Mazzino Montinari, vol. 8. Munich/Berlin: De Gruyter, 1988.

Nietzsche, Friedrich. *Kritische Studienausgabe*, ed. Giorgio Colli and Mazzino Montinari, vol. 11. Munich/Berlin: De Gruyter, 1988.

Nietzsche, Friedrich. *Kritische Studienausgabe*, ed. Giorgio Colli and Mazzino Montinari, vol. 12. Munich/Berlin: De Gruyter, 1988.

Nietzsche, Friedrich. *Kritische Studienausgabe*, ed. Giorgio Colli and Mazzino Montinari, vol. 14. Munich/Berlin: De Gruyter, 1988.

Nietzsche, Friedrich. "On Truth and Lie in an Extra-Moral Sense." In *Writings from the Early Notebooks*, ed. Raymond Geuss and Alexander Nehamas, trans. Ladislaus Löb, 253–64. Cambridge: Cambridge University Press, 2009.

Nietzsche, Friedrich. "Rhétorique et langage: Textes traduits, présentés et annotés par Philippe Lacoue-Labarthe et Jean-Luc Nancy." *Poétique* 5 (1971): 99–130.

Nietzsche, Friedrich. *Sämtliche Briefe: Kritische Studienausgabe*, ed. Giorgio Colli and Mazzino Montinari, vol. 2. Munich/Berlin: De Gruyter, 2003.

Nietzsche, Friedrich. *Sämtliche Briefe: Kritische Studienausgabe*, ed. Giorgio Colli and Mazzino Montinari, vol. 3. Munich/Berlin: De Gruyter, 2003.

Nietzsche, Friedrich. *Sämtliche Briefe: Kritische Studienausgabe*, ed. Giorgio Colli and Mazzino Montinari, vol. 5. Munich/Berlin: De Gruyter, 2003.

Nietzsche, Friedrich. *Sämtliche Briefe: Kritische Studienausgabe*, ed. Giorgio Colli and Mazzino Montinari, vol. 6. Munich/Berlin: De Gruyter, 2003.

Nietzsche, Friedrich. *Sämtliche Briefe: Kritische Studienausgabe*, ed. Giorgio Colli and Mazzino Montinari, vol. 8. Munich/Berlin: De Gruyter, 2003.

Nietzsche, Friedrich. *Selected Letters of Friedrich Nietzsche*, ed, and trans. Christopher Middleton. Chicago: University of Chicago Press, 1969.

Nolte, Ernst. *Nietzsche und der Nietzscheanismus*. Frankfurt am Main: Propyläen, 1990.

Nolte, Ernst. *Three Faces of Fascism: Action Française, Italian Fascism, National Socialism*, trans. Leila Vennewitz. London: Weidenfeld & Nicolson, 1965.

Nordhofen, Eckhard. "Die Tragik des Protestantismus." *Merkur* 834 (2019): 71–9.

Oelmann, Ute. "Norbert von Hellingrath." In *Hölderlin-Handbuch: Leben – Werk – Wirkung*, ed. Johann Kreuzer, 422–5. Stuttgart: J.B. Metzler, 2011.

Orsini, Alessandro. *Anatomy of the Red Brigades: The Religious Mind-Set of Modern Terrorists*. Ithaca, NY: Cornell University Press, 2011.

Ottmann, Henning. "Anti-Lukács: Eine Kritik der Nietzsche-Kritik von Georg Lukács." *Nietzsche-Studien* 13 (1984): 570–86.

Palmier, Jean-Michel. "La réédition d'"Humain, trop humain."" *Le Monde*, July 7, 1969.

Pannwitz, Rudolf. "Nietzsche-Philologie?" *Merkur* 117 (1957): 1073–87.

Parlato, Valentino. "Angelo, Mazzino e Fausto." In *L'impegno di una generazione: Il gruppo di Lucca dal Liceo Machiavelli alla Normale nel clima del Dopoguerra*, ed. Mario Mirri, Renzo Sabbatini, and Luigi Imbasciati, 91–3. Milan: FrancoAngeli, 2014.

Pepperle, Heinz. "Revision des marxistischen Nietzsche-Bildes?" *Sinn und Form* 38 (1986): 934–69.

Plato. *Plato's Symposium*, trans. Seth Benardete. Chicago: University of Chicago Press, 2001.

Plessner, Helmut. *Die verspätete Nation*. Frankfurt am Main: Suhrkamp, 1974.

Podach, Erich. *Friedrich Nietzsches Werke des Zusammenbruchs*. Heidelberg: W. Rothe, 1961.

Pöthig, Charis. *Italien und die DDR: Die politischen, ökonomischen und kulturellen Beziehungen von 1949 bis 1980*. Frankfurt am Main: Peter Lang, 2000.

Prosperi, Adriano. "Delio Cantimori, maestro di tolleranza." *il manifesto*, March 30, 2005.

Prosperi, Adriano. ""Io ci provo, ma quello degli storici sta diventando un mestiere inutile."" *La Repubblica*, June 29, 2015.

Pursche, Robert. "Philologie als Barrikadenkampf: Rolf Tiedemann und die

Arbeit für Walter Benjamins Nachleben." *Mittelweg 36: Zeitschrift des Hamburger Instituts für Sozialforschung* 30, no. 3 (2021): 12–40.

Raulff, Ulrich. "Das Labyrinth des Lesens und das Eselsohr der Philologie." *Süddeutsche Zeitung*, October 4, 2003.

Raulff, Ulrich. "Klickeradoms: Nietzsche liegt in Stücken." *Süddeutsche Zeitung*, November 24, 2001.

Reibnitz, Barbara von. "Die Handschrift lesen: Der Nachlass des späten Nietzsche in neuer Edition." *Neue Zürcher Zeitung*, October 30, 2002.

Reichert, Herbert W. "The Present Status of Nietzsche: Nietzsche Literature in the Post-War Era." *Monatshefte* 51 (1959): 103–20.

Reschke, Renate, and Rüdiger Schmidt-Grépály, "Über Zugänge zu Nietzsche: Renate Reschke im Gespräch mit Rüdiger Schmidt-Grépály." In *Zur Rückkehr des Autors: Gespräche über das Werk Friedrich Nietzsches*, ed. Rüdiger Schmidt-Grépály, 63–93. Göttingen: LSD, 2013.

Riedel, Manfred. *Nietzsche in Weimar: Ein deutsches Drama*. Leipzig: Reclam, 1997.

Rintelen, Enno. *Mussolini als Bundesgenosse: Erinnerungen des deutschen Militärattachés in Rom, 1936–1943*. Tübingen: R. Wunderlich, 1951.

Ritter, Henning. "Es gibt ihn nicht mehr, den gefährlichen Nietzsche." *Frankfurter Allgemeine Zeitung*, March 19, 2002.

Ritter, Henning. "Nietzsche für Philologen? Zu einer Tagung über seine philosophischen Anfänge." *Frankfurter Allgemeine Zeitung*, March 25, 1992.

Ritter, Henning. *Notizhefte*. Berlin: Berlin Verlag, 2010.

Ritter, Henning. "Stille Penelopearbeit: Nietzsche ist ein anderer geworden." *Frankfurter Allgemeine Zeitung*, April 21, 1993.

Ritter, Henning. "Tanz ohne Ketten: Zu Mazzino Montinaris unvollendetem Nietzsche-Kommentar." *Frankfurter Allgemeine Zeitung*, December 3, 1986.

Röllin, Beat, and René Stockmar. "Nietzsche lesen mit KGW IX: Zum Beispiel Arbeitsheft W II 1, Seite 1." In *Text/Kritik: Nietzsche und Adorno*, ed. Martin Endres, 1–38. Berlin: De Gruyter, 2017.

Roloff, Hans-Gert. "Karl Lachmann, seine Methode und die Folgen." In *Geschichte der Editionsverfahren vom Altertum bis zur Gegenwart im Überblick*, ed. Hans-Gert Roloff, 63–81. Berlin: Weidler, 2003.

Roos, Richard. "Les derniers écrits de Nietzsche et leur publication." *Revue Philosophique* 146 (1956): 262–87.

Roos, Richard. "Règles pour une lecture philologique de Nietzsche." In

Nietzsche aujourd'hui?, ed. Centre culturel international de Cerisy-la-Salle, vol. 2: *Passion*, 283–324. Paris: Union générale d'éditions, 1973.

Rossanda, Rossana. *Vergebliche Reise oder Politik als Education sentimentale*, trans. Barbara Kleiner. Frankfurt am Main: Suhrkamp, 1985.

Rötzer, Florian, "Jacob Taubes." In *Denken, das an der Zeit ist*, ed. Florian Rötzer, 305–19. Frankfurt am Main: Suhrkamp, 1987.

Russo, Luigi. "Antonio Gramsci e l'educazione democratica in Italia." *Belfagor* 2, no. 4 (1947): 395–411.

Russo, Rosarita. "Die Anfänge der Nietzsche-Rezeption in Italien." In *Widersprüche: Zur frühen Nietzsche-Rezeption*, ed. Andreas Schirmer and Rüdiger Schmidt, 234–44. Weimar: Hermann Böhlaus Nachfolger, 2000.

Salin, Edgar. "Der Fall Nietzsche." *Merkur* 112 (1957): 573–87.

Sartre, Jean-Paul. "Palmiro Togliatti." In *Situations, IX: Mélanges*, by Jean-Paul Sartre, 137–51. Paris: Gallimard, 1972.

Sattler, D.E. "Friedrich Hölderlin, 'Frankfurter Ausgabe': Editionsprinzipien und Editionsmodell." *Hölderlin-Jahrbuch* 19/20 (1975): 112–30.

Schelz, Sepp. "Fragen und Denken am Abgrund: Literarische Symptome einer Wiederkunft." *Deutsches Allgemeines Sonntagsblatt*, March 1, 1981.

Schieder, Wolfgang. *Mythos Mussolini: Deutsche in Audienz beim Duce.* Munich: Oldenbourg, 2013.

Schiera, Pierangelo. "Carl Schmitt und Delio Cantimori." In *Complexio Oppositorum: Über Carl Schmitt*, ed. Helmut Quaritsch, 529–35. Berlin: Duncker & Humblot, 1988.

Schirrmacher, Frank. "Lust auf Leben: Zum Tode von Mazzino Montinari." *Frankfurter Allgemeine Zeitung*, November 26, 1986.

Schirrmacher, Frank. "Nietzsches Wiederkehr." *Frankfurter Allgemeine Zeitung*, September 19, 1986.

Schlechta, Karl. *Der Fall Nietzsche: Aufsätze und Vorträge.* Munich: C. Hanser, 1959.

Schlechta, Karl. "Philologischer Nachbericht." In *Werke in drei Bänden*, by Friedrich Nietzsche, 1383–1432. ed. Karl Schlechta. Munich: Hanser, 1956.

Schmidt, Rüdiger. "Die verratenen Gedanken: Wie Nietzsche erst gefälscht und dann rekonstruiert wurde." *Süddeutsche Zeitung*, November 24/5, 2001.

Schnädelbach, Herbert. "Morbus hermeneuticus: Thesen über eine philosophische Krankheit." In *Vernunft und Geschichte: Vorträge und Abhandlungen*, by Herbert Schnädelbach, 279–84. Frankfurt am Main: Suhrkamp, 1987.

Schuster, Marc-Oliver. "Rudolf Pannwitz' kulturphilosophische Verwendung des Begriffs 'postmodern.'" *Archiv für Begriffsgeschichte* 47 (2005): 191–213.

Schutte, Anne Jacobson. "Carlo Ginzburg." *The Journal of Modern History* 48 (1976): 296–315.

Schutte, Anne Jacobson. "Periodization of Sixteenth-Century Italian Religious History: The Post-Cantimori Paradigm Shift." *The Journal of Modern History* 61 (1989): 269–84.

Sciascia, Leonardo. *The Moro Affair; And, The Mystery of Majorana*, trans. Sacha Rabinovitch. Manchester: Carcanet, 1987.

Seibt, Gustav. "Freigängerbriefe." In *Nahaufnahmen*, by Adriano Sofri, 7–10, trans. Martina Bartel. Berlin: Transit, 1999.

Seibt, Gustav. "Wie in neuen Werkausgaben mit Nietzsche, Marx und Burckhardt umgegangen wird." *Die Zeit*, October 19, 2000.

Seidel Menchi, Silvana. "'Ein Neues Leben': Contributo allo studio di Delio Cantimori." *Studi Storici* 34 (1993): 777–86.

Senger, Hans Gerhard. "Die historisch-kritische Edition historisch-kritisch betrachtet." In *Buchstabe und Geist: Zur Überlieferung und Edition philosophischer Texte*, ed. Walter Jaeschke et al., 1–20. Hamburg: F. Meiner, 1987.

Sestan, Ernesto. "Cantimori e i Giacobini." *Annali della Scuola Normale Superiore di Pisa: Lettere, Storia e Filosofia, Serie II* 37 (1968): 233–40.

Sieburg, Heinz. "Die Buchstäblichkeit der Buchstaben." In *Buchstäblichkeit: Theorie, Geschichte, Übersetzung*, ed. Achim Geisenhanslüke, 11–28. Bielefeld: Transcript, 2020.

Sieg, Ulrich. *Die Macht des Willens: Elisabeth Förster-Nietzsche und ihre Welt*. Munich: Carl Hanser Verlag, 2019.

Sina, Kai, and Carlos Spoerhase. "Nachlassbewusstsein: Zur literaturwissenschaftlichen Erforschung seiner Entstehung und Entwicklung." *Zeitschrift für Germanistik, Neue Folge* 23 (2013): 607–23.

Sisto, Michele. "Gli intellettuali italiani e la Germania socialista: Un percorso attraverso gli scritti di Cesare Cases." In *Riflessioni sulla DDR: Prospettive internazionali e interdisciplinari vent'anni dopo*, ed. Magda Martini and Thomas Schaarschmidt, 97–121. Bologna: Il mulino, 2011.

Sloterdijk, Peter. *Thinker on Stage: Nietzsche's Materialism*, trans. Jamie Owen Daniel. Minneapolis: University of Minnesota Press, 1989.

Sloterdijk, Peter, and Rüdiger Schmidt-Grépály, "Nietzsche, Autor, Reformator: Peter Sloterdijk im Gespräch mit Rüdiger Schmidt-Grépály."

In *Zur Rückkehr des Autors: Gespräche über das Werk Friedrich Nietzsches*, ed. Rüdiger Schmidt-Grépály, 27–62. Göttingen: LSD, 2013.

Sofri, Adriano. "Dal morbillo a Nietzsche." *Panorama*, July 31, 1988, 120–1.

Sofri, Adriano. "Federico il pendolare." *Panorama*, February 22, 1987, 139–43.

Sofri, Adriano. "Genosse Hiob: Über Antonio Gramsci." In *Nahaufnahmen*, by Adriano Sofri, 14–17. Berlin: Transit, 1999.

Soll, Jacob. "Empirical History and the Transformation of Political Criticism in France from Bodin to Bayle." *Journal of the History of Ideas* 64 (2003): 297–316.

Sommer, Andreas Urs. *Band 5.1 Kommentar zu Nietzsches "Jenseits von Gut und Böse."* Berlin: De Gruyter, 2016.

Sommer, Andreas Urs. *Nietzsche und die Folgen*. Stuttgart: J.B. Metzler, 2017.

Sontag, Susan. "Against Interpretation." In *Essays of the 1960s & 70s*, ed. David Rieff, 10–20. New York: The Library of America, 2013.

Staszak, Jürgen. "Beobachtungen an der Wirkungsweise des Lukácsschen Literaturkonzepts." *Weimarer Beiträge* 31 (1985): 573–9.

Stefanelli, Lea. "Il ricordo di una 'principiante.'" In *L'impegno di una generazione: Il gruppo di Lucca dal Liceo Machiavelli alla Normale nel clima del Dopoguerra*, ed. Mario Mirri, Renzo Sabbatini, and Luigi Imbasciati, 21–4. Milan: FrancoAngeli, 2014.

Steinbach, Matthias. *"Also sprach Sarah Tustra": Nietzsches sozialistische Irrfahrten*. Halle: Mitteldeutscher Verlag, 2020.

Steinbach, Matthias. "'Der Donnerer hinter der Mauer': Nietzsche-Lesarten und -Orte in der DDR." In *"Ins Nichts mit ihm!" Ins Nichts mit ihm? Zur Rezeption Friedrich Nietzsches in der DDR*, 5–20. Berlin: "Helle Panke" e.V. – Rosa-Luxemburg-Stiftung Berlin, 2016.

Steinfeld, Thomas. *Der leidenschaftliche Buchhalter: Philologie als Lebensform*. Munich: C. Hanser, 2004.

Stephan, Wolfgang. "Der Zugriff der sowjetischen Militäradministration auf Nietzsches Nachlass 1946 und seine Retter." *Nietzsche-Studien* 27 (1998): 527–34.

Tellkamp, Uwe. *The Tower: Tales from a Lost Country*, trans. Mike Mitchell. London: Penguin Books, 2016.

Thiel, Jens. "Monumentalisch – antiquarisch – kritisch? Archiv und Edition als Institutionen der Distanzierung: Der Fall des Nietzsche-Herausgebers

Karl Schlechta." In *"Einige werden posthum geboren": Friedrich Nietzsches Wirkungen,* ed. Renate Reschke and Marco Brusotti, 475–88. Berlin: De Gruyter, 2012.

"Thirty-Sixth Day: Thursday, 17 January 1946." In *Trial of the Major War Criminals before the International Military Tribunal, Nuremberg, 14 November 1945–1 October 1946,* vol. 5, 368–433. Nuremberg, Germany: International Military Tribunal, 1947.

Thomalla, Erika. *Anwälte des Autors: Zur Geschichte der Herausgeberschaft im 18 und 19. Jahrhundert.* Göttingen: Wallstein, 2020.

Thüring, Hubert. "Tertium datum: Der 'Nachlass' zwischen Leben und Werk: Zur Neuausgabe der handschriftlichen Dokumente des 'späten Nietzsche.'" *IASL online,* May 25, 2003.

Timpanaro, Sebastiano. *The Genesis of Lachmann's Method,* ed. and trans. Glenn W. Most. Chicago: University of Chicago Press, 2005.

Togliatti, Palmiro. "Utopisti e riformatori sociali." In *La politica nel pensiero e nell'azione: Scritti e discorsi 1917–1964,* by Palmiro Togliatti, 1263–75, ed. Michele Ciliberto and Giuseppe Vacca. Milan: Bompiani, 2014.

Turner, James. *Philology: The Forgotten Origins of the Modern Humanities.* Princeton: Princeton University Press, 2014.

Valenziano, Clara. "La Lucca della guerra e di Giorgio Colli." In *L'impegno di una generazione: Il gruppo di Lucca dal Liceo Machiavelli alla Normale nel clima del Dopoguerra,* ed. Mario Mirri, Renzo Sabbatini, and Luigi Imbasciati, 95–100. Milan: FrancoAngeli, 2014.

Veyne, Paul. "Histoire et Historiens." *Annales* 27 (1972): 668–9.

Vittoria, Albertina. "La commissione culturale del Pci dal 1948 al 1956." *Studi Storici* 31 (1990): 135–70.

Voegelin, Eric. "Nietzsche, the Crisis and the War." *The Journal of Politics* 6, no. 2 (May 1944): 177–212.

Wackwitz, Stephan. "Text als Mythos: Zur Frankfurter Hölderlin-Ausgabe und ihrer Rezeption." *Merkur* 492 (1990): 134–43.

Wägenbaur, Birgit. "Norbert von Hellingrath und Karl Wolfskehl: Eine biographische Skizze." In *Norbert von Hellingrath und die Ästhetik der europäischen Moderne,* ed. Jürgen Brokoff, Joachim Jacob, and Marcel Lepper, 161–89. Göttingen: Wallstein, 2013.

Wegmann, Nikolaus. "Was heißt einen 'klassischen' Text lesen? Philologische Selbstreflexion zwischen Wissenschaft und Bildung." In *Wissenschaftsgeschichte der Germanistik im 19. Jahrhundert,* ed. Jürgen

Fohrmann and Wilhelm Voßkamp, 334–450. Stuttgart: J.B. Metzler, 1994.

"Wiedervereinigung in Rom." *Der Spiegel*, April 17, 1956, 23–4.

Wilamowitz-Moellendorff, Ulrich von. "Future Philology! A Reply to Friedrich Nietzsche's 'Birth of Tragedy,'" trans. Gertrude Postl, Babette Babich, and Holger Schmid. *New Nietzsche Studies* 4, no. 1/2 (Summer/Fall 2000): 1–32.

Willer, Stefan. *Erbfälle: Theorie und Praxis kultureller Übertragung in der Moderne*. Paderborn: Wilhelm Fink, 2014.

Wysling, Hans, and Yvonne Schmidlin, eds. *Thomas Mann: Ein Leben in Bildern*. Zürich: Artemis, 1994.

Zagari, Luciano. "Ricordo berlinese di Mazzino Montinari." In *L'impegno di una generazione: Il gruppo di Lucca dal Liceo Machiavelli alla Normale nel clima del Dopoguerra*, ed. Mario Mirri, Renzo Sabbatini, and Luigi Imbasciati, 107–11. Milan: FrancoAngeli, 2014.

Index

Illustrations are indicated by page numbers in bold.